NEIL T. ANDERSON
& RICH MILLER

LETTING
GO
OF
FEAR

HARVEST HOUSE PUBLISHERS
EUGENE, OREGON

Cover by Darren Welch

Cover photos © Kristine / Lightstock

LETTING GO OF FEAR
Copyright © 2018 Neil T. Anderson and Rich Miller
Published by Harvest House Publishers
Eugene, Oregon 97408
www.harvesthousepublishers.com

ISBN 978-0-7369-7219-2 (pbk.)
ISBN 978-0-7369-7220-8 (eBook)

Library of Congress Cataloging-in-Publication Data
Names: Anderson, Neil T., 1942- author.
Title: Letting go of fear / Neil T. Anderson and Richard Miller.
Description: Eugene : Harvest House Publishers, 2018.
Identifiers: LCCN 2018005865 (print) | LCCN 2018016428 (ebook) | ISBN 9780736972208 (ebook) | ISBN 9780736972192 (pbk.)
Subjects: LCSH: Fear--Religious aspects--Christianity. | Fear of God.
Classification: LCC BV4908.5 (ebook) | LCC BV4908.5 .A54 2018 (print) | DDC 248.4--dc23
LC record available at https://lccn.loc.gov/2018005865

Printed in the United States of America

18 19 20 21 22 23 24 25 26 / BP-GL / 10 9 8 7 6 5 4 3 2 1

Acknowledgments

No book is ever written in a vacuum. We are indebted to our parents, former teachers, friends, and fellow workers. They have all contributed to who we are and the contents of this book. We want to thank many who have prayed specifically for this project.

We also want to thank Harvest House for trusting us with the message of this book, and for the fine work of editing, designing, and marketing. It has always been a delight to work with you.

Thank you to all our brothers and sisters in Christ who courageously told us their stories—some of which are in this book, and all of which touched our hearts.

We want to especially thank our wives, Joanne and Shirley, for their encouragement and contributions. Joanne was the unofficial editor of the first edition, as she has been with all of Neil's books. She is slowly slipping into the arms of Jesus as we write this second edition.

Finally, we want to thank our heavenly Father for calling us His children, Jesus Christ for giving us life and setting us free, and the Holy Spirit for leading us into all truth. We are indeed blessed with every spiritual blessing in Christ Jesus our Lord (Ephesians 1:3).

Contents

Foreword. 7

Introduction 11

   1.   Restoring the Foundation 31

   2.   Fortress of Fear 53

   3.   Fear of Death 79

   4.   Fear of Man 105

   5.   Fear of Failure 131

   6.   Fear of Satan 151

   7.   Fear of God 173

   8.   Breaking Strongholds of Fear 203

   9.   Panic Disorder 221

  10.   Casting All Anxiety on Christ 239

Appendix A:
  Guidelines for Leading This Study on Letting Go of Fear . . . 259

Appendix B:
  Establishing a Discipleship Counseling Ministry 261

Notes 269

Foreword

Julianne S. Zuehlke, MS, RN, CS and Terry E. Zuehlke, PhD, LP

The Lord God called to the man, "Where are you?" He answered, "I heard you in the garden, and I was afraid because I was naked; so I hid" (Genesis 3:9-10 NIV).

In this familiar passage the Bible clearly identifies the first negative feeling that entered the human experience. God, in His omniscience, knew the many stressful feelings we would encounter once sin entered the realm of our experience. In the garden of Eden, fear was the original disturbing emotion resulting from Adam's sense of disobedience and rebellion. Anxiety, fear, and panic have prevailed ever since. Almost everyone, at one time or another, has felt helpless in the face of these troubling feelings. Today we are living in the "Age of Anxiety."

None of us are beyond the reach of insecurity, self-doubt, and apprehension. In fact, anxiety is among the most prominent emotions treated by psychotropic medications. As Christian professional counselors, the nature and extent of these crippling emotions have been quite apparent in the lives of our clients. We know that fear and anxiety, although very common, can be extremely resistant to psychological and/or medical treatment. We frequently work with people caught in issues that seem overwhelming and chaotic to them. They become worried, frightened, and seized with panic. At the root of their issues is a strong sense of disconnection from God and from those in the body of Christ. This sense of isolation and alienation is painful, as is the sense of impatience over how to manage or control the feelings.

Letting Go of Fear provides clear answers for those seeking information on how to understand and cope with the feelings of anxiety, fear, and panic. You'll discover how a prevalent lack of understanding as to our identity in Christ and our inability to resolve personal and spiritual conflicts are manifest in these specific, negative emotions.

It is refreshing to see how Neil Anderson and Rich Miller have focused the general principles of *Freedom in Christ* on the prominent and powerful problem of negative emotions. This book addresses the origin of mental strongholds, the nature of anxiety, mankind's basic fears, and the problem of panic attacks in a balanced, helpful manner. It then provides strong biblical direction for disciple makers and their disciples to use in overcoming anxiety disorders. The conclusion provides a powerful presentation of how an understanding of the fear of the Lord is vital for our Christian growth.

Letting Go of Fear is valuable because it is biblically sound and practical. It allows us to move beyond the "head knowledge" of traditional counseling approaches and offers healing for the soul by providing perspective on our relationships with God through Jesus Christ. It illustrates how we are to revere Him and, in so doing, find in Him a sanctuary from all other fears. Adam didn't have to be afraid of God and try to hide from Him. He could have gone to God, confessed his sin, and experienced forgiveness and peace of mind. When he didn't, God came to Adam in the midst of his fear.

God is the source of our freedom from fear, and He wants to minister His truth to you and me. Read this book and you will appreciate His invitation to bring our anxieties, fears, and panicky feelings to Him. He is our "Wonderful Counselor," "Great Physician," and "Prince of Peace."

A Note from the Authors

In relating true stories and testimonies throughout the book, we have changed names to protect individual identity and privacy.

For ease of reading we have not distinguished ourselves from each other in authorship or experiences, preferring to use "I" and "we" as opposed to "I (Rich)" or "I (Neil)." The only exceptions are illustrations referring to family.

Introduction

I'm 36 years old. For as long as I can remember, I have been plagued with fears and anxieties. I was raised in an abusive family and lived under the threat of even worse treatment if I ever told. In the bondage of fear, I decided never to tell anyone.

I came home one evening and found everyone gone. I was gripped with fear and crawled under my bed. Why weren't they home? Did they think I told someone? What would happen when they came back? I could never enjoy the simple little things that accompany childhood.

My anxieties and fears followed me wherever I went. I was too afraid to try out for anything where I could possibly fail, and I dreaded every exam. My stomach would tie up in knots from anxiety. I became a perfectionist who had to achieve—whatever the cost.

This pattern of fear continued into my teenage years and young-adult life. I tried to accept Jesus twice, but I feared not being good enough. I feared the rejection and ridicule of others, so I tried to keep everyone happy. Even sleep offered no reprieve. The nightmares I suffered as a result of the abuse in my childhood continued into my adult years.

I am a parent now, and I fear for my children. Am I an adequate mother? Will my children be hurt or abducted? I know this is robbing me of the life I want to live, but I don't know what to do. I feel like I'm living two lives. On the outside I appear to be a successful teacher, wife, mother, and contributing member of society. But if people could see the condition of my soul, they would notice only pain, anxiety, and fear. Can somebody help me? Can I help myself, or is this what life is supposed to be?

Primordial Fear

No, that is not what life is supposed to be, and it wasn't from the beginning. "In the beginning God created the heavens and the earth" (Genesis 1:1). The Hubble telescope enables us to view the extravagance of creation in part, and that small glimpse is beyond our ability to comprehend. We can only marvel as we stare into space. "The heavens are telling of the glory of God; and their expanse is declaring the work of His hands" (Psalm 19:1). There are supernovas, black holes, galaxies, and stars so large that if they were depicted on a printed page, it would render the earth a barely visible dot in comparison.

All of this created matter is finite, devoid of life, and did not originate from preexisting matter. On the other hand, the creator is living and infinite, the mind behind the universe.

The Earth—and possibly other planets—has organic life in the form of plants, birds of the sky, beasts of the fields, and fish of the sea. Such life is subject to the natural law of death. It perpetuates its species by sowing seeds or bearing young for the next generation before it dies.

With all that in place, "Then the LORD God formed man of dust from the ground, and breathed into his nostrils the breath of life; and man became a living being" (Genesis 2:7). Something new and totally different was introduced into the universe. God shared His divine and eternal life with Adam, who was created in His image and likeness. His soul was in union with God. Adam could have eaten from the tree of life and lived forever, but he was forbidden to eat from the tree of the knowledge of good and evil. If he did, he would surely die (Genesis 2:17).

The devil deceived Eve, Adam's wife, and she ate from the forbidden tree. Adam made the fatal choice to join her, and both died spiritually. Their souls were no longer in union with God. Adam remained physically alive for centuries, because his soul was still in union with his body, but he eventually succumbed to the law of death. Adam was created to be physically and spiritually alive, but sin separated him from God.

Now all the descendants of Adam and Eve are subject to the law of sin and death, for we are all born dead in our trespasses and sins (Ephesians 2:1). In other words, we are all born physically alive, but spiritually dead. "Therefore, just as through one man sin entered into the world, and death through sin, and so death spread to all men, because all sinned" (Romans 5:12).

The immediate emotional consequence of being separated from God was fear (Genesis 3:10). Why was Adam afraid? There was nothing in the garden of Eden to fear. He had no neurological illness that needed medication. There were no learned phobias that had to be unlearned, or flesh patterns that had to be crucified. There is only one explanation for Adam's fear; He was separated from God. There is nothing more fearful than to be totally abandoned and utterly alone.

Throughout history people have been terrorized by the idea of impermanence. They have gone to extreme measures to overcome their mortality. Fanciful beliefs have been formulated by false religions to give them hope for an afterlife. Explorers have searched for the mystical Fountain of Youth. Scientists have experimented with drugs to stop the aging process. Some have turned to cryogenics (a branch of physics that deals with very low temperatures), hoping they can be resuscitated from their frozen state after a cure has been found for the disease that led to their death. Silicon Valley techies are trying to upload their consciousness to a computer. People attempt to alleviate their fears by saying someone is in a better place after they've died, when there is often no basis for making such an assertion.

This primordial fear exists in all humanity, and there is only one antidote. When Adam moved away from God he brought death, because sin had cut him off from the source of life. God, in His great love and mercy, sent Jesus to die for our sins—but He also came to do much more than that (see Romans 5:8-11). He came to give us eternal life, which is not the same as the temporal life that defines our physical existence. "Since the children share in flesh and blood, He Himself likewise also partook of the same, that through death He might render powerless him who had the power of death, that is, the devil, and might free those who through fear of death were subject to slavery all their lives" (Hebrews 2:14-15). Jesus, "who is our life" (Colossians 3:4), came to set captives free.

God didn't do away with the law of sin and death. He overcame it with a greater law. "Therefore there is now no condemnation for those who are in Christ Jesus. For the law of the Spirit of life in Christ Jesus has set you free from the law of sin and of death" (Romans 8:1-2). Some aspects of the Christian life can seem murky, for now we see dimly (1 Corinthians 13:12), but one absolute is clear: "He who has the Son has the life; he who does not have the Son of God does not have the life" (1 John 5:12). Paul admonishes you to "test yourselves to see if you are in the faith; examine yourselves! Or do you not recognize this about yourselves, that Jesus Christ is in you—unless indeed you fail the test?" (2 Corinthians 13:5).

Anxiety Disorders

God "delivered us from so great a peril of death, and will deliver us, He on whom we have set our hope" (2 Corinthians 1:10). Notice that He "has" and He "will" deliver us. For every child of God, the greatest object of fear has been removed if we believe the gospel, but other objects of fear remain as we seek the Lord in this fallen world. We still have to resist the devil, overcome our flesh patterns, and be transformed by the renewing of our minds (Romans 12:2). But God *will deliver us* from fears, worries, doubts, and panic attacks as we mature in Christ.

Anxiety disorders comprise the most common mental illness in the United States, affecting 40 million adults age 18 and over. Roughly half of those who struggle with an anxiety disorder also struggle with depression, which is the second most common mental illness.[1] The whole world is experiencing a "blues" epidemic in an age of anxiety, yet only about one third of those suffering receive treatment in the United

States.[2] Women are twice as likely as men to suffer from generalized anxiety disorder (GAD) or a panic disorder, but social anxiety disorder (SAD) affects both men and women equally, typically beginning in early teenage years.

How do we cast our anxiety onto Christ, as we're told to do in 1 Peter 5:7? How is the fear of God the beginning of wisdom (Proverbs 9:10), and how does the fear of God overcome all other fears? What is a panic attack, and how can it be stopped? The most repeated command in Scripture is "fear not," but little relief will come to those struggling with phobias if that is all they are told. If you are stricken with an anxiety disorder, where do you go for help? A primary care doctor? A psychologist? A psychiatrist? The internet? A priest, rabbi, or pastor? A bartender? God?

Dr. Edmund Bourne is one of the more credible practitioners seeking to help those struggling with anxiety disorders. He is the author of *The Anxiety and Phobia Workbook*,[3] which won the Benjamin Franklin Book Award for Excellence in Psychology. Dr. Bourne entered this field of study because he personally struggled with anxiety. Five years after the publication of the first edition of his workbook, his own anxiety disorder took a turn for the worse. This caused him to reevaluate his own life, as well as his approach to treatment. In 1998, he published a new book entitled *Healing Fear*. In the foreword, he wrote:

> The guiding metaphor for this book is "healing" as an approach to overcoming anxiety, in contrast to "applied technology." I feel it's important to introduce this perspective into the field of anxiety treatment since the vast majority of self-help books available (including my first book) utilize the applied technology approach...I don't want to diminish the importance of cognitive behavioral therapy (CBT) and the applied technology approach. Such an approach produces effective results in many cases, and I use it in my professional practice every day. In the

past few years, though, I feel that the cognitive behavior strategy has reached its limits. CBT and medication can produce results quickly and are very compatible with the brief therapy, managed-care environment in the mental health profession at present. When follow-up is done over one- to three-year intervals, however, some of the gains are lost. Relapses occur rather often, and people seem to get themselves back into the same difficulties that precipitated the original anxiety disorder.[4]

In other words, "They have healed the brokenness of My people superficially, saying, 'Peace, peace,' but there is no peace" (Jeremiah 6:14). Dr. Bourne's comments sound like Paul's in Colossians 2:8: "See to it that no one takes you captive through philosophy and empty deception, according to the tradition of men, according to the elementary principles of the world, rather than according to Christ."

Dr. Bourne believes that "anxiety arises from a state of disconnection."[5] We agree, and the primary disconnection is from God. We don't know whether Dr. Bourne has a saving knowledge of our Lord Jesus Christ, but in his own search for answers he came to the following conclusion:

In my own experience, spirituality has been important, and I believe it will come to play an increasingly important role in the psychology of the future. Holistic medicine, with its interest in meditation, prayer, and the role of spiritual healing in recovery from serious illness, has become a mainstream movement in the nineties. I believe there will be a "holistic psychology" in the not too distant future, like holistic medicine, [that] integrates scientifically based treatment approaches with alternative, more spiritually based modalities.[6]

While we are encouraged by any openness in the thinking of some secular therapists, we are also concerned that the spirituality implied may not be Christ-centered. New Age spirituality and Eastern religions are more entrenched in secular education than is historical Christianity. Biblical meditation plays an important role in true spirituality, but meditating at the feet of a New Age guru or any "divine" master will lead to spiritual bondage.

Safe and Secure

Our goal is to present a complete answer. If medicine will help our physical bodies function more efficiently, we will recommend it. Our primary focus, however, will be on the finished work of Christ. All of creation is groaning as we are "waiting eagerly for our adoption as sons" (Romans 8:23). Jesus said, "The time is fulfilled, and the kingdom of God is at hand; repent and believe in the gospel" (Mark 1:15).

In order for us to be safe and secure in the arms of Jesus, He had to accomplish three critical functions. First, He had to remove the barrier that separated us from God. So He took our sins upon Himself and nailed them to the cross. Second, He was resurrected in order that we may have new life "in Him." Finally, He came to undo the works of Satan (1 John 3:8), who had become the ruler of this world. Notice how Paul summarizes those three essentials in Colossians 2:13-15:

> When you were dead in your transgressions and the uncircumcision of your flesh, He made you alive together with Him, having forgiven us all our transgressions, having canceled out the certificate of debt consisting of decrees against us, which was hostile to us; and He has taken it out of the way, having nailed it to the cross. When He had disarmed the rulers and authorities, He made a public display of them, having triumphed over them through Him.

All that God needed to do in order for us to be alive and free in Christ has been accomplished by Jesus. Now we need to do our part, which is to repent and believe the gospel. Repentance removes the barriers that keep us from having an intimate relationship with God, including false guidance, pride, rebellion, habitual sin, and unforgiveness. Victory over anxiety disorders is assured if you know and believe the truth and are rightly related to the source of eternal life, the omnipotent authority of the universe, the Lord Jesus Christ.

To help you accomplish this, we have included *The Steps to Freedom in Christ* (Steps), which are laid out in *Discipleship Counseling*.[7] Essentially it is an encounter with God, the One who grants repentance and leads us to a knowledge of the truth that sets us free (2 Timothy 2:24-26). The Steps are being used all over the world to help believers resolve their personal and spiritual conflicts through genuine repentance and faith in God.

As children of God, we don't have just the words of Christ, we also have the very presence of His life within us. Things we learned before coming to Christ have to be unlearned through repentance and the renewing of our minds. Nobody can fix your past, but by the grace of God you can be set free from it. Only in Christ are you assured victory over your fears and anxious thoughts. He is the only One you can cast your anxieties upon and find the peace that passes all understanding (Philippians 4:6-7). Only in Christ do you have authority over the god of this world, as the following testimony (sent to the pastor who led this woman through the Steps) illustrates:

> For the past 35 years, I have lived from one surge of adrenaline to the next. My entire life has been gripped by paralyzing fears which seem to come from nowhere and everywhere—fears which made very little sense to me or anyone else. I invested four years of my life obtaining a degree in psychology, hoping it would enable me to understand and conquer those fears. Psychology only perpetuated my questions and insecurity. Six years of professional counseling offered little insight and no change in my level of anxiety.
>
> After two hospitalizations, trips to the emergency room, repeated EKGs, a visit to the thoracic surgeon, and

a battery of other tests, my panic attacks only worsened. By the time I came to see you, full-blown panic attacks had become a daily feature.

It has been three weeks since I've experienced a panic attack! I have gone to malls [and] church services. [I have] played for an entire worship service, and even made it through Sunday school with peace in my heart. I had no idea what freedom meant until now. When I came to see you, I had hoped that the Truth would set me free, but now I know it has! Friends have told me that even my voice is different, and my husband thinks I'm taller!

When you live in a constant state of anxiety, most of life passes you by because you are physically/emotionally/mentally unable to focus on anything but the fear which is swallowing you. I could barely read a verse of Scripture at one sitting. It was as though someone snatched it away from my mind as soon as it entered. Scripture was such a fog to me. I could only hear the verses which spoke of death and punishment. I had actually become afraid to open my Bible. These past weeks, I have spent hours a day in the Word, and it makes sense. The fog is gone. I am amazed at what I am able to hear, see, understand, and retain.

Before [I read your book] *The Bondage Breaker*, I could not say "Jesus Christ" without my metabolism going berserk. I could refer to "the Lord" with no ill effect, but whenever I said, "Jesus Christ," my insides went into orbit. I can now call upon the name of Jesus Christ with peace and confidence...and I do it regularly.

Research Results

There have been several exploratory studies that have shown promising results regarding the effectiveness of *The Steps to Freedom in Christ*. Judith King, a Christian therapist, did several pilot studies in 1996. All three of these studies were performed on participants who attended a Living Free in Christ conference and were led through the Steps at the conclusion of the conference.

The first study involved 30 participants, who filled out a 10-item questionnaire before completing the Steps. The questionnaire was re-administered three months after their participation. It assessed for levels of depression, anxiety, inner conflict, tormenting thoughts, and addictive behaviors. The second study involved 55 participants, who filled out a 12-item questionnaire before completing the Steps, which was then re-administered three months later. The third pilot study involved 21 participants, who also filled out a 12-item questionnaire before receiving the Steps, and then again three months afterward. The following table illustrates the *percentage of improvement* for each category.

	Pilot Study 1	Pilot Study 2	Pilot Study 3
Depression	64%	47%	52%
Anxiety	58%	44%	47%
Inner Conflict	63%	51%	48%
Tormenting Thoughts	82%	58%	57%
Addictive Behavior	52%	43%	39%

The Living Free in Christ conference is now available as a curriculum entitled *Freedom in Christ* (Bethany House, 2017). It has a leader's guide with all the messages written out, which the leaders can teach themselves; a participant's guide, which includes *The Steps to Freedom in Christ*; and a DVD with ten messages, should the leader prefer the course to be taught that way.

Research was also conducted by the board of the Ministry of Healing based in Tyler, Texas.[8] The study in Tyler was completed in cooperation with a doctoral student at Regent University under the supervision of Dr. Fernando Garzon (currently teaching at Liberty University in the psychology department). Most people participating in the *Freedom in Christ* course can work through the repentance process on their own using the Steps. In our experience, about 15% can't due to difficulties in their past. A personal session with a trained encourager was offered to the group in this study. These participants from our Oklahoma City, OK, and Tyler, TX, conferences were given a pretest before a Steps session and a posttest three months later, with the following results (given in *percentage of improvement*):

	Oklahoma City, OK	Tyler, TX
Depression	44%	52%
Anxiety	45%	44%
Fear	48%	49%
Anger	36%	55%
Tormenting Thoughts	51%	27%
Negative Habits	48%	43%
Sense of Self-Worth	52%	40%

Getting Started

The apostle Paul wrote, "The Spirit clearly says that in later times some will abandon the faith and follow deceiving spirits and things taught by demons" (1 Timothy 4:1 NIV). We can tell you from personal experience (as can all of our staff) that this is presently happening all over the world. We have helped thousands of people who are struggling with blasphemous, condemning, and deceiving thoughts that have proven to be a spiritual battle for their minds. By processing the Steps, they were able to get rid of those thoughts and experience a peaceful mind. Whether you agree or disagree with that analysis doesn't change the fact that "our struggle is not against flesh and blood, but against the rulers, against the authorities, against the powers of this dark world and against the spiritual forces of evil in the heavenly realms" (Ephesians 6:12 NIV).

We have included study questions at the end of each chapter for group discussion. One of the seven Steps will follow each of the first seven chapters. Each Step begins with a prayer asking God to grant you repentance leading to a knowledge of the truth that will set you free. We believe that God is the Wonderful Counselor and the only One who can do that for you.

If you are processing this book in a group, be assured that nobody needs to be embarrassed, and public disclosure is not required of anyone. The Steps are an encounter with God, not each other. If you have processed the Steps before, do it again. Many find the second time even more impacting, because they are more informed as to what they are doing—and often, new issues come to mind that need to be dealt with. Going through the Steps is a spiritual house cleaning that can't possibly hurt you, and preparing yourself for Communion is the least that could happen. (If you are leading a group study on this book, see Appendix A for some guidelines.) Please, for your sake, don't just read the book; do the book.

We believe that every child of God can be free from any anxiety disorder and can learn to live a liberated life in Christ. We believe there is a peace of God that surpasses all understanding and that will guard your hearts and your minds in Christ Jesus (Philippians 4:7). "The LORD your God is in your midst, a victorious warrior. He will exult over you with joy, He will be quiet in His love, He will rejoice over you with shouts of joy" (Zephaniah 3:17). As you work your way through this book, keep in mind the words of F.B. Meyer:

> God incarnate is the end of fear; and the heart that realizes
> that He is in the midst, that takes heed to the assurance of
> His loving presence, will be quiet in the midst of alarm.
> "No weapon that is formed against thee will prosper, and

every tongue that shall rise against thee in judgment Thou shalt condemn." Only be patient and be quiet.[9]

Discussion Questions

1. What is the primordial fear?
2. What is the difference between biological life and eternal life? How does an understanding of that difference affect you now?
3. How do we overcome the law of sin and death?
4. When you think of fear, what is the first thing that comes to your mind? Why?
5. When you think of anxiety, what is the first thing that comes to your mind? Why?
6. What are the three essentials of the gospel?
7. What would a holistic answer to anxiety disorders include?
8. Why is the fear of God the beginning of wisdom?
9. How do you cast all your anxieties upon Christ?
10. What do you hope to gain from this study?

Introduction to The Steps to Freedom in Christ

God created Adam and Eve in His image and in His likeness. They were physically and spiritually alive, and the latter means that their souls were in union with God. Living in a dependent relationship with their heavenly Father, they were to rule over the birds of the sky, the beasts of the fields, and the fish of the sea. They were accepted, secure, and significant.

Then, acting independently of God, they chose to disobey Him, and their choice to sin separated them from God (see Genesis 2:15–3:13). They immediately felt fearful, anxious, depressed, and insecure. Because Eve was deceived by Satan, and because Adam sinned, all their descendants are born physically alive, but spiritually dead (Ephesians 2:1). Since all have sinned (Romans 3:23), those who remain separated from God will struggle with personal and spiritual conflicts. Satan became the rebel holder of authority and the god of this world. Jesus referred to him as the ruler of this world, and the apostle John wrote that "the whole world lies in the power of the evil one" (1 John 5:19).

Jesus came to undo the works of Satan (1 John 3:8) and take upon Himself the sins of the world. By dying for our sins, Jesus removed the barrier that existed between God and those He created in His image. The resurrection of Christ brought new life to those who put their trust in Him.

Every born-again believer's soul is again in union with God, and that is most often communicated in the New Testament by saying "in Christ" or "in Him." The apostle Paul explained that anyone who is *in Christ* is a new creation (2 Corinthians 5:17). The apostle John wrote, "As many as received Him, to them He gave the right to become children of God, even to those who believe in His name" (John 1:12), and he also wrote, "See how great a love the Father has bestowed on us, that we would be called children of God; and such we are" (1 John 3:1).

No amount of effort on your part can save you, and neither can any religious activity, no matter how well intentioned. We are saved by faith, by what we choose to believe. All that remains for us to do is to put our trust in the finished work of Christ. "For by grace you have been saved through faith; and that not of yourselves, it is the gift of God; not as a result of works, so that no one may boast" (Ephesians 2:8-9). If you have never received Christ, you can do so right now. God knows the thoughts and intentions of your heart, so all you have to do is put your trust in God alone.

You can express your decision in prayer as follows:

> *Dear heavenly Father, thank You for sending Jesus to die on the cross for my sins. I acknowledge that I have sinned and that I cannot save myself. I believe that Jesus came to give me*

life, and by faith I now choose to receive You into my life as my Lord and Savior. May the power of Your indwelling presence enable me to be the person You created me to be. I pray that You would grant me repentance leading to a knowledge of the truth so that I can experience my freedom in Christ and be transformed by the renewing of my mind. In Jesus's precious name I pray. Amen.

Assurance of Salvation

Paul wrote, "If you confess with your mouth Jesus as Lord, and believe in your heart that God raised Him from the dead, you will be saved" (Romans 10:9). Do you believe that God the Father raised Jesus from the dead? Did you invite Jesus to be your Lord and Savior? Then you are a child of God, and nothing can separate you from the love of Christ (Romans 8:35). "And the testimony is this, that God has given us eternal life, and this life is in His Son. He who has the Son has the life; he who does not have the Son of God does not have the life" (1 John 5:11-12). Your heavenly Father has sent His Holy Spirit to bear witness with your spirit that you are a child of God (Romans 8:16). "You were sealed *in Him* with the Holy Spirit of promise" (Ephesians 1:13, emphasis added). The Holy Spirit will guide you into all truth (John 16:13).

Resolving Personal and Spiritual Conflict

Since we were all born dead (spiritually) in our trespasses and sin (Ephesians 2:1), we had neither the presence of God in our lives nor the knowledge of His ways. Consequently, we all learned to live independently of God. When we became new creations in Christ, our minds were not instantly renewed. That is why Paul wrote, "Do not conform to the pattern of this world, but be transformed by the renewing of your mind. Then you will be able to test and approve what God's will is—his good, pleasing and perfect will" (Romans 12:2 NIV). This is why new Christians struggle with many of the same old thoughts and

habits. Their minds have been previously programmed to live independently of God, and that is the chief characteristic of the flesh. As new
creations in Christ, we have the mind of Christ, and the Holy Spirit
will lead us into all truth.

To experience our freedom in Christ and grow in the grace of God
requires repentance, which literally means a change of mind. God will
enable that process as we submit to Him and resist the devil (James
4:7). *The Steps to Freedom in Christ* (Steps) are designed to help you
do that. Submitting to God is the critical issue. He is the Wonderful
Counselor and the One who grants repentance leading to a knowledge
of the truth (2 Timothy 2:24-26).

The Steps cover seven critical issues that affect our relationship with
God. We will not experience our freedom in Christ if we seek false
guidance, believe lies, fail to forgive others as we have been forgiven,
live in rebellion, respond in pride, fail to acknowledge our sin, and
continue in the sins of our ancestors. "He who conceals his transgres-
sions will not prosper, but he who confesses and forsakes [renounces]
them will find compassion" (Proverbs 28:13). "Therefore, since we have
this ministry, as we received mercy, we do not lose heart, but we have
renounced the things hidden because of shame, not walking in craft-
iness or adulterating the word of God, but by the manifestation of
truth commending ourselves to every man's conscience" (2 Corinthians 4:1-2).

Even though Satan is defeated, he still rules this world through a
hierarchy of demons who tempt, accuse, and deceive those who fail
to put on the armor of God, stand firm in their faith, and take "every
thought captive to the obedience of Christ" (2 Corinthians 10:5). Our
sanctuary is our identity and position in Christ, and we have all the
protection we need to live a victorious life. But if we fail to assume our
responsibility, thereby giving ground to Satan, we will suffer the consequences of our sinful attitudes and actions. The good news is, we can
repent and reclaim all that we have in Christ, and that is what the Steps
will enable you to do.

Processing the Steps

The best way to go through the Steps is to process them with a trained encourager. The book *Discipleship Counseling* explains the theology and process. However, you can also go through the Steps on your own. Every step is explained in this book, so you will have no trouble doing that. If you are in a group study, the leader will introduce each step after the discussion questions and ask you to pray the beginning prayer out loud. You will process the rest on your own.

If you experience some mental interference, just ignore it and continue on. Thoughts such as *This isn't going to work* or *I don't believe this*, or blasphemous, condemning, and accusing thoughts have no power over you unless you believe them. They are just thoughts, and it doesn't make any difference if they originate from yourself, an external source, or from Satan and his demons.

Such thoughts will be resolved when you have fully repented. The mind is the control center, and you will not lose control if you can maintain control of your mind. The best way to do that, if you are being mentally harassed, is to share it. Exposing the lies to the light breaks their power.

The apostle Paul wrote that "Satan disguises himself as an angel of light" (2 Corinthians 11:14). It is not uncommon for some to have thoughts or hear voices that seem friendly, offer companionship, or claim to be from God. They may even say that Jesus is Lord, but they cannot say that Jesus is their Lord. If there is any doubt about their origin, verbally ask God to show you the true nature of such spirit guides. You don't want any spirit other than the Holy Spirit to guide you.

Remember, you are a child of God and seated with Christ in the heavenlies (the spiritual realm; Ephesians 2:6). That means you have the authority and power to do His will. The Steps don't set you free. *Jesus* sets you free, and you will progressively experience that freedom as you respond to Him in faith and repentance. Don't worry about any demonic interference; most do not experience any. It doesn't make any difference if Satan attacks a little or a lot. The critical issue is your relationship with God, and that is what you are resolving. This is a ministry of reconciliation. Once these issues are resolved, Satan has no right to remain. Successfully completing this repentance process is not an end—it is a beginning of growth. Unless these issues are resolved, however, the growth process will be stalled, and your Christian life will be stagnant.

Breaking Mental Strongholds

On a separate piece of paper, write down any false beliefs and lies that surface during the Steps, especially those that are not true about yourself or God. When you are finished, for each exposed falsehood declare out loud: "I renounce the lie that *what you have believed,* and I announce the truth that *what you are now choosing to believe is true based on God's Word.*" It may be best to have the encourager keep this list for you if you are being led by another through the Steps. It is strongly recommended that you repeat the process of renouncing lies and choosing truth for 40 days, since you are "transformed by the renewing of your mind" (Romans 12:2), and it is very easy to defer to old flesh patterns when tempted.

Preparation

Processing the Steps presented in this book will play a major role in your journey of becoming more and more like Jesus so that you can be a fruitful disciple. The purpose is to become firmly rooted in Christ. It doesn't take long to establish your identity and freedom in Christ, but there is no such thing as instant maturity. Renewing your mind and conforming to the image of God is a lifelong process. May God grace you with His presence as you seek to do His will. Once you have experienced freedom in Christ, you can help others discover the joy of their salvation.

You are now ready to begin the Steps by saying the prayer and declaration below.

Prayer

Dear heavenly Father, You are present in this room and in my life. You alone are all-knowing, all-powerful, and present everywhere, and I worship You alone. I declare my dependency upon You, for apart from You I can do nothing. I choose to believe Your Word, which teaches that all authority in heaven and on earth belongs to the resurrected Christ. And being alive in Christ, I have the authority to resist the devil as I submit to You. I ask that You fill me with Your Holy Spirit and guide me into all truth. I ask for Your complete protection and guidance as I seek to know You and do Your will. In the wonderful name of Jesus, I pray. Amen.

Declaration

In the name and authority of the Lord Jesus Christ, I command Satan and all evil spirits to release their hold on me in order that I can be free to know and do the will of God. As a child of God who is seated with Christ in the heavenly places, I declare that every enemy of the Lord Jesus Christ in my presence be bound. God has not given me a spirit of fear; therefore, I reject any and all condemning, accusing, blasphemous, and deceiving spirits of fear. Satan and all his demons cannot inflict any pain or in any way prevent God's will from being done in my life today, because I belong to the Lord Jesus Christ.

Chapter One

Restoring the Foundation

Everyone who hears these words of Mine and acts on them, may be compared to a wise man who built his house on the rock. And the rain fell, and the floods came, and the winds blew and slammed against that house; and yet it did not fall, for it had been founded on the rock. Everyone who hears these words of Mine and does not act on them, will be like a foolish man who built his house on the sand. The rain fell, and the floods came, and the winds blew and slammed against that house; and it fell—and great was its fall.

Jesus, Matthew 7:24-27

In reality, the foundation upon which every one of us has built our lives is a mixture of truth, half truths, and outright lies. Adam and Eve were formed by God and placed in a perfect environment. The only fear object they had was God. The rest of humanity started out as "strangers and aliens" in a fallen world (Ephesians 2:19). We weren't children of God; we were children of flesh and blood. We had no prior knowledge of God and His ways, so we naturally conformed to this world, relying on our own strength and resources. We learned to fear many things, but had no fear of God. The apostle Paul describes the nature of the natural person in Ephesians 2:1-3:

> You were dead in your trespasses and sins, in which you formerly walked according to the course of this world, according to the prince of the power of the air, of the spirit that is now working in the sons of disobedience. Among them we too all formerly lived in the lusts of our flesh, indulging the desires of the flesh and of the mind, and were by nature children of wrath, even as the rest.

Introducing a person to Christ is not helping a bad person become a better person. It is helping a spiritually dead person become one who is alive in Christ. That person was alienated from God and is now united with Him.

Believers are no longer "in Adam"; we are now "in Christ" (1 Corinthians 15:22; see also Romans 8:9). God "rescued us from the domain of darkness, and transferred us to the kingdom of His beloved Son" (Colossians 1:13). "Therefore if anyone is in Christ, he is a new creature; the old things passed away; behold, new things have come" (2 Corinthians 5:17). "As many as received Him, to them He gave the right to become children of God" (John 1:12). "So then you are no longer strangers and aliens, but you are fellow citizens with the saints, and are of God's household, having been built on the foundation of the apostles and prophets, Christ Jesus Himself being the corner stone" (Ephesians 2:19-20).

If all that is true, then why do born-again believers often struggle with the same old fears and anxieties?

Everything we learned while being conformed to this world is still programmed into our minds. Unfortunately, there is no delete button, which is why Paul wrote, "Do not conform to the pattern of this world, but be transformed by the renewing of your mind. Then you will be able to test and approve what God's will is—his good, pleasing and perfect will" (Romans 12:2 NIV). Paul implies that after conversion we can continue being conformed to this world. We can fill our minds with the same old media, believe the same old lies, and live according to our old nature (the flesh). But Peter also advises otherwise: "As obedient children, do not be conformed to the former lusts which were yours in your ignorance" (1 Peter 1:14).

Stages of Human Development

How we conform to this world is different for every person. We are all shaped by our environment, and every child responds differently to it. We naturally learn the language of our parents and adopt most of their attitudes, which are more "caught" than "taught." How we personally interpret the events of life lays the foundation for specific fears and anxieties. As an illustration, consider the following testimony we received at our office. As you read it, ask yourself these questions: How did this person get this way? What did she learn at an early age? What events shaped her life?

> I have literally lived with crippling, chronic fear all of my life. When I was about seven years old, I had an experience in grade school that started my panic disorder. I was feeling very sick one day, and the teacher would not let me go home. I wanted to go very badly, but I felt trapped and experienced my first panic [attack].
>
> From there on it became a constant cycle. The feelings as a young girl that I felt that day were so scary that I spent the rest of my childhood and teenage years doing everything I could to avoid them. It got so bad that I actually quit school in ninth grade and was tutored at home. Then, at about age 14, I committed myself to a children's home for intense in-house therapy. It was either that or end my life.
>
> It was extremely hard to live there, but it did break the fear cycle because they forced me to push through the fear to attend classes.
>
> But when I returned home, it all gradually came back. I lived in my bedroom, which was my safe place. But

> eventually I started waking up in the middle of the night with terrible, gut-wrenching panic [attacks]. It was awful, and my parents had no clue as to what was wrong with me.
>
> I spent years visiting doctors and different specialists, to no avail. All my fear and panic stayed inside. I could be in a "number 10" panic, and most everyone around me would not even know. I think I felt such shame because of it. I didn't want anyone to know that I was sick. It put so much stress on my family, and I hated being the problem.

Notice that she felt fear and anxiety for as long as she could remember. She also had a traumatic event that began a panic disorder, which precipitated a social anxiety disorder. Anxiety disorders—and even minor struggles with anxiety and fear—are a product of our learning experiences and growth process.

Let's analyze this process through the grid of Erik Erikson's psychosocial theory of development.[1] Although it is a secular theory that has been around for many years, it has proven to be helpful in understanding how a person "naturally" develops and the hurdles that must be overcome in order to continue growing to maturity. We will add Christian interventions that should happen for those raised in a Christian home.

Erikson says there are basic stages of human development. Each stage has a particular "crisis" associated with it. If that crisis is not faced successfully, the growth process is impeded, giving way to certain fears and anxieties. He observed the following eight stages after studying various cultural groups around the world:

Stage	Age	Psychosocial Crisis
1	Infancy (0 to 1½)	Trust vs. mistrust
2	Early childhood (1½ to 3)	Autonomy vs. shame, doubt

3	Play age (3 to 5)	Initiative vs. guilt
4	School age (5 to 12)	Industry vs. inferiority
5	Adolescence (12 to 18)	Identity vs. confusion
6	Young adulthood (18 to 25)	Intimacy vs. isolation
7	Adulthood (25 to 65)	Generativity vs. self-absorption or stagnation
8	Maturity (65+)	Integrity vs. despair

Infancy

Infants learn trust when parents provide the physical care and emotional nurture they need. Bonding is enhanced through breast feeding and loving human contact. Babies who are neglected in orphanages often fail to develop, and some actually die. If neglect or abuse takes place, the child may never overcome the fear of abandonment. That sets the stage for a lifestyle of mistrust, fear, and suspicion of others, including God. Common fears at this age are the fears of falling, loud noises, strange objects, and people other than their parents. Such fears peak before age two and then generally decline.[2]

What is neglected by the secular world is the spiritual significance of baby dedication or infant baptism, depending on your church doctrine. Parents should assume spiritual authority over the child, commit them to the Lord, and renounce any spiritual claim of ownership by Satan. Jesus's family set the example in Luke 2:22: "When the days for their purification according to the law of Moses were completed, they brought Him [Jesus] up to Jerusalem to present Him to the Lord."

Early Childhood

In early childhood (the toddler years), children learn by exploring their world. They get into every drawer and cupboard. They become overwhelmed by things bigger than them, including dogs and cats. Two-year-olds want to know if they are loved and if they can have their own way. Consistent discipline is a proof of our love that should answer the second question with a firm *no*, or there will be difficult teenage years ahead. Deep-seated insecurities can form in children who are not loved and protected at this stage.

Spiritual protection of our children is overlooked by secular theories. We have counseled a number of parents who have children experiencing nightmares and spiritual visitations as early as two years old. We received a glowing testimony of a mother set free from her own horrible childhood by going through *The Steps to Freedom in Christ*. She concluded by writing: "By the way, my four-year-old was heard growling in her closet. I led her through the prayers, and she is free. We have talked at great length about who she is in Christ and all that Satan is not. Sometimes I hear her in her room, saying, 'I belong to Jesus and you have to leave me alone.' She's not having problems anymore either."

Play Age

Play age is a time when children become creative. They color, paint, build things with blocks, and create games with animals and dolls. If creativity is squelched by confinement, ridicule, or lack of opportunity, children can develop a sense of personal guilt ("I have done something wrong") and shame ("There is something wrong with me"). Shaming a child is an attack upon their character. If they become convinced that they are a bad person, they will take less risks, reveal less of themselves for fear of rejection, and will likely become emotionally inhibited. Fear of the dark, monsters, and injury can plague children of this age. Nightmares are more frequent than with toddlers.[3]

Children at this age often have imaginary friends. You don't want to stifle their creativity, but a spiritually discerning parent needs to find out if that imaginary friend is talking back to the child, in which case the "friend" is not imaginary—and definitely not a friend.

One summer I (Rich) was teaching at a Bible conference in western Pennsylvania. All five members of our family were sleeping in the same room in an old house on the conference grounds. One evening, as we were preparing to turn out the lights, our six-year-old daughter announced, "Daddy, I have an imaginary friend! Her name is Becca, and she is an orphan girl who lives in the house. She wants to come home and live in our house."

Knowing how the enemy operates, I was instantly "on alert." I prayed and asked God how best to deal with this situation. "Honey," I began, "sometimes a bad angel puts on a costume and pretends to be something it isn't. Becca is not a little orphan girl. He is a demon, and you have to tell it to go away, that it cannot be your friend and certainly is not welcome in our home." I was a little angry!

Fortunately, Michelle understood what I was talking about and did what I urged her to do. Becca never showed up again. What if my wife, Shirley, and I had said to Michelle, "Isn't that sweet, honey? Becca sounds cute." The very course of Michelle's life could have been altered at that moment.

A music director who attended our conference once asked about his four-year-old son. For the previous three months the child was terrorized every night and would come into the parents' room, saying, "There is something in my room." Of course they looked in the room and saw nothing. So they told the child to go back to bed. But if you saw something in your room at night, would you go back to sleep? It never dawned on them that their child was being harassed by the enemy. Thankfully, the situation was resolved and the child slept peacefully from then on. What would that child believe henceforth if there had been no resolution, and how would he deal with that fear? We will share more about the schemes of the devil in chapter 6.

School Age

School age (elementary) children are prime for discovering and developing the talents and abilities God has given them. Children at this age learn to play sports or musical instruments. They enjoy energetic accomplishment and competition. They may develop a keen interest in art and want to take lessons. If children lack opportunity or encouragement to explore and enjoy life academically, artistically, or athletically, a sense of inferiority can develop. Children can feel like losers and struggle with a fear of failure.

It is always appropriate to encourage children to explore, enjoy healthy activities, and develop their God-given talents. However, an overemphasis on excelling in these areas can set them up for identity problems in adolescence. If they only receive positive affirmation for "performing" in an activity, they get the message that their value comes from what they do and not in who they are. Building up a child's character should be preeminent, or the child could end up becoming an insecure and shallow athlete or artist who is able to perform, but is riddled with insecurity.

Adolescence

An identity crisis surfaces in early adolescence. Identity confusion often takes place before identity achievement.[4] In other words, the young person may vacillate from one role to another (for example, from athlete to clown to serious student to party animal and back again) for a number of years before settling the issue. The aggravating thing for parents is that adolescents are adept at playing the chameleon, switching roles to meet the expectations of those they are around. How they act at home or church may be very different from how they behave in school. The greatest anxiety of adolescence is the fear of rejection by peers. The failure to establish a firm foundation of who they are is the origin of many social anxiety disorders.

Early adolescence has been referred to as the "age of accountability." Ideally, these young people are transitioning from being children of flesh and blood to being children of God. Studies on cognitive development have shown that a twelve-year-old has matured enough physically to think like an adult. They are fully capable of understanding who they are in Christ and what it means to be a child of God. Recall that Jesus was twelve when He wandered away from His parents, went into the temple, and amazed the teachers with His understanding (Luke

2:42-47). Mary said, "Your father and I have been anxiously looking for You" (verse 48). To which Jesus replied, "Why is it that you were looking for Me? Did you not know that I had to be in My Father's house?" (verse 49). Catholic, Orthodox, and some Protestant churches have confirmation around the age of twelve. In Judaism, children have their *bar* or *bas mitzvah* on their thirteenth birthday.

After years of helping Christians all over the world resolve their personal and spiritual conflicts, we noticed that every struggling adult Christian had one thing in common. None of them knew who they were in Christ, nor understood what it means to be a child of God. If "the Spirit Himself testifies with our spirit that we are children of God" (Romans 8:16), why weren't they sensing that? When inner conflicts are resolved through genuine repentance and faith in God, Christians do become aware of God's presence, and most experience a peace they have never known before. How many anxiety disorders could be averted if we helped early teens connect with God in a liberating way? They should be able to say with confidence:

In Christ...

I Am Accepted

John 1:12	I am God's child.
John 15:15	I am Jesus's chosen friend.
Romans 5:1	I have been justified (forgiven) and have peace with God.
1 Corinthians 6:17	I am united with the Lord and one with Him in spirit.
1 Corinthians 6:20	I have been bought with a price—I belong to God.
1 Corinthians 12:27	I am a member of Christ's body, part of His family.
Ephesians 1:1	I am a saint.

Ephesians 1:5	I have been adopted as God's child.
Ephesians 2:18	I have direct access to God through the Holy Spirit.
Colossians 1:14	I have been redeemed and forgiven of all my sins.
Colossians 2:10	I am complete in Christ.

I Am Secure

Romans 8:1-2	I am free from condemnation.
Romans 8:28	I am assured that all things work together for good.
Romans 8:31	I am free from any condemning charges against me.
Romans 8:35	I cannot be separated from the love of God.
2 Corinthians 1:21-22	I have been established, anointed, and sealed by God.
Philippians 1:6	I am assured that the good work God has begun in me will be finished.
Philippians 3:20	I am a citizen of heaven.
Colossians 3:3	I am hidden with Christ in God.
2 Timothy 1:7	I have not been given a spirit of fear, but of power, love, and a sound mind.
Hebrews 4:16	I can find grace and mercy in time of need.
1 John 5:18	I am born of God, and the evil one cannot touch me.

I Am Significant

Matthew 5:13-14	I am the salt and light of the world.
John 15:5	I am joined to Christ and able to bear fruit.
John 15:16	I have been chosen by Jesus to bear fruit.
Acts 1:8	I am a personal witness of Christ's.
1 Corinthians 3:16	I am a temple of God, where the Holy Spirit dwells.
2 Corinthians 5:17-18	I am at peace with God, and He has given me the work of making peace between Himself and other people. I am a minister of reconciliation.
2 Corinthians 6:1	I am God's coworker.
Ephesians 2:6	I am seated with Christ in the heavenlies.
Ephesians 2:10	I am God's workmanship.
Ephesians 3:11-12	I may approach God with freedom and confidence.
Philippians 4:13	I can do all things through Christ who strengthens me.

Young Adulthood

Knowing the unconditional love and acceptance of God paves the way for young adults to develop intimate personal relationships. When they're aware that they are forgiven, they can walk in the light and have fellowship with one another (1 John 1:7). Such fellowship can be defined as the ability to relate to another person's deepest hopes, needs, and fears, while being vulnerable in return.[5]

Adulthood

Adulthood should be a time of productivity and fulfillment, and it likely will be if the right foundation has been laid. The house begins to crumble with age if the foundation is faulty. Unresolved issues from the past can keep piling up—and so can the medical bills, leading many to a midlife crisis. Obesity, alcoholism, and the use of opioids is pandemic due to an increase in anxiety disorders and depression.

Maturity

Finally, a person's years of maturity ought to be filled with a deep experience of joy from a life invested in the kingdom of God. This sense of contentment comes from the realization that they have paved the way for the next generation, sharing the wisdom of a life well lived.[6]

For too many senior citizens, however, there is a deep bitterness of soul, a disgust of self, and despair over life, according to Erikson. A sense of uselessness, meaninglessness, and fear of death can turn the twilight years into a nightmare. In other words, they "walked after emptiness and became empty" (Jeremiah 2:5).

Though the eight stages of development can overlap and vary in length of time, their sequence is fixed.[7] The crisis stages of mistrust, shame, guilt, inferiority, confusion, isolation, self-absorption, and despair reveal a faulty foundation, which can be rebuilt in Christ if we are willing to humble ourselves, repent, and believe the gospel.

Although we are most vulnerable to certain fears and anxieties at various stages of life, anxiety disorders can develop at almost any age. For example, the fear of abandonment could have its onset in the life of an adult or senior citizen due to a painful divorce or neglect by grown children. The fear of rejection by others could happen in middle age as the result of humiliation before fellow employees and termination from a job. Traumatic experiences occur at any age and can send even well-adjusted individuals into a tailspin of fear and anxiety.

Defining Phobias

There are three categories of controlling, irrational fears: specific phobias, social phobias, and agoraphobia.[8] As the name implies, *specific phobias* are irrational fears of specific situations or objects, such as people, snakes, spiders, heights, enclosed places, etc.

Social phobias involve the fear of being watched, embarrassed, humiliated, rejected, or scorned while doing something in the presence of other people. A common example of this type of phobia is the fear of public speaking. This type of fear would also apply to the Christian who is afraid to share his or her testimony, or to witness to an unbeliever. Other examples would include the fear of eating in public, using public restrooms, and meeting new people.

The typical means of coping with social phobias is called "phobic avoidance," the attempt to eliminate threatening circumstances from one's lifestyle. This obviously poses real problems if the individual is afraid to go to work or school. School phobia is a problem for some children who are unwilling to leave the security of home/parents and take the risk of coping with the perceived threatening environment of school.

Agoraphobia is when a person is afraid to be alone or in a situation in which help or escape would be difficult to find.

In the testimony shared earlier in this chapter, the woman evidenced a serious case of phobic avoidance by eventually quitting school and being tutored at home. She was suffering from social phobia. She had been so frightened and humiliated by her teacher that she established a pattern of doing everything she could to avoid that kind of pain again. It became so severe that she "lived in [her] bedroom." Although her testimony doesn't say this, it is likely that she became agoraphobic after the onset of her panic attacks. At any rate, fear was the controlling mechanism in her life.

Beyond Cognitive Behavioral Therapy

Since faulty and traumatic learning experiences are the basis for anxiety disorders, it would only logically follow that what has been learned has to be unlearned. Irrational thinking has to be replaced with rational thinking. Lies have to be replaced with truth. A crumbling foundation has to be rebuilt. Secular theorists are aware of this, and seek to rebuild people's foundations by helping them get in touch with reality and think rationally. The most common intervention is cognitive behavioral therapy (CBT).

CBT is based on the premise that people are feeling what they are feeling and doing what they are doing because of what they have chosen to believe. Therefore, if you want to help people change how they feel and behave, you need to help them change what they believe. We basically agree with that premise, because that is the central theme of repentance. (Repentance literally means a change of mind.) But CBT is not enough by itself for three critical reasons.

First, "natural people" can change how they feel and how they behave by how they think or what they believe, but that doesn't change who they are. The problem is, "a natural man does not accept the things of the Spirit of God, for they are foolishness to him" (1 Corinthians 2:14). Paul warns us to "walk no longer just as the Gentiles also walk, in the futility of their mind, being darkened in their understanding, excluded from the life of God" (Ephesians 4:17-18). If you want the truth to set you free, you have to know *who* the Truth is, not just *what* it is. Even a Christian therapist applying CBT with the words of Christ but without the life of Christ will not be lastingly effective.

Emotions are essentially a product of your thoughts, and every behavior is a product of what you have chosen to believe, because every action is preceded by a thought. You don't do anything without first thinking it. The thought process may be so rapid that you are barely aware of it. "For as he thinks within himself, so he is" (Proverbs 23:7). The mind is the control center, and you are transformed by renewing it. People don't always live according to what they profess, but they all live according to what they have chosen to believe. James says, "I will show you my faith by my works" (2:18).

Second, we are not the Wonderful Counselor. We can't set a captive free, nor can we heal the wounds of the broken-hearted. Only God can do that. The presence of God is the basis for Neil's book *Discipleship Counseling* (Bethany House, 2003). God is the one who "may grant them repentance leading to the knowledge of the truth, and they may come to their senses and escape from the snare of the devil, having been held captive by him to do his will" (2 Timothy 2:25-26). The Holy Spirit can lead people into all truth. Nothing will be complete or lasting if God isn't an integral part of the process. Rebuilding the foundation with better sand won't help a house last against the storms of life. The house has to be built upon the rock.

Third, no use of CBT will be complete or effective if we ignore the reality of the spiritual world. Irrational fears are rooted in lies, and Satan is the father of lies (John 8:44). If you are paying attention to a deceiving spirit, you are believing a lie. Tearing down mental strongholds is a spiritual battle. "For though we live in the world, we do not wage war as the world does. The weapons we fight with are not the weapons of the world. On the contrary, they have divine power to demolish strongholds. We demolish arguments and every pretension that sets itself up against the knowledge of God, and we take captive every thought to make it obedient to Christ" (2 Corinthians 10:3-5 NIV).

The testimony shared earlier in this chapter has a second half that illustrates the spiritual battle for the mind:

> I was not raised to know God. I searched for Him when I was 14, when I felt that I could not take it another minute. But I had no one to whom I could go. I tried praying to Him to help me, but felt that He was so far away. If He created me, I couldn't understand how He could allow me to live in such misery.
>
> From then on, I felt anger and bitterness toward Him. I chose not to seek Him.
>
> I eventually got married and, of course, my crippling fear did not get any better. It changed a lot as I got older,

probably because I had to learn how to fake it even better. I hated when friends would want to camp out for an evening because I still couldn't do it. But I would pretend. I would tell them, "Sure, what time and where?" But then the panic would set in and I would scramble for excuses to get out of it.

My sister was a Christian and was committed to praying for me. She prayed for 12 long years, never giving up. Praise God! I finally called her in the middle of the night after an evening of misery, feeling again that I could not take living inside this jail anymore. There was a world outside of me that I could never really touch or feel, and it killed me.

I wanted life so badly. And I wanted to be free, so I called her in tears and asked her how to find this Jesus she kept telling me about. She prayed with me on the phone, and I spent the rest of the night reading scriptures she had given me. They all referred to freedom in one way or another.

Freedom! I felt such hope. That started my journey of renewal. I spent all those years in such crippling fear, fear of fear. It was not knowing that scared me so bad. I learned about what physically happens when we fear something. I continued learning about anxiety and fear and what they can do. Understanding these things was what really set me on the road to peace.

I live today with chronic irritable bowel syndrome because of all the years of hiding in panic. My nerves are pretty shot inside. But my head and my spirit are at peace. I still struggle with going on long vacations. The old tapes still try to run in my head, but I override them with the truth. The truth being that Jesus is with me all the time, and I have nothing to fear.

Indeed, "I can do all things through Christ who

strengthens me" [Philippians 4:13 NKJV]. I found that verse when I first became a Christian, and I still rely on it today. Praise God!

Processing *The Steps to Freedom in Christ* enables you to bond with God, your heavenly Father. It removes the guilt and shame and establishes your identity in Christ. No one is inferior or superior to one another in the family of God. All the psychosocial crises are overcome in Christ. When personal and spiritual conflicts are resolved, you will be able to face the fears and anxieties that cripple so many people.

Discussion Questions

1. Why is the faith foundation for us so different from the faith foundation that Adam and Eve had?

2. If we are new creations in Christ, why do we still struggle with the same old fears and anxieties? How can we change that?

3. What stood out most to you in the stages of development?

4. When did you discover who you are in Christ?

5. What are the three main categories of phobias?

6. What is cognitive behavioral therapy (CBT), and in what way(s) is it compatible with Christianity?

7. Explain the three issues that separate the secular use of CBT from the Christian application of CBT:

a. _____

b. _____

c. _____

The Steps to Freedom in Christ

Counterfeit versus Real

The first step toward experiencing your freedom in Christ is to renounce (verbally reject) all involvement (past or present) with occult, cult, or false religious teachings or practices. Participation in any group that denies that Jesus Christ is Lord and/or elevates any teaching or book to the level of (or above) the Bible must be renounced. In addition, groups that require dark, secret initiations, ceremonies, vows, pacts, or covenants need to be renounced. God does not take lightly false guidance. "As for the person who turns to mediums and to spiritists, to play the harlot after them, I will also set My face against that person and will cut him off from among his people" (Leviticus 20:6). Ask God to guide you as follows:

> *Dear heavenly Father, please bring to my mind anything and everything that I have done knowingly or unknowingly that involves occult, cult, or false religious teachings and practices. Grant me the wisdom and grace to renounce any and all spiritual counterfeits, false religious teachings, and practices. In Jesus's name I pray. Amen.*

The Lord may bring events to your mind that you have forgotten, even experiences you participated in as a game or thought was a joke. The purpose is to renounce all counterfeit spiritual experiences and beliefs that God brings to your mind. Begin this Step by processing the following ten questions:

1. Do you now have, or have you ever had, an imaginary friend, spirit guide, or "angel" offering you guidance or companionship? If it has a name, renounce it by name. **I renounce...**

2. Have you ever seen or been contacted by beings you

thought were aliens from another world? Such deceptions should be identified and renounced. **I renounce...**

3. Have you ever heard voices in your head or had repeating, nagging thoughts such as "I'm dumb," "I'm ugly," "Nobody loves me," "I can't do anything right"—as if there were a conversation going on inside your head? If so, renounce all deceiving spirits and the lies that you have believed. **I renounce...**

4. Have you ever been hypnotized, attended a New Age seminar, or consulted a psychic, medium/channeler, or spiritist? Renounce all specific false prophecies and guidance they offered. **I renounce...**

5. Have you ever made a secret covenant or vow to any organization or persons other than God, or made an inner vow contrary to Scripture, such as "I will never..."? Renounce all such vows. **I renounce...**

6. Have you ever been involved in a satanic ritual or attended a concert in which Satan was the focus? Renounce Satan and all his works and ways. **I renounce...**

7. Have you ever made any sacrifices to idols, false gods, or spirits? Renounce each one. **I renounce...**

8. Have you ever attended any counterfeit religious event or entered a non-Christian shrine that required you to participate in their religious observances, such as washing your hands or removing your shoes? Confess and renounce your participation in false worship. **I confess and renounce...**

9. Have you ever consulted a shaman or witch doctor for the purpose of manipulating the spiritual world to place curses or seek psychic healing or guidance? All such activity needs to be renounced. **I renounce...**

10. Have you ever tried to contact the dead in order to send or receive messages? Renounce such practices. **I renounce…**

Continue this Step using the following *Non-Christian Spiritual Experience Inventory* as a guide. Then pray the prayer following the checklist to renounce each activity or group the Lord brings to mind. He may reveal to you counterfeit spiritual experiences that are not on the list. Be especially aware of your need to renounce non-Christian religious practices that were part of your culture growing up. Prayerfully renounce them *out loud* if you are working through these Steps on your own.

Non-Christian Spiritual Experience Inventory

Check all that you have participated in.

___ Wicca

___ Ouija board

___ Bloody Mary

___ Charlie Charlie

___ Channeling/chakras

___ Magic eight ball

___ Table or body lifting

___ Spells and curses

___ Freemasonry

___ Tarot cards

___ Automatic writing

___ Astrology/horoscopes

___ Palm reading

___ Silva mind control

___ Out-of-body experiences

___ Black and white magic/the Gathering

___ Paganism

___ Reiki

___ Occult games such as "light as a feather"

___ Reincarnation/previous life healing

___ Mediums and channelers

___ Mormonism

___ Mental telepathy/mind control

___ Christian Science

___ Church of Scientology

___ Nature worship (Mother Earth)

___ Unitarianism/universalism

___ Hinduism/transcendental/ Yoga meditation

__ Blood pacts   __ Fortune telling/divination

__ Sexual spirits   __ Buddhism (including Zen)

__ Séances and circles   __ Islam

__ Trances   __ Witchcraft/sorcery

__ Spirit guides   __ Bahaism

__ Clairvoyance   __ Spiritism/animism/folk religions

__ Ancestor worship   __ Rod and pendulum (dowsing)

__ Hypnosis   __ Jehovah's Witness

__ Satanism

Once you have completed your checklist, confess and renounce every false religious practice, belief, ceremony, vow, or pact that you were involved in by praying the following prayer aloud. Take your time and be thorough. Give God time to remind you of every specific incident, ritual, etc. as needed.

> *Dear heavenly Father, I confess that I have participated in specifically name every belief and involvement with all that you have checked above, and I renounce them all as counterfeits. I pray that You will fill me with Your Holy Spirit, that I may be guided by You. Thank You that in Christ I am forgiven. Amen.*

Chapter Two

Fortress of Fear

The adventurous life is not one exempt from fear, but on
the contrary, one that is lived in full knowledge of fears of
all kinds, one in which we go forward in spite of our fears.

Paul Tournier

An irrational fear is a thief. It erodes our faith, plunders our hope,
steals our freedom, and takes away our joy of living the abundant
life in Christ. Phobias are like the coils of a snake—the more we give
in to them, the tighter they squeeze. Tired of fighting, we succumb to
the temptation and surrender to our fears. But what seemed like an
easy way out becomes, in reality, a prison of unbelief—a fortress of fear
that holds us captive.

Fear is the most basic instinct of every living creature. An animal
without fear will likely be some predator's dinner. Fear is the natural
response when our physical safety and psychological well-being are
threatened. Rational fears are learned and vital for our survival. For
instance, falling off a chair at an early age develops a healthy respect for
heights. Phobias, on the other hand, are irrational fears that compel
us to do irresponsible things or inhibit us from doing what we should.

Fear is different from anxiety and panic attacks, because fear has
an object. Specific fears are categorized by their objects. Following are
some examples:

acrophobia	fear of high places
agoraphobia	fear of marketplaces or being in public
claustrophobia	fear of enclosed places
gephyrophobia	fear of crossing bridges
hematophobia	fear of blood
monophobia	fear of being alone
pathophobia	fear of disease
toxiphobia	fear of being poisoned
xenophobia	fear of strangers
zoophobia	fear of animals

In order for a fear object to be legitimate, it must possess two attributes: It must be perceived as imminent (present) and potent (powerful). Those who struggle with claustrophobia don't sense any fear until they are actually confronted with the possibility of being in a confined place. Just the thought of such a possibility causes some to shudder. The womb is an enclosed place, so it is safe to assume that a newborn infant doesn't have claustrophobia. Somehow, the fear of being confined is learned (as are most fears). Consequently, it can be unlearned.

Fear is based on perception. A United States customs official saw a colorful, small snake on the Arizona border. He fearlessly picked it up and deposited his trophy in a jar. Later he learned that it was a coral snake, which looks harmless, but is one of the most venomous snakes in the Western world. He became flushed with fear when so enlightened. Even though the fear object wasn't present, the memory of picking it up made him react as though it were.

Most of us have been educated to believe that poisonous snakes are legitimate fear objects. As you read this sentence, you probably sense no fear of venomous rattlesnakes, because there are none present (the threat is potent, but not imminent). But what if someone threw a rattlesnake into your room, and it landed at your feet (imminent and potent)? You would probably be terror-stricken. Now suppose a dead snake is thrown at your feet (imminent, but not potent). You wouldn't sense any fear—provided you were sure it was dead. The fear object is no longer legitimate when one of these two attributes is removed.

Most phobias are subcategories of fearing death, people, and Satan. For instance, snakes, sharks, and spiders would be less frightening if you had no fear of dying. But God has removed one of the essential attributes of the big three fears. The reality of physical death is always imminent, but the power of death has been broken. Paul teaches that the resurrection of Christ has rendered physical death no longer potent: "Death is swallowed up in victory. O death, where is your victory? O death, where is your sting?" (1 Corinthians 15:54-55). Jesus said, "I am the resurrection and the life; he who believes in Me will live even if he dies, and everyone who lives and believes in Me will never die" (John 11:25-26). In other words, those who have been born again spiritually will remain spiritually alive when they die physically. Paul could say with confidence—as can every born-again believer—"To me, to live is Christ and to die is gain" (Philippians 1:21). The person who is free from the fear of death is free to live today.

The phobias rooted in the fear of man include rejection, failure, abandonment, and even physical death. Jesus said, "Do not fear those who kill the body but are unable to kill the soul; but rather fear Him who is able to destroy both soul and body in hell" (Matthew 10:28). Peter said, "Do not fear their intimidation, and do not be troubled, but sanctify Christ as Lord in your hearts, always being ready to make a defense to everyone who asks you to give an account for the hope that is in you, yet with gentleness and reverence" (1 Peter 3:14-15). The number one reason Christians don't share their faith is the fear of "man" or, more specifically, the fear of rejection and failure. You don't fear any men or women when they are not present, so the remaining question is: What power do they have over you?

Both the Matthew and 1 Peter passages teach that it is God whom we should fear. Two of God's attributes make Him the ultimate fear object in our lives: He is omnipresent (always present) and omnipotent (all powerful). To worship God is to ascribe to Him His divine attributes. We do this to keep fresh in our minds that our loving heavenly Father is always with us and more powerful than any enemy.

The fear of God dispels all other fears, because God rules supreme over every other fear object—including Satan. Even though "your adversary, the devil, prowls around like a roaring lion, seeking someone to devour" (1 Peter 5:8), he has been defeated (he is imminent, but not potent). Jesus came for the very purpose of destroying the works of the devil (1 John 3:8). "When He had disarmed the rulers and authorities, He made a public display of them, having triumphed over them through Him" (Colossians 2:15).

We have been conditioned by our culture to be fearful of people and of "things that go bump in the night," but we have no fear of God. The scary movies of our childhood featured King Kong, Godzilla, and the Blob, along with the typical parade of psychopathic killers, jealous lovers, criminals, and macho men. Then the cultural tide shifted to the occult and alien abductions. In the popular film *The Exorcist*, the poor priest was no match for the demonized girl. What a tragic contradiction to Scripture! Most Christians fear Satan more than they fear God, which elevates Satan as a greater object of worship. Persons and objects are worshiped when their perceived power and value are elevated above ourselves. Only God should have that prominence in our lives. We are called to worship and fear God. Fear of any object or personality more than God and faith in God are mutually exclusive. The Bible says, "The fear of the LORD is the beginning of wisdom" (Proverbs 9:10). Notice the ancient wisdom recorded in Isaiah 8:12-14:

> You are not to say, "It is a conspiracy!" in regard to all that this people call a conspiracy, and you are not to fear what they fear or be in dread of it. It is the LORD of hosts whom you should regard as holy. And He shall be your fear, and He shall be your dread. Then He shall become a sanctuary.

Anxiety

Anxiety is different from fear in that it lacks an object or adequate cause. People are anxious because they are uncertain about a specific outcome, or they don't know what is going to happen tomorrow. It is perfectly normal to be concerned about those things that we value, which is why we need to distinguish between temporary anxiety and an anxious trait that persists.

A temporary state of anxiety exists when concern is shown before a specific event. One can be anxious about an examination that is yet to be taken, or the attendance at a planned function, or the threat of an oncoming storm. Such concern is normal and should move a person to pray and pursue responsible action.

A generalized anxiety disorder (GAD) is an anxious trait over an extended period of time. To be diagnosed as having this disorder, the obsessive worrying must occur more days than not for at least a six-month period. Those who struggle with GAD experience persistent anxiety and worry. They fret over two or more stressful life circumstances, such as finances, relationships, health, or ability to perform. Usually they struggle with a large number of worries and spend a lot of time and energy doing it. The intensity and frequency of the worrying is always out of proportion to the actual problem. The worrying is usually more detrimental than the negative consequences that initially concerned the people. Such anxious thinking does not protect anyone from tomorrow's sorrow. It only drains people of today's peace and joy.

Someone once said that every decision made is an attempt to reduce further anxiety. People don't like to live in an anxious state and will do almost anything to relieve it. Some adopt driven lifestyles because their minds are never at peace. Sitting silently by themselves is agonizing. Keeping busy may temporarily focus the mind, but it doesn't resolve the problem. It may actually contribute to it and create other problems, including burnout. Others dull their anxious minds with tranquilizers, alcohol, drugs, or food. Marketing temporary cures for anxiety may be the most lucrative business in America, but these cures offer only temporary escapes. Peter admonishes us to cast all our anxieties on Christ—the ultimate cure—because He cares for us (1 Peter 5:7). Anxiety will be explained in more depth in chapter 10.

Panic Attacks

Unlike fear and anxiety, one has to stretch their imagination to find anything good about panicking. It does indicate something is wrong physically, spiritually, or psychologically. Some people experience panic attacks when they become physically and emotionally aware of the symptoms of hypothyroidism, hypoglycemia, heart palpitations, or other physical abnormalities. Even though these problems may feel like it at first, they are typically not life threatening. Once these people receive a proper diagnosis, they usually return to a normal life, sometimes without medication.

Panic attacks can also occur spontaneously, without any apparent reason. Such episodes are labeled "attacks" because the panic is not preceded by any abnormal thinking or approaching danger. They may or may not occur with any existing phobias. Those who have frequent panic attacks will likely start avoiding public places for obvious reasons. Between 1 and 2 percent of the American population suffer from panic attacks alone, but 5 percent suffer from panic attacks complicated by agoraphobia. Panic attacks will be explained more fully in chapter 9. Keep in mind, however, that panic is a result, not a cause.

Analyzing Specific Fears

A phobia is an emotional reaction to an irrational belief, which has been learned from previous life experiences. Suppose you have a two-year-old child playing in your backyard. A harmless garter snake is slithering across the lawn. The toddler, who has had no prior exposure to snakes, will likely pick up this curious little object. Most mothers would probably freak out if they saw that happening. However, if the mother is a zoologist with extensive knowledge of reptiles, she would probably just smile and pick up the snake herself.

Most spiders are harmless, and letting one crawl around on your skin would do no harm. However, if it has a red hourglass shape on its abdomen, I wouldn't advise that, because black widow spiders can do some harm.

Most phobias are rooted in ignorance and half truths. A limited perspective can perpetuate fears, but a comprehensive knowledge of the truth sets a person free. Let's analyze several common fears with an eye for what is true, and which attribute has or can be removed. The fears of death, people, failure, Satan, and God will be dealt with extensively in the following five chapters.

1. Fear of never loving another or never being loved

"There is no fear in love; but perfect love casts out fear" (1 John 4:18). God's love (*agape*) for us is perfect. Agape is not dependent upon the object. God loves us, because God is love (1 John 4:16). It is His nature to love us, and that is why His love is unconditional. God loves all His children the same, and He would still love them the same if they failed to live up to certain standards. God "disciplines us for our good, so that we may share His holiness" (Hebrews 12:10), but that is a proof of His love.

It has been said that nobody commits suicide unless they have given up all hope for love. The problem is, we have been raised in various degrees of brotherly love (*phileo*), which is dependent upon the object. Apart from Christ, we learned to love others conditionally, because of who they are or what they do. Jesus said, "If you love those who love you, what credit is that to you? For even sinners love those who love them" (Luke 6:32). Not understanding the unconditional love of God leads many to ask, "How could God love somebody like me?" When we let the love of God flow through us, we are loving others because of who *we* are. "If we love one another, God abides in us, and His love is perfected in us" (1 John 4:12). The greatest commandments are to love the Lord our God with all our heart, and to love our neighbor as ourselves (Matthew 22:37-39). "We love, because He first loved us" (1 John 4:19).

The sequel to John 3:16 is 1 John 3:16-18: "We know love by this, that He laid down His life for us; and we ought to lay down our lives for the brethren. But whoever has the world's goods, and sees his brother in need and closes his heart against him, how does the love of God abide in him? Little children, let us not love with word or with tongue, but in deed and truth." Nobody can sincerely help another without helping themselves in the process. That is why it is more blessed to give than to receive. Those who are waiting for someone other than God to love them, may wait a long time. If we want someone to love us, then we should love someone. When we do nothing from selfishness or empty conceit, and with humility of mind regard one another as more important than ourselves, and do not merely look out for our own personal interests, but also the interests of others (Philippians 2:3-4)—then we are truly loving others and will feel loved ourselves. Love is the fruit of the Spirit abiding in us (Galatians 5:22).

2. Fear of being embarrassed

The possibility of embarrassing ourselves is imminent, but it shouldn't be potent. Often, this fear reveals a lack of security in Christ. Secure people have learned to laugh at themselves when they goof up, which is inevitable. We will all embarrass ourselves sometime.

The basic issue with the fear of embarrassment is often the fear of being rejected by others. The temptation is to become a "people pleaser." The apostle Paul wrote, "Am I now seeking the favor of men, or of God? Or am I striving to please men? If I were still striving to please men, I would not be a bondservant of Christ" (Galatians 1:10). People pleasers become bondservants of other people. We would care a lot less of what people think about us if we knew how little they actually do think about us. We should not fear being "fools for Christ's sake" (1 Corinthians 4:10).

3. Fear of being victimized

We cannot promise anyone that they will not be scammed, abused, robbed, or taken advantage of. For some believers in this fallen world, victimization is imminent. What we *can* promise is that no one has to remain a victim. Even if the victimization leads to physical death, we would victoriously be absent from the body and present with the Lord. We are always assured of God's presence, and His sustaining grace will never leave us or forsake us.

Suffering is part of our sanctification. There are many books and testimonies of people who have not only survived, but have flourished after tragedies. Often, such suffering shapes our lives for greater service. "We also exult in our tribulations, knowing that tribulation brings about perseverance, and perseverance, proven character; and proven character, hope; and hope does not disappoint, because the love of God has been poured out within our hearts through the Holy Spirit who was given to us" (Romans 5:3-5).

Trials and tribulations are a part of living in this fallen world. They are not meant to destroy us, but they do reveal our character. "We do not lose heart, but though our outer man is decaying, yet our inner man is being renewed day by day. For momentary, light affliction is producing for us an eternal weight of glory far beyond all comparison" (2 Corinthians 4:16-17). We can get through any trial if we don't lose hope, which is the present assurance of some future good. Imagine the worst-case scenario and ask yourself this question: *Can I live with that?* The fear is no longer potent if your answer is *yes*.

4. Fear of rejection

It is going to happen. There is no way that we can live so as not to experience some rejection from others. Yet the fear of rejection is the primary reason why some don't share their faith. It is an irrational fear that stops us from being a good witness. Denying someone the good news because we may get rejected isn't rational. In many cases, the unbelievers are not rejecting us; they are rejecting Christ. But the messengers often feel the sting. What the unbeliever may think of us, however, is radically different from what God thinks of us. "Coming to Him as to a living stone which has been rejected by men, but is choice and precious in the sight of God, you also, as living stones, are being built up as a spiritual house for a holy priesthood" (1 Peter 2:4-5).

Jesus lived the perfect life, and yet everyone rejected Him at the time of His trial. If you think rising to the pinnacle of success will bring widespread acceptance from everyone, then you need to learn the lesson of the whale. When you rise to the top and begin to blow, that is when you get harpooned! Fearing the criticism and rejection of others has caused many to never reach their potential in life. Nothing ventured leads to nothing gained.

> Who is there to harm you if you prove zealous for what is good? But even if you should suffer for the sake of righteousness, *you are blessed*. And do not fear their intimidation, and do not be troubled, but sanctify Christ as Lord in your hearts, always being ready to make a defense to everyone who asks you to give an account for the hope that is in you, yet with gentleness and reverence; and keep a good conscience so that in the thing in which you are slandered, those who revile your good behavior in Christ will be put to shame (1 Peter 3:13-16, emphasis added).

There is always a risk in reaching out to others, because of the possibility of being rejected. But it is a risk worth taking, because life without meaningful relationships isn't living at all. "Accept one another, just as Christ also accepted us to the glory of God" (Romans 15:7). Remember this verse when you come across others who need to be loved and accepted.

5. Fear of marriage

Many have seen their parents or others suffer through a bad marriage and fear the same might happen to them. They are reluctant to make a commitment to one person. What if it doesn't work?

A life governed by "what-ifs" isn't worth living. The pessimist asks, "What do I stand to lose if I do?" The person of faith asks, "What will I miss if I don't?" God works primarily in our lives through committed relationships. Nobody can keep a spouse from being the person God created them to be, and if both spouses keep that focus, the marriage will be a blessing to them.

Some people think, *If the marriage doesn't work, I can always get divorced.* If that is what you believe, then divorce is probably imminent. Marriage should not be understood as a contract that can be broken. It is a covenant relationship that aids in our sanctification if we will stay committed to our vows and mature in Christ.

6. Fear of disapproval

The need for approval begins very early in childhood, and most parents try to accommodate their children. They say, "Good job, Johnny," as they observe his scribbled mess. The trend is to give every child a trophy for showing up, regardless of how poorly they perform—but that may set them up for false expectations in the future. We have to help them (and ourselves) distinguish between the approval of self and the approval of work, which is always subject to disapproval. Even the presidents of the United States are doing well to have a 50 percent approval rating. Just because somebody rejects our work shouldn't mean that they reject us.

From whom we are seeking approval is also critical. Consider the case for Jesus in John 12:42-43: "Many even of the rulers believed in Him, but because of the Pharisees they were not confessing Him, for fear that they would be put out of the synagogue; for they loved the approval of men rather than the approval of God." The lie that fuels the fear of disapproval is believing that our sense of worth and happiness is dependent upon the approval of others.

If you want to increase your "approval rating," then follow the example of those who walked before us in faith: "Faith is the assurance of things hoped for, the conviction of things not seen. For by it the men of old gained approval" (Hebrews 11:1-2); "be diligent to present yourself approved to God as a workman who does not need to be ashamed, accurately handling the word of truth" (2 Timothy 2:15). Disapproval by others is imminent, but not potent for those who are secure in Christ.

7. Fear of divorce

Fear is a powerful motivator for good or evil. But making an effort to avoid divorce does not lead to the same behavior necessary for making a good marriage. What causes people to be dissatisfied is often unrelated to what satisfies them. Responding to another person's dissatisfactions so they won't leave you will be a never-ending trial. Trying to appease fleshly demands of a spouse will only deepen the flesh patterns. Fearing divorce has led many to buy things, take trips, and give in to demands. Trying to appease the other person will not likely work.

Spouses are satisfied when they love and are loved. Hungering and thirsting after righteousness is what truly satisfies (Matthew 5:6). Love and forgiveness is the glue that holds families together. God does allow for divorce in the cases of adultery and abandonment by an unbeliever. Should one be unfaithful, however, the remaining spouse can still be the person God created them to be.

8. Fear of becoming/being homosexual

God created us as male and female. A DNA test will reveal one's gender. The body is telling the truth. It's the soul that gets damaged, but it can be repaired. The origin of the homosexual lie often is the result of sexual abuse, dysfunctional family systems, and tempting thoughts. If someone has tempting thoughts toward another of the same sex, they may start questioning their sexuality. They falsely conclude, "If I am thinking these thoughts, then I must be one of them." If they believe that lie and act upon it, they have used their bodies as an instrument of unrighteousness, allowing sin to reign in their mortal bodies (see Romans 6:12), and have become one flesh with the other person (see 1 Corinthians 6:16). There is an opportunity in the Steps to resolve this issue. See the book *Winning the Battle Within* (Harvest House, 2008) for additional help.

9. Fear of going crazy

"God has not given us a spirit of fear, but of power and of love and of a sound mind" (2 Timothy 1:7 NKJV). God is not the source of our problem—being disconnected from Him is the basis for anxiety disorders. The fear of losing our minds is probably the most common but least exposed fear that plagues humanity. We have no idea the mental struggles that others are having. We can't read their minds, and we are unlikely to share what is going on in our own minds. Almost every inquirer (person seeking help) we have talked to thinks they are the only one that is struggling with tempting, accusing, and blasphemous thoughts. We have included the Steps in this book to help you win the battle for your mind. More will be said about this in chapter 6 ("Fear of Satan"), and chapter 10 deals with anxiety.

10. Fear of financial problems

You won't be concerned about your finances if you are living a responsible life and believe that God will supply all your needs according to His riches in glory (Philippians 4:19). Such fear is a lack of trust, but there are other issues that can precipitate this fear.

First, "If we have food and covering, with these we shall be content" (1 Timothy 6:8). But many are not content or grateful for what they have, and crave more things that only money can buy. Greed and lack of self-control can plunge individuals and couples into credit card debt. The love of money (not money itself) is "a root of all sorts of evil" (verse 10). The apostle Paul says, "Not that I speak from want, for I have learned to be content in whatever circumstances I am" (Philippians

4:11). That is a goal that every Christian can achieve. It's worth noting that rich people struggle with this fear as much as those who would seem to be poor, and in some cases more.

Second, we should be good stewards of all that God has entrusted us with (1 Corinthians 4:1-3). Life is not an entitlement; it is an entrustment. Poor stewardship can lead to hardship. If we are not assuming our responsibility for what God has entrusted to us, then we will feel anxious.

Third, if a man doesn't work, then neither should he eat (2 Thessalonians 3:10). "For we are His workmanship, created in Christ Jesus for good works, which God prepared beforehand so that we would walk in them" (Ephesians 2:10).

Security in Christ is what guarantees financial security, but having plenty of money doesn't buy any security in Christ.

11. Fear of pain or illness

Pain and illness are imminent; therefore, we need to learn how to render them impotent. God has not promised that we will die in perfect health, no matter how strong our faith is. When you are afraid to step out in faith because it may lead to pain or illness, think of the courageous missionaries who had to overcome that fear, because pain and illness would be inevitable in most mission fields.

Many in the Western world think of pain as an enemy, but it isn't. If we couldn't feel pain, we would be covered with scars in a matter of weeks. All growth entails a certain amount of pain. Giving birth to a child is painful, and so is growing in grace. Suffering is part of the sanctifying process. We learn obedience, like Jesus did, through the things which we suffer (Hebrews 5:8). God comforts us in all our afflictions, and we share in His sufferings, which enables us to give comfort to others (see 2 Corinthians 1:3-6). "Therefore we do not lose heart, but though our outer man is decaying, yet our inner man is being renewed day by day" (2 Corinthians 4:16).

12. Fear of never getting married

The apostle Paul wrote, "I say to the unmarried and to widows that it is good for them if they remain even as I" (1 Corinthians 7:8). The early church viewed celibacy as a gift for some. It is noble to remain single, but not viewed as normal in most cultures. There is a lot of social pressure to get married, and not to do so signifies failure in some people's eyes—often the parents. Pressure to get married has led some to propose or accept a proposal that leads to a situation far worse than remaining single. Being single does not mean a life of loneliness or a sign of rejection. It is better not to marry than to marry the wrong person. We find our meaning in life by fulfilling our calling, which may mean no marriage or children for reasons we may not know until later in life.

13. Fear of the future

Fear of the future is related to anxiety, because we don't know what is going to happen tomorrow. The key is to live a responsible life each day, learn to take one day at a time, and trust God for tomorrow. As with the fear of being victimized, consider the worst-case scenario and then ask yourself this question: *Can I, by the grace of God, live with whatever happens?* If you say *yes*, then there is nothing to fear.

14. Fear of confrontation

Do we care enough to confront somebody doing something that will bring damage to themselves or others? It takes courage, and confronting another must be done in the right spirit. Paul wrote, "Brethren, even if anyone is caught in any trespass, you who are spiritual, restore such a one in a spirit of gentleness; each one looking to yourself, so that you too will not be tempted" (Galatians 6:1). The goal is to restore, and the key phrase is "caught in any trespass." Discipline has to be based on observed behavior, not on the judgment of character. Confront the lie, but don't call the person a liar.

Courage is the mark of a Spirit-filled Christian. Acts 4:31 reads,

"When they had prayed, the place where they had gathered together was shaken, and they were all filled with the Holy Spirit and began to speak the word of God with boldness." Spirit-filled Christians are ambassadors for Christ who have been given the ministry of reconciliation (2 Corinthians 5:19-20). See Neil's book *Restoring Broken Relationships* (Bethany House, 2015) for further guidance.

15. Fear of being a hopeless case

You can live for seven minutes without air, seven days without water, and forty days without food, but you can't live for a moment without hope. People are afraid to get their hopes up, because they don't want to be disappointed. We have had numerous people tell us that they were afraid to ask us for help, because if it didn't work, that would render them hopeless. Where do you go if the "last resort" doesn't work? You go to God. "Why are you in despair, O my soul? And why have you become disturbed within me? Hope in God, for I shall again praise Him for the help of His presence" (Psalm 42:5).

Two-and-a-half years into Joanne's illness, I (Neil) clearly heard from God that my wife was not going to get well. Was she hopeless? Never, even though there is no known cure for dementia. God's presence has surrounded us, and Joanne has the hope of seeing her Lord and Savior face to face in a resurrected body. What is there to fear?

16. Fear of having committed the unpardonable sin

The passage in question is Matthew 12:31-32: "I say to you, every sin and blasphemy will be forgiven men, but the blasphemy against the Spirit will not be forgiven men. Anyone who speaks a word against the Son of Man, it will be forgiven him; but whoever speaks against the Holy Spirit, it will not be forgiven him, either in this age or in the age to come" (NKJV).

At one point in His ministry, the Pharisees accused Jesus of performing His miracles by the power of Beelzebul, a ruling territorial spirit. In response, Jesus said that if He were casting out demons by the power of Beelzebul, then Satan would be casting out Satan. Satan would be divided against himself, and his kingdom could not stand. Jesus then explained that, since He was casting out demons by the Spirit of God, the kingdom of God had come upon them (Matthew 12:24-28). Clearly, they were rejecting the Spirit of God by crediting Jesus's work to Beelzebul.

So why did Jesus say that a person can speak against Him, but not against the Holy Spirit? The unique role of the Holy Spirit was and is to give evidence to the work of Christ and to lead us into all truth (see John 14:17-19; 16:7-15). The only unpardonable sin is the sin of unbelief. If we refuse to accept the testimony given to us by the Holy Spirit, fight off His conviction of our sin, and never accept the truth, we will never come to Christ for salvation. In Christ, all our sins are forgiven. Therefore, no person who has received Christ as their Lord and Savior can commit the unpardonable sin (Romans 8:1). Only an unregenerate person who refuses to come to Christ will die in his or her sins.

The accuser of the brethren, however, will often try to convince Christians that they have committed the unpardonable sin so that they will live in defeat. Satan can't do anything about our identity and position in Christ, but if he can deceive us into believing we are not secure in Christ, then we will live as though we aren't. Christians can quench the Spirit. If we do, we will impede the work of God and live a less than victorious life, but we will not lose our salvation.

17. Fear of corrupt government officials

The Chapman University Survey on American Fears[1] (2017) reported that over 74 percent of the Americans polled feared corrupt government officials. That was the most common fear mentioned, followed by a fear of the American Healthcare Act, which was mentioned by about 55 percent of those who were polled. Corrupt and evil people can manipulate us through fear if we let them. Carlos Valles wrote:

> I say this to bring to the clearest possible light the fact that
> it is our fear that lays us open to manipulation. Fear is
> the handle we ourselves give to those who would turn us

around at their will. Terrorism exists because we are afraid. There are international commissions that meet regularly to analyze the spread of terrorism and propose remedies. They are not likely to do away with the plague. The ultimate remedy lies in the human heart. Fearlessness alone can free us from the snares our own fears have built.[2]

Discussion Questions

1. How does fear differ from anxiety and panic attacks?

2. What two attributes must a fear object have in order to be legitimate?

3. Which attribute has God removed from death and Satan?

4. Why is the fear of God the beginning of wisdom?

5. What is fundamentally wrong about fearing Satan more than God?

6. What is the value to us in worshiping God?

7. Which of the 17 fear objects discussed in the chapter spoke most clearly to you? Why?

8. Why can't a born-again Christian commit the unpardonable sin?

9. Why is terrorism so effective?

10. Think of an irrational fear object not mentioned in the chapter. What is the lie behind it, and which attribute (its presence or its power) can be eliminated?

The Steps to Freedom in Christ

Deception versus Truth

The Christian life is lived by faith according to what God says is true. Jesus is the truth, the Holy Spirit is the Spirit of truth, God's Word is truth, and we are to speak the truth in love (see John 14:6; 16:13;

17:17; Ephesians 4:15). The biblical response to truth is faith, regardless of whether we feel it is true or not. Christians are to forsake all lying, deceiving, stretching the truth, and anything else associated with false-hood. Believing lies will keep us in bondage. Choosing to believe the truth is what sets us free (John 8:32).

David wrote, "How blessed [happy] is the man...in whose spirit there is no deceit!" (Psalm 32:2). The liberated Christian is free to walk in the light and speak the truth in love. We can be honest and trans-parent before God, because we are already forgiven, and God already knows the thoughts and intentions of our hearts (Hebrews 4:12-13). So why not be honest and confess our sins? Confession means to agree with God. People in bondage are tired of living a lie. Because of God's great love and forgiveness, we can walk in the light and fellowship with God and others (see 1 John 1:7-9).

Begin this commitment to truth by praying the following prayer out loud. Don't let any opposing thoughts, such as *This is a waste of time,* or *I wish I could believe this, but I can't,* keep you from pressing forward. God will strengthen you as you rely on Him.

> *Dear heavenly Father, You are the truth, and I desire to live by faith according to Your truth. The truth will set me free, but in many ways I have been deceived by the father of lies, the philosophies of this fallen world, and I have deceived myself. I choose to walk in the light, knowing that You love and accept me just as I am. As I consider areas of possible deception, I invite the Spirit of truth to guide me into all truth. Please protect me from all deception as You "search me, O God, and know my heart; try me and know my anxious thoughts; and see if there be any hurtful way in me, and lead me in the ever-lasting way" (Psalm 139:23-24). In the name of Jesus I pray. Amen.*

Prayerfully consider the lists in the three exercises over the next few pages, using the prayers at the end of each exercise in order to confess any ways you have given in to deception or wrongly defended yourself. You cannot instantly renew your mind, but the process will never get started without acknowledging your mental strongholds or defense mechanisms, also known as flesh patterns.

Ways You Can Be Deceived by the World

__ Believing that having an abundance of money and possessions will make me happy (Matthew 13:22; 1 Timothy 6:10)

__ Believing that eating food, drinking alcohol, or using drugs can relieve my stress and make me happy (Proverbs 23:19-21)

__ Believing that an attractive body, phony personality, or image will meet my needs for acceptance and significance (Proverbs 31:10; 1 Peter 3:3-4)

__ Believing that gratifying sexual lust will bring lasting satisfaction without any negative consequences (Ephesians 4:22; 1 Peter 2:11)

__ Believing that I can sin and suffer no negative consequences (Hebrews 3:12-13)

__ Believing that I need more than Jesus to meet my needs of acceptance, security, and significance (2 Corinthians 11:2-4,13-15)

__ Believing that I can do whatever I want regardless of others and still be free (Proverbs 16:18; Obadiah 3; 1 Peter 5:5)

__ Believing that people who refuse to receive Jesus will go to heaven anyway (1 Corinthians 6:9-11)

__ Believing that I can associate with bad company and not become corrupted (1 Corinthians 15:33-34)

__ Believing that I can read, see, or listen to anything and not be corrupted (Proverbs 4:23-27; Matthew 5:28)

__ Believing that there are no earthly consequences for my sin (Galatians 6:7-8)

__ Believing that I must gain the approval of certain people in order to be happy (Galatians 1:10)

__ Believing that I must measure up to certain religious standards in order for God to accept me (Galatians 3:2-3; 5:1)

__ Believing that there are many paths to God, and Jesus is only one of the many ways (John 14:6)

__ Believing that I must live up to worldly standards in order to feel good about myself (1 Peter 2:1-12)

> *Dear heavenly Father, I confess that I have been deceived by <u>the items you checked above</u>. I thank You for Your forgiveness, and I choose to believe Your Word and believe in Jesus, who is the truth. In Jesus's name I pray. Amen.*

Ways You Can Deceive Yourself

__ Hearing God's Word, but not doing what it says (James 1:22)

__ Saying that I have no sin (1 John 1:8)

__ Thinking I am something or someone I'm really not (Galatians 6:3)

__ Thinking I am wise in this worldly age (1 Corinthians 3:18-19)

__ Thinking I can be truly religious but not control what I say (James 1:26)

__ Thinking that God is the source of my problems (Lamentations 3)

__ Thinking I can live successfully without the help of anyone else (1 Corinthians 12:14-20)

> *Dear heavenly Father, I confess that I have deceived myself by <u>the items you checked above</u>. Thank You for Your forgiveness. I commit myself to believe only Your truth. In Jesus's name I pray. Amen.*

Ways You Can Wrongly Defend Yourself

__ Denial of reality (conscious or unconscious)

__ Fantasy (escaping reality by daydreaming, watching TV or movies, listening to music, playing computer or video games, consuming drugs or alcohol)

__ Emotional insulation (withdrawing from people or keeping people at a distance to avoid rejection)

__ Regression (reverting back to less threatening times)

__ Displaced anger (taking out frustrations on innocent people)

__ Projection (attributing to another what I find unacceptable in myself)

__ Rationalization (making excuses for my own poor behavior)

__ Lying (protecting myself through falsehoods)

__ Hypocrisy (presenting a false image)

> *Dear Heavenly Father, I confess that I have wrongly defended myself by <u>the items you checked above</u>. Thank You for Your forgiveness. I trust You to defend and protect me. In Jesus's name I pray. Amen.*

The wrong methods we have employed to shield ourselves from pain and rejection are often deeply ingrained in our lives. You may need additional discipling or counseling to learn how to allow Jesus to be your rock, fortress, deliverer, and refuge (see Psalm 18:1-2). The more you learn how loving, powerful, and protective God is, the more likely you'll be to trust Him. The more you realize how much God unconditionally loves and accepts you, the more you'll be released to be open, honest, and (in a healthy way) vulnerable before God and others.

The New Age movement and postmodernism have twisted the concept of faith by teaching that we make something true by believing it. That is false. We cannot create reality with our minds; only God can do that. Our responsibility is to face reality and choose to believe what God says is true. True biblical faith, therefore, is choosing to believe and act upon what is true, because God has said it is true, and He is the truth. Faith is something we decide to do, not something we feel like doing. Believing something doesn't make it true. It's already true; therefore, we choose to believe it! Truth is not conditioned by whether we choose to believe it or not.

Everybody lives by faith. The only difference between Christian faith and non-Christian faith is the object of our faith. If the object of our faith is not trustworthy or real, then no amount of believing will change that. That's why our faith must be grounded on the solid rock of God's perfect, unchanging character and the truth of His Word. For two thousand years Christians have known the importance of verbally and publicly declaring truth.

Read aloud the following Statements of Truth, and carefully consider what you are professing. You may find it helpful to read them aloud every day for at least six weeks, which will help renew your mind to the truth.

Statements of Truth

1. I recognize that there is only one true and living God who exists as the Father, Son, and Holy Spirit. He is worthy of all honor, praise, and glory as the One who made all things and holds all things together. (See Exodus 20:2-3 and Colossians 1:16-17.)

2. I recognize that Jesus Christ is the Messiah, the Word who became flesh and dwelt among us. I believe that He came to destroy the works of the devil and that He disarmed the rulers and authorities and made a public display of them, having triumphed over them. (See John 1:1,14; Colossians 2:15; and 1 John 3:8.)

3. I believe that God demonstrated His own love for me in

that while I was still a sinner, Christ died for me. I believe that He has delivered me from the domain of darkness and transferred me to His kingdom, and in Him I have redemption, the forgiveness of sins. (See Romans 5:8 and Colossians 1:13-14.)

4. I believe that I am now a child of God and that I am seated with Christ in the heavenly realms. I believe that I was saved by the grace of God through faith and that it was a gift and not a result of any works on my part. (See Ephesians 2:6,8-9 and 1 John 3:1-3.)

5. I choose to be strong in the Lord and in the strength of His might. I put no confidence in the flesh, for the weapons of warfare are not of the flesh but are divinely powerful for the destruction of strongholds. I put on the full armor of God. I resolve to stand firm in my faith and resist the evil one. (See 2 Corinthians 10:4; Ephesians 6:10-17; and Philippians 3:3.)

6. I believe that apart from Christ I can do nothing, so I declare my complete dependence on Him. I choose to abide in Christ in order to bear much fruit and glorify my Father. I announce to Satan that Jesus is my Lord. I reject any and all counterfeit gifts or works of Satan in my life. (See John 15:5,8 and 1 Corinthians 12:3.)

7. I believe that the truth will set me free and that Jesus is the truth. If He sets me free, I will be free indeed. I recognize that walking in the light is the only path of true fellowship with God and man. Therefore, I stand against all of Satan's deception by taking every thought captive in obedience to Christ. I declare that the Bible is the only authoritative standard for truth and life. (See John 8:32,36; 14:6; 2 Corinthians 10:5; 2 Timothy 3:15-17; and 1 John 1:3-7.)

8. I choose to present my body to God as a living and holy sacrifice, and the members of my body as instruments of righteousness. I choose to renew my mind by the living Word of God in order that I may prove that the will of God is good, acceptable, and perfect. I put off the old self with its evil practices and put on the new self. I declare myself to be a new creation in Christ. (See Romans 6:13; 12:1-2; 2 Corinthians 5:17; and Colossians 3:9-10.)

9. By faith, I choose to be filled with the Spirit so that I can be guided into all truth. I choose to walk by the Spirit so that I will not carry out the desires of the flesh. (See John 16:13; Galatians 5:16; and Ephesians 5:18.)

10. I renounce all selfish goals and choose the ultimate goal of love. I choose to obey the two greatest commandments: to love the Lord my God with all my heart, soul, mind, and strength and to love my neighbor as myself. (See Matthew 22:37-39 and 1 Timothy 1:5.)

11. I believe that the Lord Jesus has all authority in heaven and on earth, and He is the head over all rule and authority. I am complete in Him. I believe that Satan and his demons are subject to me in Christ since I am a member of Christ's body. Therefore, I obey the command to submit to God and resist the devil, and I command Satan in the name of Jesus Christ to leave my presence. (See Matthew 28:18; Ephesians 1:19-23; Colossians 2:10; and James 4:7.)

Chapter Three

Fear of Death

The last enemy that will be abolished is death.
1 Corinthians 15:26

Ernest Becker, in his Pulitzer Prize-winning book *The Denial of Death*, writes, "The fear of death haunts the human animal like nothing else; it is the mainspring of human activity."[1] Becker describes "the emergence of man as we know him: a hyperanxious animal who constantly invents reasons for anxiety, even when there are none."[2]

How have we become a nation of worriers, especially as it relates to the fear of dying? Gavin de Becker, author of the best seller *The Gift of Fear*, puts it this way:

> Worry is the fear that we manufacture, and those who choose to do it certainly have a wide range of dangers to dwell upon. Television in most major cities devotes up to 40 hours a day [sic] to telling us about those who have fallen prey to some disaster and to exploring what calamities may be coming next. The local news anchor should begin each evening's broadcast by saying, "Welcome to the news; we're surprised you made it through another day. Here's what happened to those who didn't." Each day, we learn what the new studies reveal: "Cellular phones can kill you"; "The dangers of debit cards"; "Contaminated turkey kills family of three. Could your family be next?"[3]

"If it bleeds, it leads." Media sensationalism has burdened viewers with an unbearable load of fearful images: violent crime scenes (and violent crimes in progress!), airplane crash footage, and teary-eyed disaster victims picking through wreckage. Not surprisingly, over 90 percent of people have some fear of flying, and more than 35 million Americans avoid airplanes altogether.[4] Every hour on prime-time TV there are three murders, according to studies done by Dr. George Gerbner, director of Philadelphia's Cultural Indicators Research Project.[5] Crime-related news stories more than tripled during the first half of the 90s, even though our nation's crime rates remained about the same or decreased slightly, according to the Center for Media and Public Affairs in Washington, DC.[6] During that same period, murder stories on the evening-news shows of the three main networks increased ninefold.[7]

Although the fear of death is exacerbated by the media, it isn't the only source for our fears, and it's not the original source. Satan is the genesis for fearing death, for he had the power of death. "Since the children share in flesh and blood, [Christ] likewise also partook of the same, that through death He might render powerless him who had the power of death, that is, the devil, and might free those who through fear of death were subject to slavery all their lives" (Hebrews 2:14-15). People are in bondage to the fear of death unless they have eternal life in Christ Jesus, who holds the keys of death and Hades (Revelation 1:18). The following testimony sent to our office illustrates how the fear of death can shackle a believer in Christ, and how the truth sets a person free:

> I am 30 years old. When I was five my mother and father took me to a witch doctor to help cure my nosebleeds. My parents were to say a few prayers and then place a silver coin on my forehead. Shortly after the nosebleeds ended I became obsessed with dying. A tremendous fear came over me that would not subside.
>
> I accepted the Lord when I was 25. Two years ago the fear of dying came back full force after giving my

testimony at a women's Bible study sharing day. The fear was oppressive.

Every day I chose clothes to wear that I thought would be my death clothes. How was I going to die? The thoughts in my mind were petrifying. I would die, and my three-year-old would grow up without a mom. I would die, and my husband would marry a beautiful blonde.

Where were these thoughts coming from? I asked God to remove this fear.... I became familiar with all the "fear" Bible verses. It was so overwhelming...I thought I was going crazy.

I came across *The Bondage Breaker*...I was in bondage. I remember crying out to God to show me what was holding me back. I prayed the prayers...and when I came to the part of renouncing my sexual sins, I tried to envision every man I had ever had sex with...what they looked like or what their name was.... I prayed for these men.... I prayed that their names were written in the Lamb's book of life.... I felt the fear leaving me...the fear of being unworthy to stand before God...the fear of getting AIDS...the fear of dying.

This may sound funny, but with every prayer I almost felt a *poof* coming out of my mind. Then I slowly asked the Lord why this fear had plagued me for so long...and I remembered long ago going to the witch doctor...that, to this day, my mom claims was a man of God.

I truly believe that a curse was placed on my life when I was five. I lived 28 years infested with fear. I didn't care how I lived and became a loose woman because I was sure I would never live to see the consequences.

Thanks be to God from whom all blessings flow that there truly is freedom in Christ.

Such occult "healings" by the father of lies are not new. Around the year AD 200, Tertullian wrote about the activities of demons in his

Apology for Christianity: "Very kind too, no doubt, they are in regard to the healing of diseases. For, first of all, they make you ill; then to get a miracle out of it, they command the application of remedies either altogether new, or contrary to those in use, and straightway withdrawing hurtful influence, they are supposed to have wrought a cure."[8]

John, a missionary bush pilot in Africa, had two close calls while flying and became agoraphobic. By the end of his first term on the mission field, he was barely able to leave the house for any reason. The seeds of fear, however, were planted early in life, when he unwittingly paid attention to a deceiving spirit, as his testimony reveals.

> After so many years of deception that held me in bondage and fear, I am set free in Christ. Praise His name.
>
> At age 14, my hobby was amateur radio. I enjoyed tuning across the bands and finding faraway stations. When lights-out time came, I would turn the amateur radio off, get in bed, plug in an earphone to my AM radio, and continue listening for faraway broadcast stations.
>
> In time I located a station in New York State. At 10:00 p.m. I heard their news, station ID, and the introduction to the next program, the CBS Radio Mystery Theater. From that night on for the next four years, I was hooked to that program, falling asleep with images of suspense and fear flooding my mind. If only I had known what I was setting myself up for.
>
> Sometime thereafter a voice began to tell me just when the phone would ring and who was on the other end without fail.
>
> I was also able to tell my parents secret habits about people that I knew to be true, even when meeting an individual for the first time. Sometime in the future, often years later, my folks would remark to each other and ask me, "How did you know?"
>
> After I received my driver's license, the same voice would tell me where the speed traps were on the interstate.

My mom once told me that during my years at Bible school I was blessed with tremendous spiritual insight because of all the things I knew and could do. Spiritual insight is right; however, [it was] the wrong kind.

Not always did the voice tell me truth. The voice would actually become rough and tell me to burn my arms with my soldering iron or poke out my eye with a screwdriver. When I would climb my radio tower to repair antennas at 100 feet, the voice would often tell me to jump off.

The battle for my mind at those moments while on the tower was so intense that just trying to keep safety and good practice in the front of my mind would cause great debilitating fear.

This same fear began motivating my daily activities. Although the voice in my head would often tell me that I was stupid, ugly, dumb, fat, and would never amount to anything, 90 percent of the time it told the truth. So I just kept listening to it.

While working through the Steps, John realized that the "voice" he was listening to was not God. He had been paying attention to a deceiving spirit. The devil, who once held the power of death, is obsessed with death and dying. Suicidal thoughts are a given for those who are in spiritual bondage.

John was a changed man after going through the Steps. He was no longer being controlled by fear. When he went back to Africa to collect his possessions (for transition back to America), he told us that he had more ministry in the lives of people in those two weeks than he'd had in the three years prior to his furlough. People were so amazed by the changes in his life that he would stay up till two or three o'clock in the morning sharing what God had done for him.

A Life-Giving Spirit

"The first man, Adam, became a living soul. The last Adam became a life-giving spirit" (1 Corinthians 15:45). The Nicene Creed said of

Jesus, "Who for us men and for our salvation came down from heaven and was incarnated by the Holy Spirit and the Virgin Mary and became Man." Unlike the first Adam, Jesus never sinned, even though He was tempted in every way that we are (Hebrews 4:15). He showed us how a spiritually alive human could live a righteous life, but that is not the primary reason why He came. Jesus came to be the perfect sacrifice for our sins, which had separated us from God, and to be resurrected in order that we may have eternal life "in Christ." "In Him was life, and the life was the Light of men" (John 1:4).

From the incarnation to the crucifixion, Jesus was fully God and fully man. He was one person with two natures. Ambrose, the bishop of Milan (AD 374-397), wrote:

> In taking upon Himself a human soul, He also took upon Himself the affections of the soul. As God He was not distressed, but as a human He was capable of being distressed. It was not as God He died, but as man. It was in human voice that He cried, "My God, My God, why have You forsaken Me?" As human therefore, He speaks on the cross, bearing with Him our terrors. For amid dangers it is a very human response to think ourselves abandoned. As human, therefore, He is distressed, weeps, and is crucified.

The Apostles' Creed states that Jesus descended into *hell*, which is the Hebrew word *sheol*. In the Old Testament there is only one word for both hell and death, and that is *sheol* (in Greek, *hades*). The emphasis is on separation, not destination. It was the separation of Jesus's human nature from the Father that caused Him to cry out. Between the excruciating pain of the crucifixion and the triumph of the resurrection, Jesus took the plunge into the abyss of aloneness—complete abandonment—which is a frightening prospect. The fear that comes from being totally alone speaks to human vulnerability. We cannot rationally explain it away.

In that moment of separation, Jesus quoted from Psalm 22. His cry of agony was a prayer: "My God, My God" (Matthew 27:46; Mark 15:34). While the mocking crowd and the first thief had given up their faith in God, Jesus clung to it. What an example that is for us in our hour of greatest despair. In the midst of Jesus's own abandonment, He cried out to God.

Hell is loneliness, where no love can penetrate. It is the total absence of God, who is love. In the final judgment, those whose names are not written in the Lamb's book of life will be cast out of His presence. That is hell. But heaven is to be completely in His presence. Experiencing His presence now is a taste of heaven on earth. It is understandable why the Old Testament has only one word for hell and death, because they are essentially the same.

Fear of Being Alone

In the beginning of time God said, "It is not good that man should be alone" (Genesis 2:18 NKJV). Have you ever visited a mortuary and entered a room where the corpse of a stranger was lying motionless in an open casket? Did you feel uneasy, and maybe even a little frightened, even though you knew the dead person could do you no harm? This is not the fear of anything in particular, but the fear of being alone with death. Such a fear cannot be overcome by a rational explanation of its groundlessness. This apprehension relates to our most basic of human needs: to have a sense of belonging, to be in union with God and other living souls. It also explains why many struggle with issues of abandonment. The fear of walking alone through the woods at night or down a dark alley is diminished by the presence of another. The uneasiness of sitting alone with a corpse disappears when a friend or family member joins you in the room.

Our ultimate need is eternal life, to be in union with God. That is why the primordial fear is to be separated from Him. Our natural life has less value because it is temporal, but it's still treasured more than all other earthly possessions. We can't fulfill our purpose on earth if our soul isn't in union with our body, nor can we relate to our brothers and sisters. We were created to be in fellowship with God and one another, which is why the greatest commandment is to love God with our whole being, and the second greatest is to love our neighbor as ourselves (Matthew 22:37-39).

Life has no meaning without relationships. The value of being present with one another is determined by our capacity to love. "There is no fear in love; but perfect love casts our fear" (1 John 4:18). Imagine being raised in a family where there is no love shown to one another. It would be a house full of people who are all alone. A living hell.

Salvation Conquers Death

What Adam lost in the fall was life, and that is what Jesus came to give us (John 10:10). What He gave was Himself, because Jesus "is our life" (Colossians 3:4). "The testimony is this, that God has given us eternal life, and this life is in His Son. He who has the Son has the life; he who does not have the Son of God does not have the life. These things I have written to you who believe in the name of the Son of God, so that you may know that you have eternal life" (1 John 5:11-13). The early church understood salvation to mean union with God, and this is most often conveyed in the epistles with the prepositional phrase "in Christ," "in Him," or "in the Beloved." In the book of Ephesians alone there are 40 such prepositional phrases (11 in the first 13 verses). The problem is that we don't see it, and that is why Paul says in Ephesians 1:18, "I pray that the eyes of your heart may be enlightened, so that you will know what is the hope of His calling, what are the riches of the glory of His inheritance in the saints."

Paul's theology is centered on who we are in Christ. He writes to the struggling church in Corinth, "I have sent to you Timothy, who is my beloved and faithful child in the Lord, and he will remind you of *my ways which are in Christ, just as I teach everywhere in every church*" (1 Corinthians 4:15-17, emphasis added).

Eternal life is not something we get when we die. In fact, all we would have to look forward to is hell if we didn't have eternal life before we physically die. Jesus said, "I am the resurrection and the life; he who believes in Me will live even if he dies" (John 11:25). In other words, you will remain spiritually alive after you physically die. That is not something to fear, because "we are of good courage, I say, and prefer rather to be absent from the body and to be at home with the Lord" (2 Corinthians 5:8). Paul said, "For to me, to live is Christ and to die is gain" (Philippians 1:21).

Many people fear that physical death is the worst thing that could happen to them, but for the believer it is gain. Believers will be fully in the presence of God in a resurrected body that has no pain or suffering. However, that is not a license to commit suicide, because we are called to be good stewards of the time, talent, and treasure He has entrusted to us. "For we are His workmanship, created *in Christ Jesus* for good works, which God prepared beforehand so that we would walk in them" (Ephesians 2:10, emphasis added).

Recall from the last chapter that in order to eliminate any fear object, only one of its attributes has to be removed. Physical death is still imminent, "as it is appointed for men to die once and after this comes judgment" (Hebrews 9:27). But God has overcome the power of death. It is no longer potent, because we have eternal life in Christ. "'O death, where is your victory? O death, where is your sting?' The sting of death is sin, and the power of sin is the law; but thanks be to God, who gives us the victory through our Lord Jesus Christ" (1 Corinthians 15:55-57).

Fear of Losing Your Salvation

There has always been a struggle within the church to find the balance between God's sovereignty and human responsibility, which are both taught in Scripture. Was coming to Christ primarily God's sovereign choice, or was it our choice to believe—or both? Some would argue that it is our choice to believe or not believe, and subsequent to salvation we can choose to reject Christ and forfeit our salvation. Others would argue from passages like John 6:44 that "no one can come to Me [Jesus] unless the Father who sent Me draws him; and I will raise him up on the last day." That would seem to imply that God chose us. Ultimately, God is sovereign, but in His sovereignty He had this call recorded in Scripture: "Believe in the Lord Jesus, and you will be saved" (Acts 16:31). Rather than defend either divine election or free will, we prefer to believe that both our will and God's will are part of the salvation process.

Jesus said, "I am the door; if anyone enters through Me, he will be saved" (John 10:9). If there were a sign above the door to eternal life, it would read, "Whoever will call on the name of the Lord will be saved" (Romans 10:13). But as you step through the door and look back, there would be another sign that reads, "I have known you from the foundations of the world" (see Ephesians 1:4). We are not going to try to solve the question as to whether you are saved because God chose you or because you chose God. But we do hope to convince you that you can be secure in Christ regardless of your position on the previous question. If you can't be secure in Christ, then there is no security, because true security is relating to the eternal and changeless nature of God, not the temporal, transitory nature of this world.

For any relationship to be intimate and secure, both parties have to be faithful. We know from Scripture that God will always be faithful. He will never leave us nor forsake us (Hebrews 13:5). Jesus said, "My sheep hear My voice, and I know them, and they follow Me; and I give eternal life to them, and they will never perish; and no one will snatch them out of My hand" (John 10:27-28). The apostle Paul wrote that "having also believed, you were sealed in Him with the Holy Spirit of promise, who is given as a pledge of our inheritance, with a view to the redemption of God's own possession, to the praise of His glory" (Ephesians 1:13-14). And John wrote, "If we confess our sins, He is faithful and righteous to forgive us our sins and to cleanse us from all unrighteousness" (1 John 1:9). Many Christians question their salvation when they are struggling with sin. If sinning didn't bother them, then they *should* question their salvation. But if it is bothering them, that is a pretty good sign the Holy Spirit is in residence.

Unfortunately, there are cultural "Christians" who have little basis for their hope in God. John said of them, "They went out from us, but they were not really of us; for if they had been of us, they would have remained with us; but they went out, so that it would be shown that they all are not of us" (1 John 2:19). Jesus said, "The one who endures to the end, he will be saved" (Mark 13:13). Remember, God will always be faithful. "If we are faithless, He remains faithful, for He cannot deny Himself" (2 Timothy 2:13). God has a grip on you, and He won't let go. He will keep His end of the bargain, and it is up to us to keep our end of the bargain. If you want to be secure in Christ, then remain faithful, and you will be.

The best way to help you be assured of your salvation is to remove the barriers between yourself and God through genuine repentance. The Step at the end of this chapter deals with the "sin which so easily entangles us" (Hebrews 12:1). Romans 6 begins by identifying every believer with the life, death, burial, and resurrection of Christ. Verses 8-13 tell us what our responsibility is to overcome the law of sin and death:

> If we have died with Christ, we believe that we shall also live with Him, knowing that Christ, having been raised from the dead, is never to die again; death no longer is master over Him. For the death that He died, He died to sin once for all; but the life that He lives, He lives to God. Even so consider yourselves to be dead to sin, but alive to God in Christ Jesus. Therefore do not let sin reign in your mortal body so that you obey its lusts, and do not go on presenting the members of your body to sin as instruments of unrighteousness; but present yourselves to God

as those alive from the dead, and your members as instruments of righteousness to God.

It is our responsibility to not let sin reign in our mortal bodies, and we do that by not using our bodies as instruments of unrighteousness. The most common entrapment of sin is sexual, because "every other sin that a man commits is outside the body" (1 Corinthians 6:18). There is no way that we could commit a sexual sin without using our bodies as an instrument of unrighteousness. Therefore, when we sin in this way, we have allowed sin to reign (rule) in our mortal body. According to Paul, our bodies are members of Christ and temples of God. If we have sex with another person other than our spouse, we become one flesh with them (1 Corinthians 6:16).

It is unlikely that the entrapment of this sin and the bonding to another can be resolved by confession alone. In the Step at the end of this chapter, you will be encouraged to ask the Lord to reveal to your mind every sexual use of your body as an instrument of unrighteousness. God will, and He usually starts with your first experience and works forward. You will be instructed to renounce having sex with that person and ask God to break the mental, emotional, and spiritual bond that may have been formed. You can do this privately, so there is no reason to fear exposing yourself to others.

It is hard to convince someone that they have overcome the law of death if they haven't overcome the law of sin. Paul urges us "by the mercies of God, to present your bodies a living and holy sacrifice, acceptable to God, which is your spiritual service of worship" (Romans 12:1). If we do that first, then the next verse instructing us to be transformed by the renewing of our minds is possible. Trying to win the *battle* for our minds before breaking the *bondage* to sin is almost impossible.

Fearing the Death of a Loved One

"Precious in the sight of the LORD is the death of His godly ones" (Psalm 116:15). This verse doesn't make sense from a temporal perspective, but it does from an eternal perspective. We don't fear for the departed Christian who is now fully in God's presence. We fear being left behind, being abandoned, or losing a friend, lover, or maybe the one person we don't think we can live without.

Losses are tough and the primary cause for depression. Three times Jesus told His disciples "that the Son of Man must suffer many things and be rejected by the elders and the chief priests and the scribes, and be killed, and after three days rise again" (Mark 8:31). Peter's first response was denial (8:32). The disciples were afraid to talk about it the second time (9:32), and Jesus's followers were fearful as they approached Jerusalem (10:32).

We are going to lose significant people in our lives, and Jesus modeled how important it is to prepare ourselves and others for impermanence in this world. Denying the inevitable and being afraid to talk about it will not alleviate the fear. "Therefore, laying aside falsehood, speak truth each one of you with his neighbor, for we are members of one another" (Ephesians 4:25). Our lives are in the hands of God, and it is His presence that sustains us before and after the loss of a loved one.[9]

The loss of a child may be one of the most devastating experiences that anyone could go through. The most common social response is the divorce of the parents. The following testimony reveals the apprehension of parenting:

> My greatest fear is no different than any other parent...the fear of losing a child. I was always afraid that something may happen to them and I would not know it...I could not help them.
>
> In November of 1975, I became a mother, never to be the same.... How I loved that child...a beautiful little boy, Michael Jon. I knew if I held on too tight, he would not be able to grow...that I would smother him.
>
> How hard it is to let go, to let them fall, scrape their

knees, take those first steps. If you think about it, fear is very much a part of motherhood.

I reached a point when he was 20 years old, with a smile that would melt your heart…a zest for life…[when] I had to say, "Lord, if You can move mountains, You can take care of this boy."

This mother is strong in her faith, but ultimately the decision to follow Christ lies with each one of us. Tragically, this dear woman's son chose to take his own life during a hard time. It was two years after his suicide that she bravely shared her testimony of pain with us. She had endured more anguish in those 24 months than most people suffer in a lifetime. Her ability to go on with life and even write so openly about her grief is testimony to the healing grace of God.

After the death of his children and the loss of his health, it was not fatalism, but rather bottom-line faith, that moved Job to say, "Naked I came from my mother's womb, and naked I shall return there. The LORD gave and the LORD has taken away. Blessed be the name of the LORD" (Job 1:21). Scripture commended Job for his faith, declaring that "through all this Job did not sin nor did he blame God" (Job 1:22).

The fear of losing a loved one can easily cause one to cross the line from being a responsible and protective parent to being an irresponsible and overprotective parent. When that happens, mothering becomes smothering. Vanessa Ochs, in her book *Safe and Sound: Protecting Your Child in an Unpredictable World*, comments, "When protection turns to overprotection, regardless of how we rationalize, regardless of how and why it was motivated…it has serious, long-term consequences for a child's self-esteem and sense of well-being."[10] Ochs goes on to describe overprotection as "an insidious form of child abuse. You are locking a child's horizons in the closet. The difference is, this abuse is caused by an enormous amount of love."[11]

This kind of "protection" can masquerade as genuine love, but in reality it is motivated by fear. Because we cannot bear the thought of how much it will hurt us to see our loved ones harmed or killed, we do everything we can to control people and circumstances. In the process, we end up perpetuating a stronghold of fear in our families, producing children who are as phobic as we are.

Finding the balance is increasingly difficult for parents in a world filled with danger. We must trust in God and believe in our children. We are called to encourage—not discourage—one another. Fear would never allow children to cross the street, but responsible parents know the risk must be taken, and so they teach their kids how to do it safely. Greater risks will be required as children get older and learn to drive, go off to college, and leave home. We will develop emotional cripples and alienate our loved ones if we don't communicate trust and instill confidence in the next generation.

We should always exercise godly wisdom and caution in the face of real danger, but we can't always be with our loved ones. So we need to teach them how to live courageously and commit them to the care of the only One who can be with them every moment of the day. It is not enough to prepare our children for the physical dangers that exist; we also need to prepare them for the spiritual battle that we are all in. Just before His departure from this earth, Jesus prayed for the 11 disciples He was leaving behind (Satan had already claimed Judas), and for all those who believe in Him: "I do not ask You to take them out of the world, but to keep them from the evil one. They are not of the world, even as I am not of the world. Sanctify them in the truth; Your word is truth" (John 17:15-17).

God's people throughout the ages have suffered the most awful atrocities at the hands of cruel and evil people. In fact, being an outspoken Christian in some countries of the world today is tantamount to signing your death warrant. The prophets and saints of old "experienced mockings and scourgings, yes, also chains and imprisonment. They were stoned, they were sawn in two, they were tempted, they were put to death with the sword" (Hebrews 11:36-37).

Stephen courageously shared his faith and became the first martyr in the church. His death, recorded in Acts 7:54-60, is a testimony to the sufficiency of God's grace, even at the moment of death:

> Now when they [the Sanhedrin] heard this, they were cut to the quick, and they began gnashing their teeth at him. But being full of the Holy Spirit, he gazed intently into heaven and saw the glory of God, and Jesus standing at the right hand of God; and he said, "Behold, I see the heavens opened up and the Son of Man standing at the right hand of God." But they cried out with a loud voice, and covered their ears and rushed at him with one impulse. When they had driven him out of the city, they began stoning him; and the witnesses laid aside their robes at the feet of a young man named Saul. They went on stoning Stephen as he called on the Lord and said, "Lord Jesus, receive my spirit!" Then falling on his knees, he cried out with a loud voice, "Lord, do not hold this sin against them!" Having said this, he fell asleep.

Scripture tells us that Jesus is seated at the right hand of God (see Luke 22:69; Ephesians 1:20; Colossians 3:1), but Stephen saw Him standing. Do we dare say that Jesus made a "standing ovation" for the greatest performance of any witness ever? We teach our children to dial 911 when faced with a crisis. For the Christian, that is Psalm 91:1 and the verses that follow:

> He who dwells in the shelter of the Most High will abide in the shadow of the Almighty. I will say to the Lord, "My refuge and my fortress, my God, in whom I trust!" For it is He who delivers you from the snare of the trapper and from the deadly pestilence. He will cover you with His pinions, and under His wings you may seek refuge; His faithfulness is a shield and bulwark.
>
> You will not be afraid of the terror by night, or of the

arrow that flies by day; of the pestilence that stalks in darkness, or of the destruction that lays waste at noon. A thousand may fall at your side and ten thousand at your right hand, but it shall not approach you. You will only look on with your eyes and see the recompense of the wicked. For you have made the LORD, my refuge, even the Most High, your dwelling place. No evil will befall you, nor will any plague come near your tent.

For He will give His angels charge concerning you, to guard you in all your ways. They will bear you up in their hands, that you do not strike your foot against a stone. You will tread upon the lion and cobra, the young lion and the serpent you will trample down.

"Because he has loved Me, therefore I will deliver him; I will set him securely on high, because he has known My name. He will call upon Me, and I will answer him; I will be with him in trouble; I will rescue him and honor him. With a long life I will satisfy him and let him see My salvation" (Psalm 91).

Discussion Questions

1. What does the last Adam have in common with the first Adam, and how are they different?

2. What is hell?

3. Why do we fear death?

4. Who once held the power of death, and how has that power been overcome?

5. Why do you think people are so easily duped by false healings?

6. Why is it so important to know who we are "in Christ"?

7. What happens when we physically die?

8. How can we be assured of our salvation?

9. Why are sexual sins so difficult to overcome?

10. How can the fear of losing a loved one to death have a negative effect on how we relate to them?

The Steps to Freedom in Christ

Bondage versus Freedom

Many times we feel trapped in a vicious cycle of "sin, confess; sin, confess" that never seems to end, but God's promises say, "God is faithful, and he will not let you be tempted beyond your ability, but with the temptation he will also provide the way of escape" (1 Corinthians 10:13 ESV) and, "Submit therefore to God. Resist the devil and he will flee from you" (James 4:7). If you did not choose the way of escape and sinned, then you should confess that to God, ask Him to fill you with His Holy Spirit, and resist the devil by putting on the full armor of God (see Ephesians 6:10-17).

Sin that has become a habit may require you to seek help from a trusted brother or sister in Christ. James 5:16 says, "Confess your sins to one another, and pray for one another so that you may be healed. The effective prayer of a righteous man can accomplish much." Sometimes the assurance of 1 John 1:9 is enough: "If we confess our sins, He is faithful and righteous to forgive us our sins and to cleanse us from all unrighteousness." Remember, confession is not simply saying, "I'm sorry"; it is openly admitting, "I did it." Whether you need help from other people or just the accountability of walking in the light before God, pray the following prayer:

> *Dear heavenly Father, You have told me to put on the Lord Jesus Christ and make no provision for the flesh in regard to its lust. I confess that I have given in to fleshly lusts that wage war against my soul. I thank You that in Christ my sins are already forgiven, but I have broken Your holy law and allowed sin to wage war in my body. I come to You now*

to confess and renounce these sins of the flesh so that I might
be cleansed and set free from the bondage of sin. Please reveal
to my mind all the sins of the flesh I have committed and the
ways I have grieved the Holy Spirit. In Jesus's holy name I
pray. Amen. (See Romans 6:12-13; 13:14; 2 Corinthians
4:2; James 4:1; 1 Peter 2:11; and 5:8.)

The following list contains many sins of the flesh, but a prayerful examination of Mark 7:20-23; Galatians 5:19-21; Ephesians 4:25-31; and other passages will help you to be even more thorough. Look over the list below and ask the Holy Spirit to bring to your mind the sins you need to confess. He may reveal others to you as well. For each sin the Lord shows you, pray a prayer of confession from your heart. Use the sample prayer following the list to help you confess these sins to God.

Note: Sexual sins, marriage and divorce issues, gender identity, abortion, suicidal tendencies, perfectionism, eating disorders, substance abuse, gambling, and bigotry will be dealt with later in this Step.

__ Stealing   __ Quarreling/fighting

__ Jealousy/envy   __ Complaining/criticism

__ Sarcasm   __ Gossip/slander

__ Swearing   __ Apathy/laziness

__ Lying   __ Hatred

__ Anger   __ Drunkenness

__ Cheating   __ Avoiding responsibility

__ Greed/materialism

Others: _____

Dear heavenly Father, I confess that I have sinned against You
by __name the sins__. Thank You for Your forgiveness and cleans-
ing. I now turn away from these expressions of sin and turn

*to You, Lord. Fill me with Your Holy Spirit so that I will not
carry out the desires of the flesh. In Jesus's name I pray. Amen.*

Resolving Sexual Sin

It is our responsibility not to allow sin to reign (rule) in our physical bodies. To avoid that, we must not use our bodies or another person's body as instruments of unrighteousness (see Romans 6:12-13).
Sexual immorality is not only a sin against God, but it is a sin against
the body, which is the temple of the Holy Spirit (1 Corinthians 6:18-
19). Sex was intended by God to be the means for procreation and for
the pleasure of a husband and wife. When marriage is consummated,
the two become one flesh (Genesis 2:24). If we sexually join our bodies to another person outside of marriage, we also become "one flesh"
with that person (1 Corinthians 6:16), which creates a spiritual bond
between two people, leading to spiritual bondage—whether it is het-
erosexual or homosexual.

Sexual relations between people of the same sex are explicitly forbidden by God, but so is sex with someone of the opposite sex who is
not your spouse. To find freedom from sexual bondage, begin by praying the following prayer:

> *Dear heavenly Father, I have allowed sin to reign in my mor-
> tal body. I ask You to bring to my mind every sexual use of
> my body as an instrument of unrighteousness so that I can
> renounce those sexual sins and break those sinful bondages.
> In Jesus's name I pray. Amen.*

As the Lord brings to your mind every immoral sexual use of your
body, whether it was done to you (rape, incest, sexual molestation)
or willingly by you (pornography, masturbation, sexual immorality),
renounce every experience as follows:

> *Dear heavenly Father, I renounce <u>name the sexual experi-
> ence</u> with <u>person's name</u>. I ask You to break that sinful bond*

with <u>person's name</u> spiritually, physically, and emotionally. In Jesus's name I pray. Amen.

If you have used pornography, say the following prayer:

Dear heavenly Father, I confess that I have looked at sexually suggestive and pornographic material for the purpose of stimulating myself sexually. I have attempted to satisfy my lustful desires wrongly, and I have polluted my body, soul, and spirit. Thank You for cleansing me and for Your forgiveness. I renounce any satanic bonds I have allowed in my life through the unrighteous use of my body and mind. Lord, I commit myself to destroy any objects in my possession that I have used for sexual stimulation and to turn away from all media that are associated with my sexual sin. I commit myself to the renewing of my mind and thinking pure thoughts. Fill me with your Holy Spirit, that I may not carry out the desires of the flesh. In Jesus's name I pray. Amen.

After you have finished, commit your body to God by praying:

Dear heavenly Father, I renounce all these uses of my body as an instrument of unrighteousness, and I admit to any willful participation. I choose to present my physical body to You as an instrument of righteousness, a living and holy sacrifice, acceptable to You. I choose to reserve the sexual use of my body for marriage only. I reject the devil's lie that my body is not clean or that it is dirty or in any way unacceptable to You as a result of my past sexual experiences. Lord, thank You that You have cleansed and forgiven me and that You love and accept me just the way I am. Therefore, I choose now to accept myself and my body as clean in Your eyes. In Jesus's name I pray. Amen.

Special Prayers and Decisions for Specific Situations

The following prayers will enhance your growth process and help you make critical decisions. On their own they are unlikely to bring complete resolution or recovery, but they are an excellent starting point. You will then need to work on renewing your mind. Please don't hesitate to seek godly counsel for additional help when needed.

Marriage

Dear heavenly Father, I choose to believe that You created us male and female and that marriage is a spiritual bond between one man and one woman who become one in Christ. I believe that bond can only be broken by death, adultery, or desertion by an unbelieving spouse. I choose to stay committed to my vows and to remain faithful to my spouse until physical death separates us. Give me the grace to be the spouse You created me to be and enable me to love and respect my partner in marriage. I will seek to change only myself and accept my spouse as You have accepted me. Teach me how to speak the truth in love, to be merciful as You have been merciful to me, and to forgive as You have forgiven me. In Jesus's name I pray. Amen.

Divorce

Dear heavenly Father, I have not been the spouse You created me to be, and I deeply regret that my marriage has failed. I choose to believe that You still love and accept me. I choose to believe that I am still Your child, and I know Your desire for me is that I continue serving You and others in Your Kingdom. Give me the grace to overcome the disappointment and emotional scars I carry, and I ask the same for my ex-spouse. I choose to forgive my ex-spouse, and I choose to forgive myself for all the ways I contributed to the divorce. Enable me to learn from my mistakes and guide me so that I don't repeat the same old flesh patterns. I choose to believe the truth that I am still accepted, secure, and significant in Christ. Please guide me to healthy relationships in Your church and keep me from seeking a marriage on the rebound. I trust You to supply all my needs in the future, and I commit myself to follow You. In Jesus's name I pray. Amen.

Gender Identity

Dear heavenly Father, I choose to believe that You have created all humanity to be either male or female (Genesis 1:27) and commanded us to maintain a distinction between the two genders (Deuteronomy 22:5; Romans 1:24-32). I confess that I have been influenced by the social pressures of this fallen world and the lies of Satan to question my biological gender identity and that of others. I renounce all the accusations and lies of Satan that would seek to convince me I am somebody other than who You created me to be. I choose to believe and accept my biological gender identity, and I pray that You would heal my damaged emotions and enable me to be transformed by the renewing of my mind. I take up the full armor of God (Ephesians 6:13) and the shield of faith to extinguish all the temptations and accusation of the evil one (Ephesians 6:16). I renounce any identities and labels that derive from my old nature, and I choose to believe that I am a new creation in Christ. In the wonderful name of Jesus I pray. Amen.

Abortion

Dear heavenly Father, I confess that I was not a proper guardian and keeper of the life You entrusted to me, and I confess that I have sinned. Thank You that because of Your forgiveness, I can forgive myself. I commit my child to You for all eternity and believe that he or she is in Your caring hands. In Jesus's name I pray. Amen.

Suicidal Tendencies

Dear heavenly Father, I renounce all suicidal thoughts and any attempts I've made to take my own life or in any way injure myself. I renounce the lies that life is hopeless and that I can find peace and freedom by taking my own life. Satan is a thief and comes to steal, kill, and destroy. I choose to remain alive in Christ, who said He came to give me life and give it abundantly. Thank You for Your forgiveness that allows me to forgive myself. I choose to believe that there is always hope in Christ and that my heavenly Father loves me. In Jesus's name, I pray. Amen.

Drivenness and Perfectionism

Dear heavenly Father, I renounce the lie that my sense of worth is dependent upon my ability to perform. I announce the truth that my identity and sense of worth are found in who I am as Your child. I renounce seeking the approval and acceptance of other people for my affirmation, and I choose to believe the truth that I am already approved and accepted in Christ because of His death and resurrection for me. I choose to believe the truth that I have been saved, not by deeds done in righteousness, but according to Your mercy. I choose to believe that I am no longer under the curse of the law, because Christ became a curse for me (Galatians 3:13). I receive the free gift of life in Christ and choose to abide in Him. I renounce striving for perfection by living under the law. By Your grace, heavenly Father, I choose from this day forward to walk by faith in the power of Your Holy Spirit, according to what You have said is true. In Jesus's name I pray. Amen.

Eating Disorders or Self-Mutilation

Dear heavenly Father, I renounce the lie that my value as a person is dependent upon my appearance or performance. I renounce cutting or abusing myself, vomiting, misusing laxatives, or starving myself as a means of being in control, altering my appearance, or trying to cleanse myself of evil. I announce that only the blood of the Lord Jesus Christ cleanses me from sin. I realize I have been bought with a price, and my body, the temple of the Holy Spirit, belongs to God. Therefore, I choose to glorify God in my body. I renounce the lie that I am still evil or that any part of my body is evil. Thank You that You accept me just the way I am in Christ. In Jesus's name I pray. Amen.

Substance Abuse

Dear heavenly Father, I confess that I have misused substances (alcohol, tobacco, food, or prescription or street drugs) for the purpose of pleasure, to escape reality, or to cope with difficult problems. I confess that I have abused my body and programmed my mind in harmful ways. I have quenched the Holy Spirit as well. Thank You for Your forgiveness. I renounce any satanic connection or influence in my life through my misuse of food or chemicals. I cast my anxieties onto Christ, who loves me. I commit myself to yield no longer to substance abuse; instead, I choose to allow the Holy Spirit to direct and empower me. In Jesus's name I pray. Amen.

Gambling

Dear heavenly Father, I confess that I have been a poor steward of the financial resources that have been in my possession. I have gambled away my future by chasing a false god. I have not been content with food and clothing, and the love of money has driven me to behave irrationally and sinfully. I renounce making provision for my flesh in regard to this lust. I commit myself to stay away from all gambling casinos, gambling websites, bookmakers, and lottery sales. I choose to believe that I am alive in Christ and dead to sin. Fill me with Your Holy Spirit so that I don't carry out the desires of the flesh. Show me the way of escape when I am tempted to return to my addictive behaviors. I stand against all of Satan's accusations, temptations, and deceptions by putting on the armor

of God and standing firm in my faith. I choose to believe that
You will meet all my needs according Your riches in glory. In
Jesus's name I pray. Amen.

Bigotry

Dear heavenly Father, You have created all humanity in
Your image. I confess that I have judged others by the color of
their skin, their national origin, their social or economic sta-
tus, their cultural differences, or their sexual orientation. I
renounce racism, elitism, and sexism. I choose to believe that
"there is neither Jew nor Greek, there is neither slave nor free
man, there is neither male nor female; for you are all one in
Christ Jesus" (Galatians 3:28). Please show me the roots of
my own bigotry so that I may confess it and be cleansed from
such defilement. I pledge myself "to walk in a manner worthy
of the calling to which [I] have been called, with all humil-
ity and gentleness, with patience, bearing with one another
in love, eager to maintain the unity of the Spirit in the bond
of peace" (Ephesians 4:1-3 ESV). In Jesus's name I pray. Amen.

Chapter Four

Fear of Man

He that fears you present, will hate you absent.

Thomas Fuller (1654–1734), Gnomologia

In Hannah Hurnard's classic book *Hinds' Feet on High Places*, the main character, a woman named Much-Afraid, encounters the Shepherd, a picture of Christ. He tenderly places the sharp thorn of love into her heart and invites her to join him on a journey into the mountains.

Much-Afraid is thrilled to know that at the end of her journey she will be healed of her lameness and ugliness and will receive love in return. She eagerly accepts the Shepherd's invitation and sets off for her cottage to prepare for her departure from the Valley of Humiliation.

She is especially excited to go because her relatives, the Fearings, have been pressuring her to stay and marry her cousin Craven Fear, whom she despises. The following excerpt from the book illustrates graphically the terror that can control someone who is in bondage to the fear of man:

> She walked singing across the first field and was halfway over the next when suddenly she saw Craven Fear, himself, coming toward her. Poor Much-Afraid; for a little while she had completely forgotten the existence of her dreadful relatives, and now here was the most dreaded and detested of them all slouching toward her. Her heart filled with a terrible panic. She looked right and left, but

there was no hiding place anywhere, and besides, it was all too obvious that he was actually coming to meet her, for as soon as he saw her he quickened his pace, and in a moment or two was right beside her.

With a horror that sickened her very heart she heard him say, "Well, here you are at last, little Cousin Much-Afraid. So we are to be married, eh, what do you think of that?" And he pinched her, presumably in a playful manner, but viciously enough to make her gasp and bite her lips to keep back a cry of pain.

She shrank away from him and shook with terror and loathing. Unfortunately this was the worst thing she could have done, for it was always her obvious fear which encouraged him to continue tormenting her. If only she could have ignored him, he soon would have tired of teasing and of her company and would have wandered off to look for other prey. In all her life, however, Much-Afraid had never been able to ignore Fear. Now it was absolutely beyond her power to conceal the dread which she felt.

Her white face and terrified eyes immediately had the effect of stimulating Craven's desire to bait her. Here she was, alone and completely in his power.[1]

Many of us can relate to Much-Afraid's plight. It painfully reminds us of times we were bullied as children. Separated from the protection of parents or friends, we were intimidated into submission by somebody who was bigger, stronger, smarter, or more aggressive.

Maybe the bully was your brother or sister. Sadly, for many, it was a parent. Maybe for you it still is. Maybe the one you fear is your boss or your spouse. It could even be your own child who has manipulated the reins of household control away from you.

Although we will be confronted by people and situations that frighten us in this life, it is clear from Scripture that we are not to be controlled by the fear of man. Jesus said, "What I tell you in the darkness, speak in the light; and what you hear whispered in your ear, proclaim upon the housetops. Do not fear those who kill the body but are unable to kill the soul; but rather fear Him who is able to destroy both soul and body in hell" (Matthew 10:27-28).

Jesus lived in the real world, and in His humanity He experienced the reality of our situation and what people can do to each other. They can ridicule us, reject us, and ruin our reputations. They can do us physical harm and even take our lives. Jesus experienced all of those things, but He was never controlled by the fear of man. Jesus showed us how a Spirit-filled believer can live a righteous life, one that is totally dependent upon God, and worship Him alone. "The fear of man brings a snare, but he who trusts in the LORD will be exalted" (Proverbs 29:25).

The Courage of Conviction

The fear of man led to the sad demise of King Saul of Israel. Saul boasted to Samuel about carrying out the command of God (1 Samuel 15:13), but he had kept the spoils of war for himself, which God had forbidden. When confronted by Samuel for not obeying the voice of God, Saul said to him, "I have sinned; I have indeed transgressed the command of the LORD and your words, because I feared the people and listened to their voice" (1 Samuel 15:24). He was a man of shallow convictions, who only paid lip service to the commandments of God. One doesn't overcome the fear of man with a half-hearted commitment to God. The courage to live out our convictions is a challenge believers face every day.

Suppose you have a very intimidating boss, but you aren't afraid of him as you read this book because he probably isn't present. He often asks you at work to do things that violate your conscience, such as lying for him. What would happen if you decided that you couldn't do that anymore? What power does he have over you? In this case he could ridicule you, curse you, or fire you and hire someone else who will cater to his demands.

We don't suggest you quit your job or be rebellious, but we do think you should be willing to lose your job rather than compromise who you are. You could say something like, "Sir, I want to be the best employee that I can be and work for the success of the company, but I can't lie for you." If you lose your job for standing firm in your convictions, then trust God that He has something better for you than to cower under such intimidation. The only power that people have over you is what you give to them, because nobody can keep you from being the person God created you to be.

We should always look for and offer an alternative to demands placed upon us that would violate our convictions. Daniel was given a privileged position in the court of the king, who appointed them a daily ration from his choice food and wine. "But Daniel made up his mind that he would not defile himself with the king's choice food or with the wine which he drank" (Daniel 1:8), which put his direct supervisor in a tough position. The commander favored Daniel, but said to him, "I am afraid of my lord the king, who has appointed your food and your drink" (verse 10). Rather than be openly rebellious, Daniel offered a creative alternative: "Please test your servants for ten days, and let us be given some vegetables to eat and water to drink. Then let our appearance be observed in your presence and the appearance of the youths who are eating the king's choice food; and deal with your servants according to what you see" (verses 12-13). After ten days, Daniel and his companions were clearly healthier than those who followed the king's menu, and everyone got what they wanted (verses 15-16).

Sometimes there is no alternative when our faith is put to the test. Peter and some of the apostles were put in prison for teaching the truth, but miraculously escaped and continued to teach in the temple. They were brought before the council, and the high priest reminded them that they had been ordered not to teach about Jesus. "But Peter and the apostles answered, 'We must obey God rather than men'" (Acts 5:29).

The Bondage of People Pleasing

The apostle Paul said of himself, "Am I now seeking the favor of men, or of God? Or am I striving to please men? If I were still trying to please men, I would not be a bond-servant of Christ" (Galatians 1:10). People pleasers are bond-servants of people. Everybody wants others to like them, but we are being ruled by others if we try to live up to their expectations. We should make it our ambition to please the Lord, because "when a man's ways are pleasing to the LORD, He makes even his enemies to be at peace with him" (Proverbs 16:7).

In a slave-master (or employer-employee) working relationship, you should "do your work heartily, as for the Lord rather than for men, knowing that from the Lord you will receive the reward of the inheritance. It is the Lord Christ whom you serve" (Colossians 3:23-24). In other words, whether you work at a company, at home, or for the government, you will have someone in a position of authority over you—but in reality, you are working for God. That should make you a better employee and a better ambassador for Christ. However, you can be taken advantage of, which is why Paul adds, "Masters, grant to your slaves justice and fairness, knowing that you too have a Master in heaven" (Colossians 4:1).

The following testimony from a woman in full-time ministry illustrates how you can sometimes be mistreated unless you speak up:

> I was working for a Christian missionary organization in the area of communications, which was my expertise. I, however, was wanting more responsibilities when my leader asked me to assist the director in her assorted duties. I gladly accepted.
>
> Within the next six months I personally had taken on the added job of helping local people minister in a nearby country that was spiritually oppressed. It was a needed ministry and one I personally owned in my heart.

A few months later I was approached again with the opportunity to add the title of office manager to my plate. I accepted, knowing that I was probably the best person for the job and that there was no one else to take the position since our staff was small at the time.

Within another six months my leader approached me again with the idea of being personnel coordinator as well. I accepted; however, this time I felt trapped—like I had to take on this added responsibility or let the leadership and the organization down.

After working five different jobs for a few months, I conferred with my leader and told him I needed to get rid of some responsibilities, because I felt I could not handle them all. I was not doing any of them well.

He said I needed to get a handle on time management and left it at that. I felt like, yes, it was my fault that I could not handle the jobs given to me. So I cried out to God to help me and went back to all my jobs feeling trapped by the leadership as well as by my own feelings of needing acceptance. If I could do these jobs well, then I would know that I was really accepted by the people over me and also by God. I could not let anybody down. I had taken on a perfectionist outlook. I had to do everything right.

I had to make it work. I worked long, stressful hours every day. I left work feeling inadequate, like I just was not good enough. I never could measure up to my own expectations, much less those of others, and I felt like a failure.

The Courage to Say No

This woman's struggle with saying no is symptomatic of people pleasing. People pleasers are looking for affirmation from others and fear rejection and disapproval. When do we say no to the responsibilities offered to (or dumped on) us by those in authority over us? And when do we submit and simply accept those tasks as from the hand of

God? What criteria do we use to gauge our decision to remain with a company or seek employment elsewhere? When are feelings of entrapment the result of our own wrong attitudes or a warning that we are being taken advantage of? Can we trust God to supply all our needs if we lose employment for the sake of living righteously?

These are tough questions for those fearing rejection and looking for the approval of others. Unless they turn to God or He mercifully intervenes, they will eventually succumb to fear, depression, physical illness, and incompetence. Fortunately, God's merciful intervention was the case for this woman, whose testimony concludes as follows:

> Finally I was transferred to another part of the world but with the same organization. God had heard my prayer and rescued me. He took me out of a situation I could not handle. It was His grace and mercy.
>
> At this new location, the leadership was very wise and discerning. That first week they saw how burned out and hurt I was. They did not give me any added responsibilities, but gave me love and acceptance. God used this time to bring healing to my heart and soul. He taught me what it meant to be accepted for who I was. I learned to just be.
>
> God loved me in my disappointments and fears and showed me that I didn't have to strive anymore for acceptance from Him or others—that I was wonderful in who He made me to be. I did not have to try and be anything else but me. I came to realize that God loved me for who I was, His daughter, and not because of what I could do for Him.

The Comfort of God's Presence

We are more prone to be governed by the fear of man if we are not secure in the unconditional love and acceptance of God. It is also easy to overlook the omnipresence and omnipotence of our invisible God when confronted by various fear objects we can see. That is why we need to continually worship God, which is to ascribe to Him His divine attributes. We need to keep our minds filled with the knowledge of His almighty presence.

God brought this point home when He reproved His people through the prophet Isaiah for their faintheartedness in the face of human enemies:

> I, even I, am He who comforts you. Who are you that you are afraid of man who dies and of the son of man who is made like grass, that you have forgotten the LORD your Maker, who stretched out the heavens and laid the foundations of the earth, that you fear continually all day long because of the fury of the oppressor, as he makes ready to destroy? But where is the fury of the oppressor? (Isaiah 51:12-13).

God presents a stark contrast between mere mortals and Himself. The bottom line is that natural people live and die like grass, and God is the creator of heaven and earth (including the grass!). Why be afraid of man, who may oppress temporarily, when God is the eternal, all-powerful comforter? As long as we live on planet Earth, people will be present, but what power do they have over us that cannot be overcome in Christ? None. Not even death, which was the case for the martyred missionary Jim Elliot, who said, "He is no fool who gives what he cannot keep to gain that which he cannot lose." We may be rejected by people, but we will always be "a chosen race, a royal priesthood, a holy nation, a people for God's own possession" (1 Peter 2:9).

In our opening story from *Hinds' Feet on High Places*, Much-Afraid took her eyes off the Shepherd and was overwhelmed with Fear. She found help from the All-Powerful One when she cried out in fear and pain:

> [Craven Fear] caught hold of her, and poor Much-Afraid

uttered one frenzied cry of terror and pain. At that moment Craven Fear loosed his grasp and cringed away.

The Shepherd had approached them unperceived and was standing beside them. One look at his stern face and flashing eyes and the stout Shepherd's cudgel grasped in his strong, uplifted hand was more than enough for the bully. Craven Fear slunk away like a whipped cur, actually running from the village instead of toward it, not knowing where he was going, urged by one instinct alone, to find a place of safety.[2]

Being driven by the fear of man and living by faith in God cannot be operative in our lives at the same time. We will always struggle with tempting thoughts and fearful feelings, but they do not have to keep us from making the choice to walk by faith in God. That is courage—making that choice to walk by faith and to do what's right in the face of fear. Being alive and free in Christ doesn't mean we will never feel fear; it means that such fears no longer have any power over us if we exercise our faith in God.

The Courage to Share Our Faith

Paul preached the gospel of grace, knowing that it ran crosscurrent with the preaching of the Judaizers who wanted to bring new Gentile converts under the yoke of the law. Paul ferociously attacked their false teaching and accepted some painful shots while protecting the church from heresy. How many believers are scared into silence when they ought to be proclaiming from the rooftops what God has done for them in Christ? How many times do we sense the inner urging of the Spirit of God to witness for Christ, but we keep quiet with the excuse that we don't want to appear pushy, preachy, or insensitive?

Do we value our own safety and security more than the soul of another person? Most of us would emphatically say no—but when an opportunity arises to share our faith, we are paralyzed by fear. Where does that fear come from? "God has not given us a spirit of fear, but of power and of love and of a sound mind" (2 Timothy 1:7 NKJV).

Phobias drain our confidence and make physically strong people feel weak and paralyzed. It takes away love for others and drives us into a whirlpool of self-centeredness. Fear of mankind and love of mankind are mutually exclusive. Love is self-giving, but fear is self-protecting. Love moves toward others; fear causes us to shrink from others. Fear steals our wisdom and clear thinking, replacing them with confusion and error.

Dr. Bill Bright's personal life and ministry as founder of Cru (formerly known as Campus Crusade for Christ) is a testimony to the power of the Holy Spirit in witnessing. In his book *Witnessing Without Fear*, he wrote:

> Witnessing for our Lord is something we all know we should do...Yet witnessing is an activity we frequently shrink from. To intrude in someone else's life seems not only threatening but blatantly presumptuous. We fear offending the other person, fear being rejected, fear doing an inadequate job of representing our Lord and even being branded a "fanatic."[3]

Dr. Bright suggests three main reasons for believers' timidity in evangelism: spiritual lethargy (not being filled with the Spirit due to sin), lack of proper training, and listening to the devil's lies.[4] It stands to reason that if the gospel is the power of God for salvation, then the enemy will do all he can to keep God's people from being the ambassadors He has called them to be. Satan is the father of lies, and if we believe him, we will keep silent. Following are some of the specific lying "lines" the enemy tries to feed us, according to Dr. Bright:

- "Mind your own business—you don't have any right to force your views on others."

- "You're going to offend this person. Don't say anything."
- "That person will think you're a fanatic."
- "This person will say no, and you'll be embarrassed."[5]

Notice that each one of the devil's lies is targeted at our own insecurities. We naturally want other people to like and respect us. We feel more comfortable when things are peaceful and free of conflict or controversy. Far too often we keep quiet, or we talk about everything under the sun except Jesus and our faith in Him. "But even if you should suffer for the sake of righteousness, you are blessed. And do not fear their intimidation, and do not be troubled, but sanctify Christ as Lord in your hearts, always being ready to make a defense to everyone who asks you to give an account for the hope that is in you, yet with gentleness and reverence" (1 Peter 3:14-15).

Courage Under Fire

How do you find the courage to face fear and do what's right when the stakes are much higher? It is one thing to be embarrassed for a moment by a stranger; it is something much riskier when a job (and its salary or opportunity for advancement) is involved. Even more tenuous is a situation where a close relationship with a loved one is in jeopardy—or when one's personal health, safety, or life is at stake.

As long as we perceive that somebody or something has the power to destroy anything we value, we will be in bondage to that fear object. And that fear will paralyze us into a life of compromise or withdrawal.

The apostle Paul didn't shrink in the face of opposition. Consider his litany of afflictions in 2 Corinthians 11:23-26:

> Are they servants of Christ?—I speak as if insane—I more
> so; in far more labors, in far more imprisonments, beaten
> times without number, often in danger of death. Five times
> I received from the Jews thirty-nine lashes. Three times
> I was beaten with rods, once I was stoned...[in] dangers

from robbers, dangers from my countrymen, dangers
from the Gentiles, dangers in the city, dangers in the wilderness, dangers on the sea, dangers among false brethren.

Such a man is untouchable, unshakable, and unstoppable. The
devil could not deter him from preaching the gospel, and neither could
godless people. He was a living, breathing example of what John wrote
about in Revelation 12:11: "They overcame him [the devil] because of
the blood of the Lamb and because of the word of their testimony, and
they did not love their life even when faced with death."

Freedom from Control and Abuse

If you believe that your sense of worth is dependent upon the
approval and acceptance of others, you will be in subjection to them.
As long as we believe that people have something we need for our own
physical or psychological well-being, we will fear the possibility that
they will withhold it.

A forty-year-old wife and mother of three children was so afraid of
her mother that she would do anything she said. Everything she did
at home was motivated by the approval or disapproval of her mother.
A huge inheritance hung over her head. Her brother had walked away
from their mother's manipulative control years earlier and had been
disinherited.

She was encouraged to write or speak to her mother for the purpose of respectfully informing her that she could no longer live that
way. Being subject to her mother's manipulative control was destroying her marriage and compromising her walk with God. She too was
disinherited for three years. But it gets lonely when nobody will play
your control game any longer, so the mother finally capitulated and
sought reconciliation.

Nobody has the right to usurp God's role in our lives. The fruit
of the Spirit is self-control—not "spouse control" or "child control."
That doesn't mean we shouldn't be submissive to governing authorities.
We should be, but without compromising who we are. Submission is

trusting God to work through someone less than perfect—husbands, wives, parents, and employers—and by so doing, find favor with God (1 Peter 2:13-17; 3:1-7).

If you are being harassed or abused in the workplace, you need to appeal appropriately up the chain of command for redress. Yes, there are risks for being a whistle blower, but if someone doesn't report the abuse, it will only continue. Evil will flourish if good people do nothing.

Fear is what keeps the mentally, emotionally, and sexually abused victims from seeking help. Often they are threatened by the abusers that worse will come if they say anything. They fear being blamed for destroying the family. Wives will stay in abusive situations, because they fear losing financial support. Abusers need to be turned in to responsible authorities. There are laws in our land to protect battered wives (and husbands) and abused children. You will never help an abuser by allowing him or her to continue in their sickness and sin. Getting help for yourself and the abuser is the most loving thing you can do.

At times like these, the church ought to provide sanctuary for victims of abuse, even to the point of offering a safe place to go until the danger has passed or the abuse has ceased. Christ wants to manifest His caring presence and protection for the oppressed through His people.

Unfortunately, the church has at times been a culprit under the false pretense of "touch not mine anointed" (1 Chronicles 16:22 KJV). We have counseled numerous victims of sexual sins within the church, who were told by church officials to keep their mouths shut in order to protect the officials' reputations. Some were warned not to bring an accusation against an elder. The Catholic Church is paying a horrible price for covering up sexually deviant priests. Fear had kept their victims from reporting their sins for years. Spiritual abuse is a double offense, because victims are not only being abused, but the abuse is committed by the ones they were supposed to go to for protection. The same goes for parents. Imagine what it must feel like to be blamed for damaging the family's or church's reputation when you are the victim.

A few brave souls may have to stand alone when attacked by evil people. Alexander the coppersmith did Paul much harm (2 Timothy 4:14), for which he will answer to God. Paul recounts how difficult it was to be deserted by everyone, but also how God had and would continue to rescue him:

> At my first defense no one supported me, but all deserted me; may it not be counted against them. But the Lord stood with me and strengthened me, so that through me the proclamation might be fully accomplished, and that all the Gentiles might hear; and I was rescued out of the lion's mouth. The Lord will rescue me from every evil deed, and will bring me safely to His heavenly kingdom; to Him be the glory forever and ever. Amen (verses 16-18).

Healing Damaged Emotions

Chances are you have been rejected, criticized, or falsely accused—and possibly have been physically, emotionally, or sexually abused. Our churches are full of wounded people, and so are many homes. Wounds that are not healed are often inflicted on others. Unless there is a way to free ourselves from the past, we will continue to wound one another. We can't promise that anyone reading this book will not be victimized by sick people in the future, but we can assure you that you don't have to be a victim anymore. We can't fix your past, and God doesn't either. Instead, He sets you free from it. How does He do that?

First, we are not just a product of our past; we are a product of Christ's work on the cross. We are a new creation in Christ. "The old things passed away; behold, new things have come" (2 Corinthians 5:17). God doesn't recognize us according to our flesh patterns or the defense mechanisms that were erected before forgiveness and new life were given to us (2 Corinthians 5:16). "Those who belong to Christ Jesus have crucified the flesh with its passions and desires" (Galatians 5:24).

Second, we are not in bondage to past traumas. Instead, we are in bondage to the lies we believed as a result of those traumas, such as *This is all my fault*; *God doesn't love or care for me*; *no one will believe me*; *I deserved this*; etc. Such lies are often deeply embedded and require the Holy Spirit to lead us into all truth. Jesus said, "If you continue in My word, then you are truly disciples of Mine; and you will know the truth, and the truth will make you free" (John 8:31-32).

Third, we have to forgive those who have offended us. Forgiving another is to set a captive free, only to realize that we were the captive ones. Those who hold on to their bitterness are bound to the past. As the saying goes, to remain bitter is like swallowing poison, while hoping the other person will die. "See to it that no one comes short of the grace of God; that no root of bitterness springing up causes trouble, and by it many be defiled" (Hebrews 12:15). Forgiving others as Christ has forgiven you is the most Christlike thing you can do, and you are doing it for your sake.

These three issues are why we have included the Steps in this book. To experience your freedom, you have to repent and believe the gospel, and that is what the Steps are designed to help you do. The Step at the end of this chapter is on forgiveness. For your sake and for the sake of those you live with, please take the time to forgive others as Christ has forgiven you.

Victory over Fear

Church history is filled with stories of martyrs who would not be swayed by the fear of man or death. Read about the "cloud of witnesses surrounding us" (Hebrews 12:1):

> What more shall I say? For time will fail me if I tell of Gideon, Barak, Samson, Jephthah, of David and Samuel and the prophets, who by faith conquered kingdoms, performed acts of righteousness, obtained promises, shut the mouths of lions, quenched the power of fire, escaped the edge of the sword, from weakness were made strong,

became mighty in war, put foreign armies to flight. Women received back their dead by resurrection; and others were tortured, not accepting their release, so that they might obtain a better resurrection; and others experienced mockings and scourgings, yes, also chains and imprisonment. They were stoned, they were sawn in two, they were tempted, they were put to death with the sword; they went about in sheepskins, in goatskins, being destitute, afflicted, ill-treated (men of whom the world was not worthy), wandering in deserts and mountains and caves and holes in the ground. And all these, having gained approval through their faith, did not receive what was promised, because God had provided something better for us, so that apart from us they would not be made perfect (Hebrews 11:32-40).

"What was promised" was the gospel, and that was yet future for the Old Testament saints. One of the greatest signs of maturity is the ability to postpone rewards. Be assured that God will always make it right in the end for those who put their trust in Him. Faith in God is the victory.

The following testimony shows one timid soul's victory over fear, and how it saved his marriage:

Seven years after I became a Christian, I was sitting in a church service, and the pastor asked a question: "Is there anyone else here that would like to follow Jesus in obedience through baptism?"

That was the beginning of my real fear. It meant getting up in front of the congregation, giving a testimony of how I became a believer, and then getting immersed in a tank. Getting immersed wasn't the problem. Speaking in front of the congregation was a minor problem. But losing my wife was a major problem.

As it turned out, my wife wouldn't even attend. She

was upset that I was becoming a "clone" like all the other people in that church. At least that was her viewpoint.

Well, the day came, and I was very scared, to say the least. But I knew courage was needed, and I would have to get through it to get it over with.

I was very blessed that God gave me boldness to share my faith from then on. No one could shut me up!

And then the real fears began.

I had started a business, and we were looking forward as a family to the American dream—earning a million dollars. Then things started to go very badly in the business, because I shared my faith with a customer. He became very angry with me for leaving my old church. The next thing I knew he took away the business he was giving us, which was one-third of our revenue.

We were doing over a million dollars in business that year.

Again, fear struck. I was afraid I would lose my job, house, and family. Several people prayed for me, and though I did lose the business, God gave me a better job with less working hours and more pay.

As I was progressing along in my Christian walk, a friend of mine told me to share something with my wife. You see, our marriage started getting worse because of my walk with Christ. She didn't want any part of it. He said that I needed to confront her with a question the next time she started to criticize me about Jesus.

Well, I told him, "You are crazy! She will just want a divorce this time."

Again, fear developed very strongly.

The question was, "Why do you reject Jesus?" I said, "That would be all I needed to do. She would ask for a divorce."

Sure enough, that night she started criticizing me

about my faith. I asked her the question, and as expected, she said it was about time for a divorce—the thing I dreaded most to hear.

But she started listening to me that night and started to read her Bible!

To make a long story short, within one month she received the Lord and has been as committed as I am (and sometimes much more!).

As I was reflecting on this two years ago when I was reading your book *The Bondage Breaker*, God showed me what the root of my fears was during a prayer time. When I was eight years old I was awakened suddenly in bed with an intense fear. I thought a snake was in bed with me. I was paralyzed for a moment until I had the courage to count to three then bolt out of bed and back into the living room where my parents were.

Naturally, they came back into the room with a flashlight to show me nothing was there. But do you see the correlation (i.e., snake and Satan)? The fears don't come back much anymore, but when they do, because of your ministry, I know now I have the authority in Christ to send them away, using the Word of God as my sword. Thanks for being faithful to help us live free in Christ.

Discussion Questions

1. What person or type of person has caused you the most fear? Why?

2. Think of a time when you were intimidated in an effort to make you compromise your convictions. What alternative could you have offered at the time?

3. How does your experience of living under the authority of others change when you choose to believe it is actually "the Lord Christ whom you serve" (Colossians 3:24)?

4. From one of the testimonies we shared, what should the exhausted woman working for a missionary organization have done on her first assignment?

5. Why is it hard for some people to say no?

6. What is the contrast between fearing God and fearing man?

7. Why is it that being driven by the fear of man and living by faith in God are mutually exclusive?

8. How are the fear of mankind and the love of mankind mutually exclusive?

9. Why are people afraid to report abuse?

10. How can you overcome past abuses?

The Steps to Freedom in Christ

Bitterness versus Forgiveness

We are called to be merciful just as our heavenly Father is merciful (Luke 6:36) and to forgive others as we have been forgiven (Ephesians 4:31-32). Doing so sets us free from our past and doesn't allow Satan to take advantage of us (2 Corinthians 2:10-11). Ask God to bring to your mind the people you need to forgive by praying the following prayer aloud:

> *Dear heavenly Father, I thank You for the riches of Your kindness, forbearance, and patience toward me, knowing that Your kindness has led me to repentance. I confess that I have not shown that same kindness and patience toward those who have hurt or offended me (Romans 2:4). Instead, I have held on to my anger, bitterness, and resentment toward them. Please bring to my mind all the people I need to forgive so I may now do so. In Jesus's name I pray. Amen.*

On a separate sheet of paper, list the names of people who come to your mind. At this point don't question whether you need to forgive them or not. Often we hold things against ourselves as well, punishing ourselves for wrong choices we've made in the past. Write "myself" at the bottom of your list if you need to forgive yourself. Forgiving yourself is accepting the truth that God has already forgiven you in Christ. If God forgives you, you can forgive yourself.

Also write down "thoughts against God" at the bottom of your list. Obviously, God has never done anything wrong, so He doesn't need our forgiveness—but we need to let go of our disappointments with our heavenly Father. People often harbor angry thoughts against Him because He did not do what they wanted Him to do. Those feelings of anger or resentment toward God need to be released.

Before you begin working through the process of forgiving those on your list, review what forgiveness is and what it is not. The critical points are highlighted in bold print below.

Forgiveness is not forgetting. People who want to forget all that was done to them will find they cannot do it. When God says that He will remember our sins no more, He is saying that He will not use the past against us. Forgetting is a long-term by-product of forgiveness, but it is never a means toward it. Don't put off forgiving those who have hurt you, hoping the pain will go away. Once you choose to forgive someone, then Christ will begin to heal your wounds. We don't heal in order to forgive; we forgive in order to heal.

Forgiveness is a choice, a decision of the will. Since God requires you to forgive, it is something you can do. Some people hold on to their anger as a means of protecting themselves against further abuse, but all they are doing is hurting themselves. Others want revenge. The Bible teaches, "'Vengeance is Mine, I will repay,' says the Lord" (Romans 12:19). Let God deal with the person. Let him or her off your hook, because as long as you refuse to forgive someone, you are still hooked to that person. You are still chained to your past, bound up in your bitterness. By forgiving, you let the other person off your hook, but he or she is not off God's hook. You must trust that God will deal with the person justly and fairly, something you simply cannot do. "But you don't know how much this person hurt me!" you say. No other human really knows another person's pain, but Jesus does, and He instructs us to forgive others for our own sake. Until you let go of your bitterness and hate, the person is still hurting you. Nobody can fix your past, but you can be free from it. What you gain by forgiving is freedom from your past and those who have abused you.

Forgiveness is agreeing to live with the consequences of another person's sin. We are all living with the consequences of someone else's sin. Our only choice is to do so in the bondage of bitterness or in the freedom of forgiveness. But where is the justice? The cross makes forgiveness legally and morally right. Jesus died once for all our sins. We are to forgive as Christ has forgiven us. He did that by taking upon Himself the consequences of our sins. God "made Him who knew no sin to be sin on our behalf, so that we might become the righteousness of God in Him" (2 Corinthians 5:21). We cannot wait for the other person to ask for our forgiveness. Remember, Jesus did not wait for those who were crucifying Him to apologize before He forgave them. Even while they mocked and jeered at Him, He prayed, "Father, forgive them; for they do not know what they are doing" (Luke 23:34).

Forgive from your heart. Allow God to bring to the surface your painful memories, and acknowledge how you feel toward those who've hurt you. If your forgiveness doesn't touch the emotional core of your life, it will be incomplete. Too often we're afraid of the pain, so we bury our emotions deep down inside us. But we need to let God bring them to the surface so He can begin to heal those damaged emotions.

Forgiveness is choosing not to hold someone's sin against him or her anymore. It is common for bitter people to bring up past offenses with those who have hurt them. They want them to feel as bad as they do. But you must let go of the past and choose to reject any thought of revenge. This doesn't mean you continue to put up with abuse. God does not tolerate sin, and neither should you. You will need to set up scriptural boundaries that put a stop to further abuse. Take a stand against sin while continuing to exercise grace and forgiveness toward those who hurt you. If you need help setting scriptural boundaries to protect yourself from further abuse, talk to a trusted friend, counselor, or discipler.

Don't wait until you feel like forgiving. You will never get there. Make the hard choice to forgive even if you don't feel like it. Once you choose to forgive, Satan will lose his hold on you, and God will begin to heal your damaged emotions. Start with the first person on your list and make the choice to forgive him or her for every painful memory that comes to your mind. Stay with that individual until you are sure you have dealt with all the remembered pain. Then work your way down the list in the same way. As you begin forgiving people, God may bring to your mind painful memories you've totally forgotten. Let Him do this even if it hurts. God is surfacing those painful memories so you can face them once for all time and let them go.

Don't excuse the offender's behavior, even if it is someone you are really close to. Don't say, "Lord, please help me to forgive." He is already helping you and will be with you all the way through the process. Don't say, "Lord, I want to forgive," because that bypasses the hard choice we have to make. Say, "Lord, I *choose* to forgive these people and what they did to me." For every painful memory that God reveals for each person on your list, pray as follows:

> *Dear heavenly Father, I choose to forgive <u>name the person</u> for <u>declare what they did or failed to do</u>, because it made me feel <u>share the painful feelings (i.e., rejected, dirty, worthless, inferior, etc.)</u>.*

After you have forgiven every person for every painful memory, then pray as follows:

Lord Jesus, I choose not to hold on to my resentment. I relinquish my right to seek revenge and ask You to heal my damaged emotions. Thank You for setting me free from the bondage of my bitterness. I now ask You to bless those who have hurt me. In Jesus's name I pray. Amen.

Note: During this step God may have brought to your mind people that you have knowingly or unknowingly wounded. See below for instruction on how to seek the forgiveness of others.

Seeking the Forgiveness of Others

Jesus said, "If you are offering your gift at the altar and there remember that your brother has something against you, leave your gift there before the altar and go. First be reconciled to your brother, and then come and offer your gift. Come to terms quickly with your accuser" (Matthew 5:23-25 ESV). If someone has hurt you, then go to God. You don't need to go to the offender to forgive them, and in many cases that would be inadvisable. Your need to forgive another is primarily an issue between you and God. However, if you have offended another, you must go to them, ask for their forgiveness, and make amends when appropriate. The following are steps to seeking forgiveness:

1. Be certain about what you did that was wrong and why it was wrong.

2. Make sure you have forgiven the other person for whatever they have done to you.

3. Think through exactly how you will ask them to forgive you.

4. Be sure to state that what you did was wrong.

5. Be specific and admit that you did it.

6. Don't offer any excuses or try to defend yourself.

7. Place no blame on any others.

8. Don't expect that they will ask *you* to forgive them, and don't let that be what motivates you to seek their forgiveness.

9. Your confession should lead to the direct question, "Will you forgive me?"

10. Seek the right place and the right time, but the sooner the better.

11. Ask for forgiveness in person, face to face whenever possible and safe.

12. Unless there is no other option, do not write a letter. It can be misunderstood, others may see it who are not involved, and it could be used against you in a court case or otherwise.

"If possible, so far as it depends on you, live peaceably with all" (Romans 12:18 ESV)—but keep in mind that it doesn't always depend on you. If the other person doesn't want to be reconciled, it won't happen. Reconciliation between two people requires repentance and forgiveness by both parties. Rarely is there one who is completely innocent. However, if you have forgiven the other person and genuinely asked their forgiveness, then you have done all God requires of you. Be at peace with God.

Prayer for Restoration of Broken Relationships

Dear heavenly Father, I confess and repent of my sins against my neighbor (spouse, parents, children, relatives, friends, neighbors, or brothers and sisters in Christ). Thank You for Your forgiveness. I forgive them for what they have done to me, and I choose not to hold it against them in the future. I ask that You bless them and enable them to live with the consequences of my sin against them. I pray that You would heal the wounds from the sins I have inflicted on them. I ask the same for myself, that I may be set free from the consequences of their sin or that You would give me the grace to live with the consequences without bitterness. I pray that You would heal my wounds and set me free so that I can live in peaceful coexistence with my neighbors and with You. In Jesus's name I pray. Amen.

Chapter Five

Fear of Failure

The danger is not that we should fall…but
that we should remain on the ground.

John Chrysostom

The late Mel Farr's best friends were his sons and his brothers, but worry was his most constant companion. It's what made him go to the University of Detroit at night after practicing all day with the Detroit Lions football team. It's what made him spend his off-season from training to become one of the first black auto dealers in the United States. It's what woke him up at three o'clock some mornings.

Farr told a journalist, "Guess what I do then? I get up and go to work. It's not work that kills the man. It's worry that kills the man. I'd much rather work than worry."

At age 52, Farr was the most successful black auto dealer in America and owner of the nation's second-largest African-American-owned private business. His fourteen franchises in five states grossed more than $500 million in sales annually. While he was pleased with what he'd accomplished since graduating from high school in Beaumont, Texas, it was the prospect of failure that drove him. "The minute you think you're there is when you stop trying. It's very difficult to stop something once it starts going down. My motivation is the fear of failure."[1]

Fear of failure is the motivation for most type A personalities and for everyone who is trying to please a significant other. A denominational leader told me in a private conversation, "As I talk to our pastors I have come to the conclusion that their number-one motivation in ministry is the fear of failure." I wondered at the time if that was true. So when I taught a doctor of ministry class, I had the students fill out a sentence completion questionnaire at the beginning of the week. One sentence they were to complete was, *The thing I fear the most is...* The students were all pastors in a doctoral program that required a master of divinity degree and a minimum of five years of ministry experience. Every response indicated a fear of failure. I was surprised and asked them why nobody said anything about fearing God. I heard a lot of excuses!

Fear of failure motivates some to climb the corporate ladder and others not to risk trying anything at all, thereby avoiding any possibility of failure. Fear has an object, but in this case, what exactly is it? How would you define failure? How would you define success? One person's success is another person's failure. One student could feel like a failure getting a "B" on an exam, while another student would be thrilled with that accomplishment. You could be a complete success in the eyes of God and a total failure in the eyes of the world, and vice versa.

A Biblical Definition of Success

Who is more successful: the best janitor a school ever had or the principal of that school? Which parent is more successful: the father of a corporate president or the mother of a handicapped child? Which student is most successful: the one who gets a perfect report card or the severely dyslexic student who barely manages to graduate with the aid of a tutor? You can't know the answer to those questions, because no two people have the same opportunity or potential.

God has not equally distributed gifts, talents, or intelligence to His children. Some have perfect pitch, while others are tone deaf. Some can do math, but others struggle adding and subtracting. Some can dunk a basketball, while others can't dribble. Suppose God did create two children exactly the same intellectually and athletically. One was born in

Connecticut to wealthy parents; the other was born in a remote jungle to parents who couldn't read or write. What would constitute success for either one?

Paul said, "We are not bold to class or compare ourselves with some of those who commend themselves; but when they measure themselves by themselves and compare themselves with themselves, they are without understanding" (2 Corinthians 10:12). To say, "I'm not as bad as him," or "I did better than her," is a common defense mechanism, but it reveals a lack of understanding. We can't determine our success or failure by comparing ourselves with others. There must be some other standard of evaluation for success by which we can motivate ourselves.

The first instruction in the Bible concerning success came just before Joshua led the Israelites into the Promised Land:

> Only be strong and very courageous; be careful to do according to all the law which Moses My servant commanded you; do not turn from it to the right or to the left, so that you may have success wherever you go. This book of the law shall not depart from your mouth, but you shall meditate on it day and night, so that you may be careful to do according to all that is written in it; for then you will make your way prosperous, and then you will have success (Joshua 1:7-8).

First Principle of Success

Joshua's success did not depend on favorable circumstances in the Promised Land, nor on the cooperation of the Philistines. The Israelites would be successful and prosperous if they understood and believed God's Word and lived accordingly. The first biblical principle of success is *to know God and His ways*. "Thus says the LORD, 'Let not a wise man boast of his wisdom, and let not the mighty man boast of his might, let not a rich man boast of his riches; but let him who boasts boast of this, that he understands and knows Me, that I am the LORD who exercises lovingkindness, justice and righteousness on earth; for I delight in these things,' declares the LORD" (Jeremiah 9:23-24; see also 1 Corinthians 1:31).

The ultimate failure is to never know God.

Nobody set the standard for success higher than the apostle Paul. He had intelligence, social status, and drive. He was the ultimate achiever and leading candidate for "theologian of the year" when Christ struck him down. Listen to how he describes his "before and after" drive for success:

> If anyone else has a mind to put confidence in the flesh, I far more: circumcised the eighth day, of the nation of Israel, of the tribe of Benjamin, a Hebrew of Hebrews; as to the Law, a Pharisee; as to zeal, a persecutor of the church; as to the righteousness which is in the Law, found blameless. But whatever things were gain to me, those things I have counted as loss for the sake of Christ. More than that, I count all things to be loss in view of the surpassing value of knowing Christ Jesus my Lord, for whom I have suffered the loss of all things, and count them but rubbish so that I may gain Christ (Philippians 3:4-8).

Paul is not the only person to climb the "corporate ladder," only to discover that it was leaning against the wrong wall. The feeling of success that comes from winning the race, getting the promotion, or graduating at the top of the class is very fleeting. What happens when you reach your goal? Does it satisfy? Do you need to climb one rung higher? "For what does it profit a man to gain the whole world, and forfeit his soul? For what will a man give in exchange for his soul?" (Mark 8:36-37).

What *does* satisfy? Take your highest standard of success in terms of appearance, performance, status, or possessions and then ask yourself, "If I were able to accomplish or possess it, would that bring lasting satisfaction?"

A middle-aged couple started attending our church because they were having problems in their marriage. He was a corporate attorney who had engineering and law degrees. He drove his attractive wife to church in a very expensive sports car. He even joined the choir, but resisted making a decision for Christ. He made an appointment with me and told me of a conversation he had with one of our members, who had said, "Why don't you become a Christian? You would be such a positive witness." A witness to what? His success as a natural man? Even he could see through that. The problem was, he had reached the top of the ladder and did not want to humble himself by beginning on the bottom rung of another ladder. He wanted to push the ladder over to the right wall and stay on top. He never did make a decision for Christ, and eventually he left the church and his wife for another woman. He was not a successful man.

There are no box scores in heaven keeping tabs on all the toys and trophies we accumulate in this world. Neither God nor the angels in heaven give a holy hoot about man-made achievements on earth, but there is one thing the angels do shout about: "I tell you, there is joy in the presence of the angels of God over one sinner who repents" (Luke 15:10).

There is only one thing that completely and continuously satisfies while living on earth. Jesus said, "Blessed are those who hunger and thirst for righteousness, for they shall be satisfied" (Matthew 5:6). Nothing else can satisfy like living a righteous life and being intimately related to our heavenly Father.

Second Principle of Success

It seems to have taken three years in the desert for Paul to overcome the loss of everything he once counted to be gain (see Galatians 1:15-18). Moving our ladder over to the right wall can be a humbling experience. God took away Paul's eyesight for a period of time and told him to get the help he needed from the people he once persecuted. God made sure that Paul started on the bottom rung, as we all have to do.

That is what brokenness is all about. With new life and a new purpose, Paul then set out in the right direction with a determination to become all that God created him to be:

> Not that I have already obtained it or have already become perfect, but I press on so that I may lay hold of that for which also I was laid hold of by Christ Jesus. Brethren, I do not regard myself as having laid hold of it yet; but one thing I do: forgetting what lies behind and reaching forward to what lies ahead, I press on toward the goal for the prize of the upward call of God in Christ Jesus (Philippians 3:12-14).

Paul was again motivated to succeed, but with the right goal. He pressed on to lay hold of whatever Christ wanted for him. Christ had chosen Paul for a purpose, as He has chosen all of us.

The second principle of success is *to become the people God created us to be*. That is also God's will for our lives (i.e., our sanctification [1 Thessalonians 4:3]). The fact that nobody and nothing can keep us from being the person God has created us to be is good news. The only thing or person that can keep us from being successful is ourselves.

We may not have enough time to accomplish what we want in life, but we have precisely enough time to do God's will. We may not be able to reach the position we wanted, but what position is higher than being seated with Christ in the heavenlies (Ephesians 2:6)? We can try to make a name for ourselves in the world, but what name could we make for ourselves that remotely compares to being called children of God (1 John 3:1)?

Scripture doesn't provide any instruction on career choices. There are no verses helping us to decide whether we should be engineers, teachers, or chefs—but He does guide us in our journey upward. Our professional niche in the world is dependent upon our God-given capabilities and favorable opportunities. The will of God is more concerned about what kind of *person* you are as an engineer, teacher, or chef. It is part of our calling to serve in certain roles, but the roles do not determine who we are. In other words, it isn't what we do that determines who we are; it is who we are that determines what we do.

So who are we? "Beloved, now we are children of God, and it has not appeared as yet what we will be. We know that when He appears, we will be like Him, because we will see Him just as He is. And everyone who has this hope fixed on Him purifies himself, just as He is pure" (1 John 3:2-3).

Scripture doesn't provide instruction for setting career goals either. However, setting career goals can be a good thing if they provide direction for your present-day work. Setting unrealistic goals for the future and hoping they will come true is setting yourself up for failure.

Suppose you have these personal goals: to own a small business, be a good witness in the community, live in a comfortable home in the right part of town, and have a nest egg set aside for retirement. Sounds like the American dream. With a lot of hard work, your business is showing a good profit, and you are well on your way to achieving your goals.

Then one day you discover that your trusted bookkeeper has been stealing money from the business. Instead of being financially prosperous, you find yourself facing the possibility of bankruptcy. To save the business, you mortgage your home and borrow money from your retirement savings. About the time your creditors have been paid off, the market goes bad and you have to lay off employees. Finally, you sell the business and seek employment elsewhere. Your house is mortgaged and your pension is gone—and so is your business. Despite your best efforts, what you may have feared the most has happened. Are you a failure?

Did those trials and tribulations keep you from being the person God created you to be? Did those circumstances, which you had no ability to control, take away your hope for the future? The apostle Paul wouldn't think so. He wrote, "We also exult in our tribulations, knowing that tribulation brings about perseverance; and perseverance, proven character; and proven character, hope; and hope does not disappoint, because the love of God has been poured out within our hearts through the Holy Spirit who was given to us" (Romans 5:3-5). It is hard for us to envision that God may actually thwart our career goals in order to make us the people we are called to be. The worldly idea of success can ruin a good person. Thank God He loves us enough to keep us from ruin.

The trials and tribulations can exacerbate the fear of failure if we have the wrong goal. But they actually contribute to the right goal of proven character, and that is where our hope lies. The successful Christian can survive any crisis by the grace of God and become the better for it.

Fred was a real estate agent who had the goal of selling two houses per week. His average the previous year had been one-and-a-half homes per week, so he thought he would give himself an additional incentive. He wanted to be the salesperson of the year, and the added income would enable him to buy the house he dreamed of. After one month, he had sold only three houses. Fear of failure motivated him to try harder, but his efforts didn't bear fruit. The pressure he put on himself started to show up in very negative ways. He became irritable and controlling, believing he needed to push others to cooperate with him so he could accomplish his goal.

Then the unthinkable happened. Fred was fired for his bad attitude at the office. How could he tell his wife? All his dreams went up in smoke. He became so depressed that all he could do was sit around the house, believing that he was a failure. Finally he swallowed his pride and called his pastor for an appointment.

After hearing his story, his pastor said, "Fred, you're a good person, but have you considered the possibility that you may have had the wrong goal? All God asks of us is to be the people He created us to be. There is nothing wrong with being the salesperson of the year and winning a trip to Hawaii or buying a better house to live in, but that alone wouldn't satisfy you, nor would it mean you were successful. Chasing your dream may have actually prevented you from being the salesperson, husband, and father God wanted you to be. Paul said, 'Do not merely look out for your own personal interests, but also for the interests of others. Have this attitude in yourselves which was also in Christ Jesus' (Philippians 2:4-5)."

God has not called us to fail. He wants us to prosper in our faith. John wrote, "Beloved, I pray that in all respects you may prosper and be in good health, just as your soul prospers" (3 John 2). A young lady flew across the country to see me because she was in spiritual bondage. She quoted that verse and asked, "Why isn't God prospering me?" It turned out that she had had two abortions and tried unsuccessfully three times to overcome her chemical addictions in a secular treatment program. In reality, she was prospering (or not) just as her soul was prospering. Her idea of prosperity was to have the riches of this world.

The so-called "prosperity gospel" isn't a gospel at all. It is just materialism. God wants our souls to prosper. What would you exchange for love, joy, peace, patience, kindness, goodness, faithfulness, gentleness, and self-control (Galatians 5:22-23)? A new house? A cabin in the hills? A promotion at work? The fruit of the Spirit is there for the picking. All we have to do is live by the Spirit.

Third Principle of Success

"As obedient children, do not be conformed to the former lusts which were yours in your ignorance, but like the Holy One who called you, be holy yourselves also in all your behavior; because it is written, 'You shall be holy, for I am holy'" (1 Peter 1:14-16). Who we are is more important than what we do, because our potential for greatness emanates from who we are. Scripture teaches character before career, maturity before ministry, and being before doing. Those who have their priorities straight will accomplish great things, "for we are His workmanship, created in Christ Jesus for good works, which God prepared beforehand so that we should walk in them" (Ephesians 2:10).

Jesus said, "Let your light shine before men in such a way that they may see your good works, and glorify your Father who is in heaven" (Matthew 5:16). We have all been given by God a certain life endowment that He expects us to use to His glory. Paul wrote, "Let a man regard us in this manner, as servants of Christ and stewards of the mysteries of God. In this case, moreover, it is required of stewards that one be found trustworthy" (1 Corinthians 4:1-2). *Being a good steward of the time, talent, gifts, and treasures that God has entrusted to us will help us be successful,* and that is the third principle of success.

In the parable of the talents (Matthew 25:14-30), we learn that God has given some people five talents, others two, and still others only one. In the story Jesus told, the one given five talents gained five more, and the one given two talents gained two more. The one given one talent dug a hole in the ground and buried it. On the day of accountability, God ordered the worthless and unfaithful slave, who did nothing, to be cast from His presence, and what he had was to be given to someone who had been faithful with what had been entrusted to them.

The church is mostly comprised of believers who possess only one talent. They are the backbone of the church, the foot soldiers in the trenches. The part they play may not seem as important as that of more gifted people, but it is just as essential. Every part of the body is needed, and no part can say, "'I have no need of you.' On the contrary, it is much truer that the members of the body which seem to be weaker are necessary; and those members of the body which we deem less honorable, on these we bestow more abundant honor, and our less presentable members become much more presentable" (1 Corinthians 12:21-23).

Since some are endowed with greater gifts, we will not be held accountable for producing the same fruit as someone else, but God will hold us accountable for what we have been given. Our success is dependent upon our faithfulness. A life well lived looks forward to hearing, "Well done, good and faithful slave. You were faithful with a few things, I will put you in charge of many things; enter into the joy of your master" (Matthew 25:21).

A Biblical Definition of Failure

The Bible is a book of failures. Moses struck the rock in anger and failed to reach the Promised Land. Elijah slew 450 prophets of Baal, but ran from Jezebel. David slew Goliath, but then slept with Bathsheba and arranged for her husband to be killed. Peter told the Lord to His face that he would go to prison and even be willing to die for Him, then he turned around and denied Him three times.

Many of the heroes mentioned in Hebrews 11 would be considered flops by the world's definition of success. But they weren't mentioned because of their accomplishments; they were commended for their faithfulness. *Failure is being unfaithful.*

To stumble and fall is not failure. To stumble and fall again is not failure. "For a righteous man falls seven times, and rises again" (Proverbs 24:16). Failure comes when you say, "I was pushed," and then fail to get up again.

A highly esteemed corporate executive was retiring, and a man half his age was picked to replace him. He asked the grizzled old man, "Sir, how do you account for your tremendous success?" "No mistakes," he replied. Puzzled by the answer, the young executive asked, "How do you get to the place where you make no mistakes?" "I learned from years of experience," he said. "What kind of experience?" The old man paused for a moment and then said, "A lot of mistakes." A mistake is never a failure unless you fail to learn from it.

There are two kinds of failures: moral failure and the failure to pursue our God-given potential. Moral failure must be acknowledged for the sake of our relationship with God and cannot be blamed on anyone but ourselves. The opposite of confession is often rationalization, not silence. Confession means to agree with God. It is not saying, "I'm sorry"; it is saying, "I did it." It is closely akin to walking in the light, which is to live in moral agreement with God. It is the absence of guile and hypocrisy. John wrote, "If we confess our sins, He is faithful and righteous to forgive us our sins and to cleanse us from all unrighteousness. If we say that we have not sinned, we make Him a liar and His word is not in us" (1 John 1:9-10).

So you have sinned. Confess it, get back up again, and keep moving forward. If your sin has been evident to others, then your confession should also be made to those who know. "If we walk in the Light as He Himself is in the Light, we have fellowship with one another, and the blood of Jesus His Son cleanses us from all sin" (1 John 1:7).

Many who are afraid to fail never try, or they quit before the race is over. Failure is taking the path of least resistance. President Theodore Roosevelt had poor health and poor eyesight, but that never stopped him. He knew what it took to succeed.

> It is not the critic who counts, nor the man who points out how the strong man stumbled or where the doer of deeds could have done better. The credit belongs to the man who is actually in the arena, whose face is marred by the dust and sweat and blood; who strives valiantly; who errs and comes short again and again; who knows the great enthusiasms, the great devotions, and spends himself in a worthy cause; who, at the best, knows in the end the triumph of high achievement; and who, at the worst, if he fails, at least fails while daring greatly, so that his place shall never be with those cold and timid souls who know neither victory nor defeat.[2]

As you may have heard, success is 90 percent attitude and 10 percent aptitude. "Therefore, do not throw away your confidence, which has a great reward. For you have need of endurance, so that when you have done the will of God, you may receive what was promised"

(Hebrews 10:35-36). Those who accomplish something meaningful in their lives look back and say it was persistence that got them there.

Taking the Risk

Stepping out in faith is a risk—but life itself is a risk. We all like the security of the trunk, but the fruit of the tree is always out on the end of the limb. William Arthur Ward wrote:

> To laugh is to risk appearing a fool,
> To weep is to risk appearing sentimental.
> To reach out for another is to risk involvement,
> To expose feelings is to risk exposing your true self.
> To place your ideas and dreams before a crowd is to risk
> their loss.
> To love is to risk not being loved in return,
> To live is to risk dying,
> To hope is to risk despair,
> To try is to risk failure.
> But risks must be taken because the greatest hazard in life
> is to risk nothing.
> The person who risks nothing, does nothing, has noth-
> ing, is nothing.
> He may avoid suffering and sorrow,
> But he cannot learn, feel, change, grow or live.
> Chained by his servitude he is a slave who has forfeited
> all freedom.
> Only a person who risks is free.[3]

If you were to make a list for a "rogues' gallery" of the most offensive people in the world, who would be on the top of your list? Now compare it with the Lord's list in Revelation 21:7-8:

> He who overcomes will inherit these things, and I will be
> his God and he will be My son. But for the cowardly and
> unbelieving and abominable and murderers and immoral

persons and sorcerers and idolaters and all liars, their part
will be in the lake that burns with fire and brimstone,
which is the second death.

We would expect murderers, sorcerers, and idolaters to be on the
list, but how many would guess that the list would be headed by those
who are cowardly and unbelieving? God does not look with favor on
those who limp along in unbelief and never take the risk of living by
faith because they fear failure.

Just before God's people entered the Promised Land, God said:

> Be strong and courageous...Only be strong and very cou-
> rageous...Have I not commanded you? Be strong and
> courageous! Do not tremble or be dismayed, for the LORD
> your God is with you wherever you go...Only be strong
> and courageous (Joshua 1:6,7,9,18).

When the early church was threatened, they turned to God in
prayer: "When they had prayed, the place where they had gathered
together was shaken, and they were all filled with the Holy Spirit and
began to speak the word of God with boldness" (Acts 4:31). It is the
mark of a Spirit-filled Christian to be strong in the Lord and courageous. "For God has not given us a spirit of timidity, but of power and
love and discipline" (2 Timothy 1:7).

Susan Jeffers was raised to believe that she couldn't. Then one day
this timid soul decided she wouldn't—no, she couldn't—live that way
any longer. She wrote the following:

> Part of my problem was the nonstop little voices inside my
> head that kept telling me, "You'd better not change your
> situation. There's nothing else out there for you. You'll
> never make it on your own." You know the one I'm talk-
> ing about—the one that keeps reminding you, "Don't
> take a chance. You might make a mistake. Boy, will you
> be sorry!"

My fear never seemed to abate, and I didn't have a moment's peace. Even my doctorate in psychology didn't seem to do me much good. Then one day, as I was dressing for work, I reached the turning point. I happened to glance in the mirror, and I saw an all-too-familiar sight—eyes red and puffy from tears of self-pity. Suddenly rage welled up inside of me, and I began shouting at my reflection, "Enough...enough...enough!" I shouted until I had no more energy (or voice) left.

When I stopped, I felt a strange and wonderful sense of relief and calm I had never felt before. Without realizing it at the time, I had gotten in touch with a very powerful part of myself that before that moment I hadn't even known ever existed. I took another look in the mirror and smiled as I nodded my head yes. The old familiar voice of doom and gloom was drowned out, at least temporarily, and a new voice had come to the fore—one that spoke of strength and love and joy and all good things. At that moment I knew I was not going to let fear get the best of me. I would find a way to rid myself of the negativism that prevailed in my life. Thus my odyssey began.[4]

In Susan's book *Feel the Fear and Do It Anyway*, she shares two fundamental truths about fear. First, "the fear will never go away as long as you continue to grow." Every step in your maturing process will be met with new challenges and obstacles to overcome. You can't wait until the fear goes away, because it never will, which leads to the second truth: "The only way to get rid of the fear of doing something is to go out and do it."[5] As someone once said, "Do the thing you fear the most and the death of fear is certain."

Remember, nobody can keep you from being the person God has called you to be. It is normal to feel the fear, but step out anyway, as the following sayings by Kent M. Keith suggest:

People are illogical, unreasonable, and self-centered. Love them anyway.

If you do good, people will accuse you of selfish ulterior motives. Do good anyway.

If you are successful, you win false friends and true enemies. Succeed anyway.

The good you do today will be forgotten tomorrow. Do good anyway.

Honesty and frankness make you vulnerable. Be honest and frank anyway.

The biggest men with the biggest ideas can be shot down by the smallest men with the smallest minds. Think big anyway.

People favor underdogs, but follow only top dogs. Fight for a few underdogs anyway.

What you spend years building may be destroyed overnight. Build anyway.

People really need help but may attack you if you do help them. Help people anyway.

Give the world the best you have and you'll get kicked in the teeth. Give the world the best you have anyway.[6]

Discussion Questions

1. How does the world define success?

2. What causes people to feel like a failure?

3. Why shouldn't we compare ourselves to others?

4. What is the first principle of success? Why is it first?

5. Why is pride such an obstacle to finding true success?

6. What is the second principle of success, and how do we accomplish it?

7. What is the third principle of success? Why does "being" come before "doing," and character before career?

8. How would you define failure from a biblical perspective?

9. Why do Christians fail to pursue their God-given potential?

10. Why should we take the risk of living by faith?

The Steps to Freedom in Christ

Pride versus Humility

Pride comes before a fall, but God gives grace to the humble (James 4:6; 1 Peter 5:1-10). Humility is confidence properly placed in God, and we are instructed to "put no confidence in the flesh" (Philippians 3:3). We are to "be strong in the Lord and in the strength of His might" (Ephesians 6:10). Proverbs 3:5-7 urges us to trust in the Lord with all our hearts and to not lean on our own understanding. Use the following prayer to ask for God's guidance:

> *Dear heavenly Father, You have said that pride goes before destruction and an arrogant spirit before stumbling. I confess that I have focused on my own needs and desires and not those of others. I have not always denied myself, picked up my cross daily, and followed You. I have relied on my own strength and resources instead of resting in Yours. I have placed my will before Yours and centered my life around myself instead of You. I confess my pride and selfishness and pray that all ground gained in my life by the enemies of the Lord Jesus Christ would be canceled as I repent and overcome these sinful flesh patterns. I choose to rely upon the Holy Spirit's power and guidance so that I will do nothing from selfishness or empty conceit. With humility of mind, I choose to regard others as more important than myself. I acknowledge You as my Lord and confess that apart from You I can do nothing of lasting significance. Please examine my heart and show me the specific ways I have lived my life in pride. In the gentle and*

humble name of Jesus I pray. Amen. (See Proverbs 16:18; Matthew 6:33; 16:24; Romans 12:10; and Philippians 2:3.)

Pray through the list below and use the following prayer to confess any sins of pride the Lord brings to mind.

___ Having a stronger desire to do my will than God's will

___ Leaning too much on my own understanding and experience rather than seeking God's guidance through prayer and His Word

___ Relying on my own strengths and resources instead of depending on the power of the Holy Spirit

___ Being more concerned about controlling others than in developing self-control

___ Being too busy doing "important" and selfish things rather than seeking and doing God's will

___ Having a tendency to think that I have no needs

___ Finding it hard to admit when I am wrong

___ Being more concerned about pleasing people than pleasing God

___ Being overly concerned about getting the credit I feel I deserve

___ Thinking I am more humble, spiritual, religious, or devoted than others

___ Being driven to obtain recognition by attaining degrees, titles, and positions

___ Often feeling that my needs are more important than another person's needs

___ Considering myself better than others because of my academic, artistic, athletic, or other abilities and accomplishments

___ Not waiting on God

___ Other ways I have thought more highly of myself than I should

For each of the above areas that has been true in your life, pray as follows:

> *Dear heavenly Father, I agree I have been proud by __name__ __what you checked above__. Thank You for Your forgiveness. I choose to humble myself before You and others. I choose to place all my confidence in You and put no confidence in my flesh. In Jesus's name I pray. Amen.*

Chapter Six

Fear of Satan

The devil, however, as he is the apostate angel, can only go to this length, as he did at the beginning, to deceive and lead astray the mind of man into disobeying the commandments of God, and gradually to darken the hearts of those who would endeavor to serve him.

Irenaeus (circa AD 130–200)

God said, 'Let Us make man in Our image, according to Our likeness; and let them rule over the fish of the sea and over the birds of the sky and over the cattle and over all the earth, and over every creeping thing that creeps on the earth'" (Genesis 1:26). Dominion over this world was given to Adam and Eve and their descendants. "God blessed them; and God said to them, 'Be fruitful and multiply, and fill the earth, and subdue it'" (Genesis 1:28). Because of sin, however, they lost that dominion, and Satan became the "ruler of this world" according to Jesus (see John 12:31; 14:30; 16:11). Consequently, "the whole world lies in the power of the evil one" (1 John 5:19). Paul called him "the prince of the power of the air" (Ephesians 2:2). In the book of Revelation, he is called "the great dragon...the serpent of old who is called the devil and Satan, who deceives the whole world" (12:9).

From the dawn of history, people all over the world have feared Satan and his horde of demons. Pagans in animistic cultures have made sacrifices (including human) to appease the deities. They consult medicine men, quack doctors, shamans, and spiritists to ward off evil spirits or to gain their favor for healing and fortune. Every missiologist says that spiritism is the most dominant religious orientation in the world. Such cultic and occultic practices were strictly forbidden in the Old Testament for God's people, but the kingdom of darkness, ruled by Satan, went unchallenged in the world until the Messiah came. Satan tried again to stop God's plan, as he had attempted in the garden of Eden, by tempting Jesus through the same three channels he tempted Eve (i.e., through "the lust of the flesh and the lust of the eyes and the boastful pride of life" [1 John 2:16]). The last temptation recorded in Matthew 4:8-11 reveals Satan's greatest desire:

> The devil took Him to a very high mountain and showed Him all the kingdoms of the world and their glory; and he said to Him, "All these things I will give to You, if You fall down and worship me." Then Jesus said to him, "Go, Satan! For it is written, 'You shall worship the Lord your God, and serve Him only.'" Then the devil left Him; and behold, angels came and began to minister to Him.

Jesus didn't refute Satan's claim to the kingdoms of this world. He came to establish His own kingdom. When two kingdoms are in conflict, the ultimate question is, who has the right to rule? Two sovereigns cannot rule over the same realm at the same time. Thus, authority is *the* issue in spiritual warfare.

The Bible portrays a battle between the kingdom of God and the kingdom of darkness, between good and evil, between true prophets and false prophets, between the Spirit of truth and the father of lies, and between the Christ and the antichrist. The conflict began in the garden of Eden and is recorded throughout the Bible, up to the final showdown in the book of Revelation. Every believer is a participant in the battle: "For our struggle is not against flesh and blood, but against the rulers, against the powers, against the world forces of this darkness, against the spiritual forces of wickedness in the heavenly places" (Ephesians 6:12).

Kingdoms in Conflict

To set up the kingdom of God on earth, Jesus chose twelve disciples and invited them to follow Him. They observed Jesus demonstrate His authority over the natural world and the spiritual world by calming the seas, healing the sick, and casting out demons. Then Jesus "called the twelve together, and gave them power and authority over all the demons and to heal diseases. And He sent them out to proclaim the kingdom of God and to perform healing" (Luke 9:1-2). It was a tough learning experience that produced mixed results, and Jesus sternly rebuked them for their lack of faith (9:40-41) and their pride (9:46-48).

Then Jesus appointed 70 others and sent them out with the same authority and power, and they returned triumphantly. "The seventy returned with joy, saying 'Lord, even the demons are subject to us in Your name'" (Luke 10:17). The Lord was pleased, but also warned them in verses 18-20:

> I was watching Satan fall from heaven like lightning. Behold, I have given you authority to tread upon serpents and scorpions, and over all the power of the enemy, and nothing will injure you. Nevertheless do not rejoice in this, that the spirits are subject to you, but rejoice that your names are recorded in heaven.

That is a sober warning to us as well. Satan was the consummation of perfection in his original wisdom and beauty (Ezekiel 28:11-19), but pride was his downfall. Five proclamations beginning with "I will" detail Satan's sin in Isaiah 14:12-15. He wanted the glory that belonged to God alone. In his rebellion against God he took a third of the angels with him (Revelation 12:4). He rules over this world through that hierarchy of demons. Throughout church history, accomplished men and women of God have likewise fallen when they have been caught up in their own brilliance. One of the chosen disciples had his own rebellious plan, with devastating consequences: "Satan entered into Judas" (Luke 22:3).

At the Lord's Supper "there arose also a dispute among them as to which one of them was regarded to be greatest" (Luke 22:24). That sin of pride may have been what prompted Jesus to say, "Simon, Simon, behold, Satan has demanded permission to sift you like wheat; but I have prayed for you, that your faith may not fail; and you, when once you have turned again, strengthen your brothers" (verses 31-32). Satan had an argument. "You kicked me out of heaven for my pride, now how about Peter?" Peter didn't take a third of the disciples with him, and he wasn't setting himself up to be like God, but he did get sifted. After Peter boasted that he was willing to go to prison and even die for Jesus, the Lord told him that the rooster wouldn't crow that day until Peter had denied him three times (verses 33-34). It happened just as Jesus predicted (verses 55-62).

Jesus died for our sins and was resurrected in order that we may have eternal life, but that is not all He accomplished. "When He had disarmed the rulers and authorities, He made a public display of them, having triumphed over them" (Colossians 2:15). "The Son of God appeared for this purpose, to destroy the works of the devil" (1 John 3:8). That is the gospel that animists and spiritists need to hear, and it is just as much a part of the gospel as the forgiveness of sin. The cross was a dagger to the heart of Satan.

Jesus said to His disciples, "All authority has been given to Me in heaven and on earth. Go therefore and make disciples of all the nations, baptizing them in the name of the Father and the Son and the Holy Spirit, teaching them to observe all that I commanded you; and lo, I am with you always, even to the end of the age" (Matthew 28:18-20). They were told to wait in Jerusalem, where they would receive power when the Holy Spirit came upon them—and that happened at Pentecost

(Acts 1:4-5; 2:1-4). Under the New Covenant, Satan and His demons have no authority or power over any believer. God "rescued us from the domain of darkness, and transferred us to the kingdom of His beloved Son, in whom we have redemption, the forgiveness of sins" (Colossians 1:13-14).

Authority and Power

Authority is the right to rule, and power is the ability to rule. Because of our position in Christ, we have both. Our names are recorded in heaven, but never forget that we live by His authority and His power. We have the authority to do God's will, not our own will. This authority is over the kingdom of darkness, not over each other. We have the power to do God's will as long we are living by faith in the power of the Holy Spirit. That power is not operative when we live according to the flesh, which is relying on our own strength and resources.

Rejoice that you are a child of God, because Satan can't do anything about your identity and position in Christ—but if he can deceive you into believing that isn't true, you will live as though it isn't.

The conferring of God's power and authority to believers is taught by Paul in Ephesians 1:18-23 and Colossians 1:29:

> I pray that the eyes of your heart may be enlightened, so that you will know what is the hope of His calling, what are the riches of the glory of His inheritance in the saints, and what is the surpassing greatness of His power toward us who believe. These are in accordance with the working of the strength of His might which He brought about in Christ, when He raised Him from the dead and seated Him at His right hand in the heavenly places, far above all rule and authority and power and dominion, and every name that is named, not only in this age but also in the one to come. And He put all things in subjection under His feet, and gave Him as head over all things

to the church, which is His body, the fullness of Him who fills all in all (Ephesians 1:18-23).

Striving according to His power, which mightily works within [us] (Colossians 1:29).

In the Ephesians passage, "rule and authority and power and dominion" describe different orders of angels according to rabbinic thought at the time. The "heavenly places" refers to the spiritual realm that exists all around us. Every believer is seated with Christ in the heavenlies (Ephesians 2:6). The throne of God is the ultimate authority of the universe. Jesus sits at the Father's right hand, and we are united there with Him. "The Spirit Himself testifies with our spirit that we are children of God, and if children, heirs also, heirs of God and fellow heirs with Christ" (Romans 8:16-17). We are not heirs to the riches of this world. That is what Satan offered to Jesus (Matthew 4:8-9). "Listen, my beloved brethren: did not God choose the poor of this world to be rich in faith and heirs of the kingdom which He promised to those who love Him?" (James 2:5). Rejoice in that!

Exercising God's Authority

A local counselor had been working with a young lady for years, but was making no progress. He had no training in spiritual warfare and little knowledge of the spiritual world. So he asked if I would sit in on a session and provide some assessment. I told her within five minutes that there was a spiritual battle for her mind, and she said, "Praise God, someone finally understands what I'm going through." I met with her the next week. She was physically imposing and poorly groomed due to the extreme abuse she had suffered. We had been together no more than ten minutes when she got disoriented, rose from her chair, and started slowly walking toward me with a menacing look. What would you do?

I said in a calm but firm voice, "I'm a child of God. You can't touch me." She stopped in her tracks. I said, "Sit down," and she did. I wasn't speaking to the young lady. What I said is an application of 1 John 5:18: "He who was born of God keeps him, and the evil one does not touch him." Saying those words is not a formula to be applied defensively when under attack. It comes from the inner assurance that we are the temple of God, who has all authority in heaven and on earth. I was not putting up a fearful defense. I was making an offensive stand for the sake of the young lady.

It is important to note that the authority we have in Christ does not increase with the volume of our voice. We don't shout at the devil. We calmly take our place in Christ. It is no different than exercising parental authority. We are not exercising our God-given authority as parents if we attempt to control our children by shouting, threatening, and screaming at them. We are actually undermining it, because we are operating in the flesh. Parents who rely on intimidation do so because it brings temporary control as their children capitulate in fear. That is also Satan's strategy. He tries to frighten us so that we respond in the flesh, when we should be walking by faith in the power of the Holy Spirit. Fear of Satan and faith in God are mutually exclusive.

When we glorify God in our bodies, we are manifesting the presence of God. We are the arms, legs, and mouthpiece for Jesus. God propagates His kingdom through believers who are obedient to Him. In contrast, demons are dismembered spirits. They have to work through animate objects to propagate the kingdom of darkness, preferring swine over nothing (Mark 5:12). It is the eternal purpose of God to make His wisdom "known through the church to the rulers and authorities in the heavenly places" (Ephesians 3:10).

In the story above it would appear to a natural observer that I was counseling a mentally ill person. From a spiritual perspective, it was the Holy Spirit within me that was confronting an evil spirit (i.e., "the spirit that is now working in the sons of disobedience" [Ephesians 2:2]). God was making His wisdom known through me to Satan's demonic hierarchy.

Satan is the puppet master of the world. He is like the Wizard of

Oz, an impotent voice speaking through a megaphone. "Your adversary, the devil, prowls around like a roaring lion, seeking someone to devour. But resist him, firm in your faith" (1 Peter 5:8-9). This lion (the devil) has no teeth, but he is gumming the cowardly and unbelieving to death.

When I (Neil) was a little boy on the farm, my dad, brother, and I visited our neighbors. They had an ornery little dog that scared the socks off me. When we got out of the pickup, the dog came barking, and I climbed to the top of the pickup, stricken by fear. My dad and brother were standing near the dog, but he was barking at me. What power did that dog have to put me on top of the pickup? Only what I gave it. On the next trip to their farm my dad said, "It is just a little dog. Why don't you stand your ground?" Beads of sweat started to appear on my forehead, but I was determined not to run. When the dog came barking this time, I kicked a rock at it, and it fled. In the same way, we're told to "resist the devil and he will flee from you" (James 4:7).

Two kids riding in the back seat of a car started screaming when a bee flew through the window. The father reached back and grabbed the bee in his hand, and it stung him. Then he released the bee, and the kids started screaming again. The father said, "There is nothing to be afraid of. The bee has no stinger. Look and see. It's in my hand." Jesus is saying to all who will hear, "Fear not. I have disarmed the devil. Look at my hands, my feet, and my side."

Nighttime Terrors

It should surprise no one that most spiritual attacks happen when we are alone, and mostly at night. One of Job's friends had such an encounter:

> Now a word was brought to me stealthily, and my ear received the whisper of it. Amid disquieting thoughts from the visions of the night, when deep sleep falls on men, dread came upon me, and trembling, and made

all my bones shake. Then a spirit passed by my face; the hair of my flesh bristled up. It stood still, but I could not discern its appearance; a form was before my eyes; there was silence, then I heard a voice: "Can mankind be just before God? Can a man be pure before his Maker?" (Job 4:12-17).

In this passage, "a word" was not "a word from the Lord." God doesn't come to us "stealthily." That was a message from the "accuser of our brethren" (Revelation 12:10), who was saying in essence, "You are right in telling Job that he is suffering because of his sin." In truth, Job was suffering because "there is no one like him on the earth, a blameless and upright man, fearing God and turning away from evil" (Job 1:8). Good people do suffer for the sake of righteousness.

Christians all over the world are having demonic visitations at night. They are suddenly aroused from deep sleep by an overwhelming sense of fear that makes their hair bristle. Some report feeling a pressure on their chest, and when they try to physically respond, they seemingly can't—as though something were grabbing their throats. This is where faith must kick in, because the only presence they feel is evil. If we call upon the name of the Lord we will be saved (Romans 10:13), but how can we do that if a spirit is preventing us from saying anything?

Actually, the devil can't prevent you, but it will seem that way if you are ignorant of his schemes. This is not a physical battle, even though it may feel like a superior power is pinning you to the bed. Paul said, "The weapons of our warfare are not of the flesh, but divinely powerful for the destruction of fortresses" (2 Corinthians 10:4). God knows the thoughts and intentions of our hearts, so we can always turn to Him inwardly. The moment we do, we will be free to call upon the Lord. If we just say, "Jesus," the attack will stop. If we submit to God first, we will be able to resist the devil, and he will flee from us (James 4:7).

While conducting conferences all over the world, we have asked attendees if they have had an experience like the one described in Job.

We have never seen less than a third of the people say they have. In high profile ministries, the percentage is usually near 100. When I first went public with our ministry, I would experience that kind of attack at 3:00 a.m. the night before every conference, and it continued for four years. It may have been a little scary at first, but it was no longer frightening once I learned how to deal with it. I started to realize the significance of some ministries by the opposition I was experiencing before the conferences happened.

I have also asked conference attendees if they were alertly awakened at a precise time in the morning, like 3:00 a.m., but didn't necessarily sense any fear. If it always happens at a precise time, then it is unlikely a natural phenomenon, unless someone set an alarm. Having helped people get out of satanism and recover from satanic ritual abuse has given us the opportunity to hear what these victims have participated in and have been exposed to. They report that 3:00 a.m. is prime time for Satanists. Chances are we have been targeted when we always wake up at that time, but so what? "You are from God, little children, and have overcome them; because greater is He who is in you than he who is in the world" (1 John 4:4). If you are not experiencing any opposition to your ministry, you may not have a ministry.

Satan's Schemes

Satan is most commonly known—and most often experienced by believers—as the tempter. The following chart shows what Satan's motives are in tempting us:

Channels of Temptation
1 John 2:15-17

	Lust of the flesh (Appetites & Cravings)	Lust of the eyes (Self-interest)	Pride of life (Self-promotion)
Eve	"The woman saw that the tree was good for food" (Genesis 3:6)	"It was a delight to the eyes" (Genesis 3:6)	"The tree was desirable to make one wise" (Genesis 3:6)

Satan	"Indeed, has God said, 'You shall not eat from any tree of the garden?'" *(Genesis 3:1)*	"You surely will not die!" *(Genesis 3:4)*	"You will be like God" *(Genesis 3:5)*
Questions	The Will of God *(Galatians 6:8)*	The Word of God *(Matthew 16:24-26)*	The Worship of God *(1 Peter 5:5-11)*
Destroys	Dependence upon God	Confidence in God	Obedience to God
Jesus	"Man does not live by bread alone, but man lives by everything that proceeds out of the mouth of the LORD" *(Deuteronomy 8:3)*	"You shall not put the LORD your God to the test" *(Deuteronomy 6:16)*	"You shall fear only the LORD your God; and you shall worship Him" *(Deuteronomy 6:13)*

Satan tempts us to live independently of God, which is the chief characteristic of our flesh. We always have a choice as to whether we are going to walk according to the Spirit or according to the flesh (see Galatians 5:16-25). "No temptation has overtaken you but such as is common to man; and God is faithful, who will not allow you to be tempted beyond what you are able, but with the temptation will provide the way of escape also, so that you will be able to endure it" (1 Corinthians 10:13). Temptations always begin with a thought, and the key is to take the way of escape the moment it hits your mind. We aren't tempted to eat health foods; we are tempted to satisfy the desires of the flesh. With the temptations come thoughts such as the following: *Everybody is doing it. You know you want to. Have a little fun. Who would know? You will get away with it.* As soon as you give in to those tempting thoughts, Satan changes his strategy from tempter to accuser: *You sicko—and you call yourself a Christian. You're no good. You will never get over this. You're a failure. You will never have victory over sin.* Every believer has struggled with such thoughts, but we have the ultimate victory. "Now the salvation, and the power, and the kingdom of our God and the authority of His Christ have come, for the accuser of our brethren has been thrown down, he who accuses them before our God day and night" (Revelation 12:10).

If we are tempted, we know it. If we are accused by the enemy, we know it. If we are deceived, however, we don't know it. If we know it, we are no longer deceived. The father of lies has deceived the whole world (Revelation 12:9). That is why Jesus prayed, "I do not ask You to take them out of the world, but to keep them from the evil one. They are not of the world, even as I am not of the world. Sanctify them in the truth; Your word is truth" (John 17:15-17). The first thing we do when we put on the armor of God is gird our loins with truth (Ephesians 6:14). That is how we keep from being deceived. Then we put on the breastplate of righteousness. That is how we stand against the devil's accusations.

The Battle for Our Minds

We shared in an earlier chapter how mental strongholds/flesh patterns/defense mechanisms have been developed in our minds. Thoughts have been raised up against the knowledge of God, but the second half of 2 Corinthians 10:5 shows us what we ought to do now (using a verb in the present tense): "We take captive every thought [*noema*] to make it obedient to Christ" (NIV). The word *noema* only occurs a few times in Scripture, of which five instances are in this epistle. Unfortunately, *noema* has been translated as "thought," "mind," and "schemes" in the same epistle, which is a little confusing for the average reader. To grasp the spiritual meaning of the word, pay special attention to the context in which it occurs.

Paul wrote concerning the need to forgive, "Anyone you forgive, I also forgive. And what I have forgiven—if there was anything to forgive—I have forgiven in the sight of Christ for your sake, in order that Satan might not outwit us. For we are not unaware of his schemes [*noema*]" (2 Corinthians 2:10-11 NIV). Have you ever lain awake at night tormented by thoughts about someone you haven't forgiven? The unwillingness to forgive others affords Satan access to the church. It is the number-one issue we seek to resolve when leading people through *The Steps to Freedom in Christ.*

Concerning salvation, Paul wrote, "[Satan] has blinded the minds [*noema*] of unbelievers, so that they cannot see the light of the gospel that displays the glory of Christ, who is the image of God" (2 Corinthians 4:4 NIV; see also 3:14, in which "minds" is also *noema*). We would better understand the need for prayer, and thus pray differently, if we understood how Satan blinds the minds or thoughts of unbelievers. Evangelism was most effective in the early church when believers understood how to free people from demonic influences. Being able to do so became a test of righteousness and orthodoxy (see Luke 9:37-43).

The following is the final occurrence of *noema* in this epistle: "I am afraid that just as Eve was deceived by the serpent's cunning, your minds [*noema*] may somehow be led astray from your sincere and pure devotion to Christ" (2 Corinthians 11:3 NIV). Satan deceived Eve, and she believed his lies. The tendency is to think that if we are nice Christian people, such deception can't happen to us, but Eve was *sinless* at the time she was deceived. Good people *can* be deceived.

Another use of the word *noema* is found in Philippians 4:6-7: "Do not be anxious about anything [i.e., don't be double-minded], but in every situation, by prayer and petition, with thanksgiving, present your requests to God. And the peace of God, which transcends all understanding, will guard your hearts and your minds [*noema*] in Christ Jesus" (NIV). In order to stand against Satan's mental assaults, we must choose to think on "whatever is true, whatever is noble, whatever is right, whatever is pure, whatever is lovely, whatever is admirable—if anything is excellent or praiseworthy—think about such things" (verse 8 NIV). Then we must put our righteous thoughts into practice, "and the God of peace will be with [us]" (verse 9 NIV).

In one sense, it doesn't make any difference whether the thoughts are coming from our flesh patterns, the world, or the father of lies. We examine every thought, and if it is not true, we don't think it—and we don't believe it. On the other hand, it is extremely important that we learn to separate our thoughts from the enemy's thoughts, or we are going to be deceived and defeated.

We have discipled hundreds and hundreds of believers who are hearing voices or struggling with condemning and blasphemous thoughts. In almost every case it has proven to be a spiritual battle for their minds. This should not surprise the church, because we have been warned: "The Spirit clearly says that in later times some will abandon the faith and follow deceiving spirits and things taught by demons" (1 Timothy 4:1 NIV). Such people are not going to grow in their faith until that is dealt with through genuine repentance and faith in God, and that includes submitting to God and resisting the devil—in that order (James 4:7).

We are not the only ones seeing this battle for people's minds. All psychiatrists and professional counselors have clients who have these mental struggles. Most secular therapists would understand such symptoms as the product of a chemical imbalance, but honest questions need to be asked. How can a chemical produce a personality or a thought? How can our neurotransmitters randomly create a thought that we are opposed to thinking? There is no natural explanation.

Secularists would likely say that the voices stopped or were diminished when the client was given antianxiety medication. That is possible—but the whole mental process probably stopped or was diminished as well. All they did was narcotize it. The whole cognitive process was dulled or deadened. Take away the medication, and the thoughts return. So nothing was cured; it was only covered up. The cause was never determined, and only the symptoms were dealt with. Having no mental peace is a primary reason why people drink or take drugs. A person can drown out those thoughts for a short period of time, but reality sets in the next day.

Can the evil one actually implant a thought in our minds? Consider 1 Chronicles 21:1, which says, "Then Satan stood up against Israel and moved David to number Israel." This was no verbal exchange. These were David's thoughts—or at least he thought they were. Satan is not going to try to persuade someone like David, who had a whole heart for God, to sacrifice his babies to a pagan god. But he will try to entice God's people to rely on their own human resources instead of God's resources. David made that fatal mistake even though the captain of his guard saw it as sin and tried to persuade him otherwise. Thousands died as a result of David being deceived.

Consider the deception of Judas: "Supper being ended, the devil having already put into the heart of Judas Iscariot, Simon's son, to betray Him" (John 13:2 NKJV). Judas was a thief (see John 12:4-6), and that may be why he was vulnerable, but that flesh pattern does not explain the origin of his plan to betray Jesus. That idea came from Satan.

Consider the early church's account of Ananias and Sapphira, who kept for themselves some of their profits, but wanted the others to think they had given all they had. "But Peter said, 'Ananias, why has Satan filled your heart to lie to the Holy Spirit and to keep back some of the price of the land?'" (Acts 5:3). The word "filled" in this passage is the same as in Ephesians 5:18, where we are admonished to "be filled with the Spirit." Whatever we yield ourselves to, with that we shall be filled (controlled by). If every believer were struck dead for lying, as Ananias and Sapphira were, our churches would be empty. Why such severity of discipline in this case? Apparently, God had to send an early warning to the church, because He knows what the real battle is. If the father of lies enters your life, marriage, home, or church undetected and persuades you to believe a lie, he will gain some control over your life.

The tendency of the Western church is to dismiss Ananias as an unbeliever, but that is not what the early church believed, nor present-day theologians. F.F. Bruce, a New Testament scholar, wrote that Ananias was a believer.[1] Ernst Haenchen wrote that Ananias was a "Jewish Christian" and commented, "Satan has filled his heart. Ananias has lied to the Holy Spirit, inasmuch as the Spirit is present in Peter (and in the community). Hence, in the last resort it is not simply two men who confront one another, but in them the Holy Spirit and Satan, whose instruments they are."[2] Remember that Peter himself was strongly rebuked by Jesus for being a mouthpiece of Satan (Matthew 16:23), even though he was unquestionably a devoted follower of Jesus.

The wife of a seminary professor was struggling with pneumonia, and she wasn't responding to treatment. When they removed a liter of fluid from her lungs, they discovered the cancer. She became phobic, and her husband asked if I would come to their home to see her. She told me privately, "I'm not sure I'm a Christian." She was a very devoted believer, and I asked why she would even think that way. She said, "I have been struggling with condemning and blasphemous thoughts about God, even when I am in church." I asked her, "Did you want to think those thoughts? Did you make a conscious choice to think those thoughts?" She emphatically said, "No!" I explained, "Then they are not your thoughts."

With her maturity, it only took a half hour to win this battle for her mind, and she never questioned her salvation again. She had been fearful because she was facing death and questioning her salvation. She had wondered, "How can I be a Christian and have those kinds of thoughts?" If such thinking came from her core nature, then her salvation would be questionable—but it didn't, and nobody had ever explained that to her. Martin Luther wrote, "The devil throws hideous thoughts into the soul—hatred of God, blasphemy, and despair."[3]

A godly pastor of a 4000-member Baptist church had surgery for prostate cancer. It was deemed so successful that radiation and chemo weren't considered necessary. He announced the news to his congregation, and everyone was thankful. Two months later he was sitting at his desk when the thought came to his mind, *The cancer is back. You're going to die.* He became so fearful that he decided to resign, but before he did he called a pastor friend who advised him to read *Victory Over the Darkness* and *The Bondage Breaker*, and to meet with an encourager to go through *The Steps to Freedom in Christ*. He did, and the Lord set him free. When the lies were gone, the fear was gone.

How do we make sense of people hearing voices that others don't hear and seeing things that others don't see? In order to physically hear something, there has to be a source for the sound, which produces a compression and rarefaction of air molecules traveling at the speed of sound. The sound hits our eardrums and sends a signal to our brains. One cannot speak and be heard in outer space, because sound requires the physical medium of air. And in order to physically see something, there has to be a light source reflecting off a material object back to our optic nerve, which sends a signal to our brain. What these people are struggling with cannot be explained in the natural realm, "for our struggle is not against flesh and blood" (Ephesians 6:12).

On two separate occasions Jesus supernaturally revealed what the Pharisees were doing (John 7:19-20; 8:37-47). We know that God is omnipresent and omniscient, and He knows the thoughts and intentions of our hearts, but the Pharisees didn't believe that Jesus was the Son of God. For Jesus to have the kind of knowledge He had, they assumed He had a demon. They realized that esoteric knowledge had to have a spiritual origin. In our present time, New Age practitioners believe Jesus was the ultimate psychic, an avatar. Just change the terminology from "demon" to "spirit guide" and "medium" to "psychic" or "channeler," and a gullible public takes the bait, believing it is all harmless.

We have no idea what is going on in the minds of other people unless they have the courage to reveal what they are thinking or hearing, or if we have the wisdom to ask the right questions. In our Western culture, most are not likely to take that risk, because they fear being deemed mentally ill and in need of medication. Such was the case for the following lady who was on the pastoral staff of a local church:

> I thought my story was unique, but I often wondered if anyone else had the spiritual conflicts I was suffering with. My problem began a couple of years ago. I was experiencing terribly demonic nightmares and had nights in which

I felt the presence of something or someone in my room. One night I woke up feeling like someone was choking me, and I could not speak or say the name of Jesus. I was terrified.

I sought help from church leaders and pastors. They had no idea how to encourage me. Eventually fear turned into an anxiety disorder, and my thoughts were so loud, destructive, and frightening that I visited my primary care provider. I thought for sure she would understand my belief that this was a spiritual battle. When I expressed the idea that the enemy was attacking me, she responded by diagnosing me with a bipolar disorder and told me that I would be on medication for the rest of my life. She also gave me a prescription for antidepressants and antianxiety meds. I was devastated.

I told my husband the diagnosis, and he assured me that it wasn't true. I decided not to take the medication. I just didn't have any peace about it. My pastors prayed over me, but nothing changed. I began Christian counseling, which helped a bit, but it was nowhere near worth the $400 per month that I paid. When I told my Christian counselor about what was happening in my mind and about my fears, she too said, "I think it is time for medication." It seemed like everyone thought I was crazy. No one believed that my problem was spiritual.

Thankfully, I came across one of your books and read stories of people I could relate to. I knew there was an answer. It was in that book that I first heard of *The Steps to Freedom in Christ*. Honestly, I was afraid of the Steps at first. I didn't know what to expect, but one of our pastors had recently met Dr. Anderson and was learning how to lead people through the Steps. He offered to help me, and I accepted.

Going through the Steps was one of the most difficult,

yet incredible things I've ever done. I experienced a lot of interference, such as a headache and confusion, but having the Holy Spirit reveal to me all that I needed to renounce was incredible. When I prayed and asked God to bring to my mind the sins of my ancestors, I was shocked at all that came up. I don't even know my ancestors! I later asked my mother about the things that came to my mind during the session, and she confirmed that my family had been involved in those things. I was amazed by how the Holy Spirit brought out the truth.

After going through the Steps, my mind was completely silent. It was amazing. There were no nagging thoughts. I was totally at peace. I wanted to cry with joy. After that I wasn't afraid of being alone, and the nightmares were gone. I didn't have to play the radio or television to drown out the terrible thoughts. I could sit in silence and be still.

We live in a hostile world, and the best way to get under God's protective authority is to develop a submissive spirit and a servant's heart. "Every person is to be in subjection to the governing authorities. For there is no authority except from God, and those that exist are established by God" (Romans 13:1). Satan rebelled against God and tempts others to do likewise, as he did with Eve. That is why we've included the Step on "Rebellion versus Submission" at the end of this chapter. "For rebellion is as the sin of divination, and insubordination is as iniquity and idolatry" (1 Samuel 15:23).

Discussion Questions

1. How did the kingdom of darkness begin?
2. How has the kingdom of darkness affected the world?
3. Is spiritual warfare a major theme of the Bible? Why or why not?

4. What are the limits and scope of every believer's authority and power?

5. Why does Satan seek to frighten us?

6. Have you ever had a nighttime terror attack or been alertly awakened at 3:00 a.m.? How did you handle it? How should you handle it if it happens again?

7. What is Satan trying to accomplish in each of the three channels of temptation?

8. Why is deception the most dangerous snare of the devil?

9. From where do you think the "voices" that people hear and the blasphemous, condemning, and accusing thoughts originate?

10. How can we tell whether a thought is our own or coming from a deceiving spirit?

The Steps to Freedom in Christ

Rebellion versus Submission

We live in rebellious times. Many people sit in judgment of those in authority over them, and they submit only when it is convenient or for fear of being caught. The Bible instructs us to pray for those in authority over us (1 Timothy 2:1-2) and submit to governing authorities (Romans 13:1-7). Rebelling against God and His established authority leaves us spiritually vulnerable. The only time God permits us to disobey earthly leaders is when they require us to do something morally wrong or attempt to rule outside the realm of their authority. To have a submissive spirit and servant's heart, pray the following prayer:

> *Dear heavenly Father, You have said that rebellion is like the sin of witchcraft and arrogance like the evil of idolatry. I know that I have not always been submissive, but instead*

have rebelled in attitude and in action against You and against those You have placed in authority over me. Please show me all the ways I have been rebellious. I choose now to adopt a submissive spirit and a servant's heart. In Jesus's name I pray. Amen. (See 1 Samuel 15:23.)

It is an act of faith to trust God to work in our lives through less-than-perfect leaders, but that is what God is asking us to do. Should those in positions of leadership or power abuse their authority and break the laws designed to protect innocent people, you need to seek help from a higher authority. Many governments require certain types of abuse to be reported to a governmental agency. If that is your situation, we urge you to get the help you need immediately.

Don't, however, assume that someone in authority is violating God's Word just because he or she is telling you to do something you don't like. God has set up specific lines of authority to protect us and give order to society. It is the position of authority that we respect. Without governing authorities, every society would be chaos.

From the list below, allow God to show you any specific ways you have been rebellious, then use the prayer that follows to confess those sins He brings to mind.

__ Civil government, including obedience to traffic laws and tax laws or attitude toward government officials (Romans 13:1-7; 1 Timothy 2:1-4; 1 Peter 2:13-17)

__ Parents, stepparents, or legal guardians (Ephesians 6:1-3)

__ Teachers, coaches, or school officials (Romans 13:1-4)

__ Employers (past and present) (1 Peter 2:18-23)

__ Husband (1 Peter 3:1-4) or wife (Ephesians 5:21; 1 Peter 3:7) [Note to husbands: Ask the Lord if your lack of love for your wife could be fostering a rebellious spirit within her. If so, confess that as a violation of Ephesians 5:22-33.]

__ Church leaders (Hebrews 13:7)

__ God (Daniel 9:5,9)

For each way you have been rebellious that the Spirit of God brings to your mind, use the following prayer to specifically confess that sin:

Heavenly Father, I confess that I have been rebellious toward <u>state name or position</u> by <u>specifically confess what you did or did not do</u>. Thank You for Your forgiveness. I choose to be submissive and obedient to Your Word. In Jesus's name I pray. Amen.

Chapter Seven

Fear of God

The Lord also said to Moses, "Go to the people and
consecrate them today and tomorrow, and let them
wash their garments; and let them be ready for the third
day, for on the third day the Lord will come down on
Mount Sinai in the sight of all the people. You shall set
bounds for the people all around, saying, 'Beware that
you do not go up on the mountain or touch the border
of it; whoever touches the mountain shall surely be put
to death. No hand shall touch him, but he shall surely
be stoned or shot through; whether beast or man, he
shall not live.' When the ram's horn sounds a long blast,
they shall come up to the mountain."...So it came
about on the third day, when it was morning, that there
were thunder and lightning flashes and a thick cloud
upon the mountain and a very loud trumpet sound, so
that all the people who were in the camp trembled.

Exodus 19:10-13,16

The introduction of the Mosaic Law came with some fanfare, and it
was effective! Nobody had to teach those folks the fear of God, and
surely none questioned His existence. "When the sound of the trumpet
grew louder and louder" (Exodus 19:19), nobody tested the boundary
for fear of the Lord. Fear can be an effective means of keeping people

from stepping over the line. Laws are ineffective if there are no conse-quences for breaking them. In this passage of Exodus, God had just made a covenant between Himself and the Israelites. "Now then, if you will indeed obey My voice and keep My covenant, then you shall be My own possession among all the peoples, for all the earth is Mine; and you shall be to Me a kingdom of priests and a holy nation" (verses 5-6). By agreeing to obey the Law, they ratified the covenant, which was conditional. "If you will indeed obey...then..." Would the Israel-ites continue to fear the Lord and obey His commands? Some did, but most didn't. So God sent prophets to confront their disobedience and call them back to God, but many of the prophets were ignored and rid-iculed, and some were even stoned to death.

Moses was the author of the Pentateuch, the first five books of the Old Testament. So he knew the story of creation, the fall, and the dis-obedience that began with Adam and continued to his day. Sin had separated Adam and Eve from God, who is holy and just, but God is also merciful and immediately set in place the plan to undo the works of Satan. "The LORD God said to the serpent, 'Because you have done this, cursed are you more than all cattle, and more than every beast of the field; on your belly you will go, and dust you will eat all the days of your life; and I will put enmity between you and the woman, and between your seed and her seed; He shall bruise you on the head, and you shall bruise him on the heel'" (Genesis 3:14-15).

Thus began the earthly battle between good and evil. There would be enmity between Satan's seed (the spiritual descendants of Satan; see John 8:44 and Ephesians 2:2) and Eve's seed (those who are in the family of God). "He," referring to Christ, would deal a deathblow to Satan's head at the cross.

However, until the fatal blow was struck to the head, God's people had no recourse but to keep pushing down one hump of the slither-ing serpent after another. As soon as one manifestation of wickedness was suppressed, another one would arise. There would be some Old

Testament revivals like the one under Hezekiah, but the kingdom of darkness spread like cancer. One cancerous cell can eventually destroy a whole body, and such is the nature of sin. "A little leaven leavens the whole lump" (1 Corinthians 5:6). "Satan, who deceives the whole world" (Revelation 12:9), began with Eve and continues to this day. "The whole world lies in the power of the evil one" (1 John 5:19), and it has since Adam sinned.

By the time we get to chapter 6 of Genesis, "the LORD saw that the wickedness of man was great on the earth, and that every intent of the thoughts of his heart was only evil continually. The LORD was sorry that He had made man on the earth, and He was grieved in His heart" (verses 5-6). That would have been the end of mankind, "but Noah found favor in the eyes of the LORD" (verse 8). Noah and his descendants were saved, but the wicked perished in the flood (see Genesis 7). Throughout the time of the Old Testament, God made sure that there would be a remnant of godly people, or at least one, to preserve the seed of the woman. Satan tried desperately to prevent the birth of the Messiah by working through Pharaoh, who ordered the killing of the male offspring of all Hebrew women (Exodus 1:16), and through Herod, at the time of Jesus's birth, who gave the order to slay all the male children in Jerusalem who were two years old and under (Matthew 2:16). But God preserved Moses (and thus the nation of Israel) and placed him in Pharaoh's court, and an angel warned Joseph and Mary to flee to Egypt. Scripture traces the bloodline from Adam and Eve to the birth of Jesus, the Redeemer.

Generations passed after the flood, and the fear of the Lord didn't remain. "They said, 'Come, let us build for ourselves a city, and a tower whose top will reach into heaven, and let us make for ourselves a name'" (Genesis 11:4). God saw the people's arrogance and pride, and He thwarted their plans by confusing their language and scattering them (verses 7-8). Then another hump in the snake surfaced in the area of the Dead Sea: "Now the men of Sodom were wicked exceedingly and sinners against the Lord" (Genesis 13:13). Judgment was inevitable, and Abraham was concerned that God would "sweep away the righteous with the wicked" (Genesis 18:23). He asked God if He would spare Sodom and Gomorrah if there were 50 righteous people. God said He would, and then Abraham bargained for 45, then 40, then 30, then 20, and finally 10—but 10 righteous people weren't found, and that was the end of Sodom and Gomorrah.

Why the Righteous Fear God

Conservative scholars believe the events in the book of Job took place around the time of Abraham. Satan, whose name means "adversary," had been roaming about on earth, and he slipped in with the angels when they presented themselves to God. God said to Satan, "Have you considered My servant Job? For there is no one like him on the earth, a blameless and upright man, fearing God and turning away from evil." Satan replied, "Does Job fear God for nothing?" (Job 1:8-9). The *accuser* was suggesting that Job had selfish motives for serving God, and that God had put a hedge of protection around him and all that he had. "Then the Lord said to Satan, 'Behold, all that he has is in your power, only do not put forth your hand on him'" (verse 12). What is immediately apparent here is that while Satan can wreak havoc, his reach is limited by God.

Job suffered mightily, yet he is a lasting role model of patience and endurance. "As an example, brethren, of suffering and patience, take the prophets who spoke in the name of the Lord. We count those blessed who endured. You have heard of the endurance of Job and have seen the outcome of the Lord's dealings, that the Lord is full of compassion and is merciful" (James 5:10-11).

The book of Job raises the age-old question, "If God is all-powerful and omnipresent, why do bad things happen to good people?" There is no way to answer that question if the only two players are God and man. One or the other is going to have to take the blame, and that is why Job's three friends argued that he was suffering because of his sin. The book of Job teaches that not all suffering is due to sin. Some of God's people will suffer for the sake of righteousness, as did Job and many of the prophets. But for those who suffer in that way, God will make it right in the end. Job's fortunes were more than restored, and he looked triumphantly into the future: "As for me, I know that my Redeemer lives, and at the last He will take His stand on the earth. Even after my skin is destroyed, yet from my flesh I shall see God" (Job 19:25-26).

Job was a patient man, but his patience was minuscule compared to God's patience. Why did a just God wait so long when Job saw nothing but evil? Peter provides part of the answer: "Do not let this one fact escape your notice, beloved, that with the Lord one day is like a thousand years, and a thousand years like one day. The Lord is not slow about His promise, as some count slowness, but is patient toward you, not wishing for any to perish but for all to come to repentance" (2 Peter 3:8-9).

A righteous God will not tolerate sin forever. Cutting out the cancer is the loving thing to do if you want to spare the rest of the body. Judgment will come, and God's people could be present when it comes upon the land. So what can they do? God told Solomon:

> If I shut up the heavens so that there is no rain, or if I command the locust to devour the land, or if I send pestilence among My people, and My people who are called by My name humble themselves and pray and seek My face and turn from their wicked ways, then I will hear from heaven, will forgive their sin and will heal their land (2 Chronicles 7:13-14).

God "will convict the world concerning sin and righteousness and judgment" (John 16:8). We are not instructed to petition God to do that. What He is looking for is righteous believers who petition Him to withhold judgment, allowing more time for the unrighteous to repent:

> "The people of the land have practiced oppression and committed robbery, and they have wronged the poor and needy and have oppressed the sojourner without justice. I searched for a man among them who would build up the wall and stand in the gap before Me for the land, so that I would not destroy it; but I found no one. Thus I have poured out My indignation on them; I have consumed them with the fire of My wrath; their way I have brought upon their heads," declares the Lord God (Ezekiel 22:29-31).

Notice the phrase, "Their way I have brought upon their heads." They reaped what they sowed. Then, as well as now, people not only questioned God's ways, but even blamed Him for the calamity they brought upon themselves. "A person's own folly leads to their ruin, yet their heart rages against the Lord" (Proverbs 19:3 niv). Here is how God answers that:

> "The house of Israel says, 'The way of the Lord is not right.' Are My ways not right, O house of Israel? Is it not your ways that are not right? Therefore I will judge you, O house of Israel, each according to his conduct," declares the Lord God. "Repent and turn away from all your transgressions, so that iniquity may not become a stumbling block to you. Cast away from you all your transgressions which you have committed and make yourselves a new heart and a new spirit! For why will you die, O house of Israel? For I have no pleasure in the death of anyone who dies," declares the Lord God. "Therefore, repent and live" (Ezekiel 18:29-32).

Our merciful God spared Noah, and He would have spared Sodom and Gomorrah if there were ten righteous people. Even to this day, He is waiting until the gospel goes out to all the nations, "and then the end will come" (Matthew 24:14). Many believers hope He is coming soon, but how many have friends, family members, and associates who don't know the Lord? When He returns, the door to heaven is shut.

In Awe of God

The fear of God is a dire warning about coming judgment for the wicked, but it also speaks to His majesty, as the following passages make clear:

> For as we cannot look at the sun for its brightness when the winds have cleared away the clouds, neither can we gaze at the terrible majesty of God breaking forth upon us from heaven, clothed in dazzling splendor. We cannot imagine the power of the Almighty, and yet he is so just and merciful that he does not destroy us. No wonder men everywhere fear him! (Job 37:21-24 TLB).

> You who fear the LORD, praise Him; all you descendants of Jacob, glorify Him, and stand in awe of Him, all you descendants of Israel (Psalm 22:23).

> Let all the earth fear the LORD; let all the inhabitants of the world stand in awe of Him. For He spoke, and it was done; He commanded, and it stood fast. The LORD nullifies the counsel of the nations; He frustrates the plans of the peoples. The counsel of the LORD stands forever, the plans of His heart from generation to generation (Psalm 33:8-11).

> O LORD, our Lord, how majestic is Your name in all the earth, who have displayed Your splendor above the heavens!...When I consider Your heavens, the work of Your fingers, the moon and the stars, which You have ordained;

> what is man that You take thought of him, and the son of
> man that You care for him? (Psalm 8:1,3-4).

God is awesome in majesty, glory, splendor, and holiness. Human language falls woefully short in describing the glory of the Lord. In the hearts of those who fear Him, there is an unspoken language of faith, a bowing down with humility before One infinitely greater and more magnificent than self. Ethan, the psalmist, revealed that God is even revered by the spiritual beings who surround Him:

> The heavens praise your wonders, LORD, your faithfulness
> too, in the assembly of the holy ones. For who in the skies
> above can compare with the LORD? Who is like the LORD
> among the heavenly beings? In the council of the holy ones
> God is greatly feared; he is more awesome than all who sur-
> round him. Who is like you, LORD God Almighty? You,
> LORD, are mighty, and your faithfulness surrounds you
> (Psalm 89:5-8 NIV).

The sheer magnitude of His glory and greatness does not diminish over time. Familiarity does not breed contempt of the Almighty. Heavenly beings who have been in His presence since their creation do not cease day and night to proclaim, "Holy, holy, holy is the Lord God, the Almighty, who was and who is and who is to come" (Revelation 4:8). No mortal has seen God the way angels do, but a few have had a partial glimpse of His glory, and it left them profoundly changed.

Moses asked God to show him His glory. God said, "You cannot see My face, for no man can see Me and live!" (Exodus 33:20), but God did pass His glory by Moses. When he came down from the mountain to speak to the people, "the skin of his face shone" (34:29), and the people were afraid to come near Moses. Moses put a veil over his face as the glory slowly departed (verse 33).

Isaiah also saw a manifestation of God:

> In the year of King Uzziah's death I saw the Lord sitting
> on a throne, lofty and exalted, with the train of His robe
> filling the temple. Seraphim stood above Him, each hav-
> ing six wings: with two he covered his face, and with two
> he covered his feet, and with two he flew. And one called
> out to another and said, "Holy, Holy, Holy, is the LORD of
> hosts, the whole earth is full of His glory." And the foun-
> dations of the thresholds trembled at the voice of him who
> called out, while the temple was filling with smoke. Then
> I said, "Woe is me, for I am ruined! Because I am a man
> of unclean lips, and I live among a people of unclean lips;
> for my eyes have seen the King, the LORD of hosts" (Isa-
> iah 6:1-5).

The prophet Isaiah, a godly man worshiping in the temple, was
brought face to face with his own sin in the presence of the Holy One.
He cried out in holy fear, as we all would. After the fear of God gripped
him, the forgiving love of God touched him through one of His angels:
"Then one of the seraphim flew to me with a burning coal in his hand,
which he had taken from the altar with tongs. He touched my mouth
with it and said, 'Behold, this has touched your lips; and your iniquity
is taken away and your sin is forgiven'" (Isaiah 6:6-7).

There are two important takeaways from this passage. First, if any
one of us were brought fully into God's presence, we would instantly
fall on our faces and be aware of how far short we fall from the glory of
God. The only sin we would be aware of is our own. Then comes the
forgiveness. How could we not come before His presence with thanksgiving? Second, the seraphim weren't being forced to worship God,
and neither are we. Upon seeing a beautiful sunset, we aren't forced to
acknowledge its loveliness, but we can do so voluntarily.

I remember standing before General Sherman and General Grant,
which are two of the largest giant sequoia trees in the world. It would
take 25 men standing in a circle to put their arms around the trunk

of General Sherman. I just stood there looking up in awe. Of course, I didn't say, "Praise you." But I did say, "It's huge! Look how big that thing is!" I was proclaiming its attributes.

Worshiping God is ascribing to Him His divine attributes. If we were fully in His presence, we couldn't help but do otherwise. Worship of God naturally flows from us during times of personal revival. We have seen love and gratitude for God flow from those who have genuinely repented by going through the Steps when they realize they are free, forgiven, loved, and safe in the arms of Jesus.

Some Bible translations have substituted the word "reverence" for fear. Indeed, we do revere God and stand in awe of Him, but there is more to fearing God than reverence. Such reverence should lead you to "work out your salvation with fear and trembling; for it is God who is at work in you, both to will and to work for His good pleasure" (Philippians 2:12-13).

"The fear of the LORD is the beginning of wisdom, and the knowledge of the Holy One is understanding" (Proverbs 9:10). It is a wise person who seeks first His kingdom and His righteousness, because all they need will be given to them (Matthew 6:33). It is a wise man who trusts in the Lord with all his heart, leans not on his own understanding, and acknowledges God in all his ways, because then his path will be straight (Proverbs 3:5-6). Those who fear the Lord are enabled to see the world from God's perspective. Those who don't fear the Lord see a pretty woman, but a wise man sees a prostitute and flees from immorality (Proverbs 5:3-5). Those who fear the Lord can spot a wolf in sheep's clothing (Matthew 7:15). Those who fear the Lord live in the shelter of the Most High, and He "delivers [them] from the snare of the trapper and from the deadly pestilence" (Psalm 91:1,3). God opens the eyes of those who fear Him, as He did for Elisha's servant when he saw the enemy surrounding them:

> Now when the attendant of the man of God had risen
> early and gone out, behold, an army with horses and

chariots was circling the city. And his servant said to him, "Alas, my master! What shall we do?" So he answered, "Do not fear, for those who are with us are more than those who are with them." Then Elisha prayed and said, "O LORD, I pray, open his eyes that he may see." And the LORD opened the servant's eyes and he saw; and behold, the mountain was full of horses and chariots of fire all around Elisha (2 Kings 6:15-17).

We have more than angels surrounding us. "You are from God, little children, and have overcome them [false prophets and deceiving spirits]; because greater is He who is in you than he who is in the world" (1 John 4:4). This fallen world may be ruled by Satan and his horde of demons, but we aren't. God is always present and all-powerful. God is the only legitimate fear object, and those who see the world from God's perspective know it. When the world threatens us, the nightly news is all bad, and the devil spins his web, "you are not to say, 'It is a conspiracy!' in regard to all that this people call a conspiracy, and you are not to fear what they fear or be in dread of it. It is the LORD of hosts whom you should regard as holy. And He shall be your fear, and He shall be your dread. Then He shall become a sanctuary" (Isaiah 8:12-14).

In the Old Testament, the term "sanctuary" referred to the tabernacle of Moses and later to the temple of Solomon. A sanctuary was a place where God manifested His presence to His people. It was a holy place of communion with the Almighty. Under the grace of God, our sanctuary is "in Christ," which is a spiritual position, not a physical location.

Drawing Near to God

It would be tragic if our whole orientation toward God was to avoid punishment. Nobody wants to draw near a consuming fire. When I (Neil) was in the seventh grade, the school had a program called "religious day instruction." Every Tuesday the classes were shortened so the students could attend the church of their choice for the last hour. It wasn't forced. Students could go to the library and study if they chose. I went to the church of my mother's choice. One beautiful fall day I decided to skip and went to the park to play. I thought I had gotten away with it, but I hadn't. The next day the principal called me in and sternly reprimanded me. His closing comment was, "I have arranged for you to be away from school Thursday and Friday."

I was shocked. Expelled from school for two days because I skipped religious day instruction! I was not looking forward to telling my parents. On the bus ride home, I was thinking of ways to avoid the punishment I feared was looming. I could pretend that I was sick for two days or leave for school and go hide in the woods. Eventually, I realized that I couldn't get away with it, so I had no choice but to face the music. I went to my mother because I believed there would be some mercy there. "Mom," I said, "I have been expelled from school for two days because I skipped religious day instruction." My mother looked surprised and maybe disappointed at first, then a smile broke out on her face, and she said, "Oh Neil, I forgot to tell you. We called the principal on Tuesday asking for you to be dismissed on Thursday and Friday to help us pick corn."

Would I have dreaded going home and facing my authoritative parents if I had known I was excused? I would have raced home and gladly greeted them. Many believers live as though they are walking on glass or eggshells, waiting for the hammer of God to fall upon them. Christians, the hammer already fell! It fell on Christ. We are no longer "sinners in the hands of an angry God," to quote a sermon title by Jonathan Edwards (1703–1758). We are saints in the hands of a loving God who called us out of darkness into the kingdom of His beloved Son. We have been invited to come boldly before His presence with confidence (Ephesians 3:12), "with a sincere heart in full assurance of faith, having our hearts sprinkled clean" (Hebrews 10:22). If you knew that and truly believed it, you would go running to your heavenly Father.

Zechariah had a remarkable vision of Joshua the high priest

standing before the angel of the Lord in filthy garments (3:1-3). Under the Law, sacrifices were made to atone for sins, and on the day of atonement the high priest would go into the holy of holies to atone for all the sins of Israel. Nobody else dared go in, and the high priest would go through elaborate rituals of ceremonial cleansing before he entered. They would tie a rope to his leg and sew bells on his garment for fear that he would be consumed. The rope would be used to pull him out if the bells stopped ringing. Coming before the presence of God in filthy garments spelled doom. Not only that, but Satan was standing at Joshua's right hand to accuse him. Then a remarkable thing happened:

> The LORD said to Satan, "The LORD rebuke you, Satan! Indeed, the LORD who has chosen Jerusalem rebuke you! Is this not a brand plucked from the fire?" Now Joshua was clothed with filthy garments and standing before the angel. He spoke and said to those who were standing before him, saying, "Remove the filthy garments from him." Again he said to him, "See, I have taken your iniquity away from you and will clothe you with festal robes" (Zechariah 3:2-4).

Aren't you a child of God saved from the fires of hell? Haven't you been clothed in His righteousness? Consider the supreme court in heaven. God, our Father, is the judge. Satan is the prosecuting attorney. We are the accused, and Jesus is our defense attorney. I don't think we are going to lose this case. "He is able also to save forever those who draw near to God through Him, since He always lives to make intercession for them" (Hebrews 7:25). The verdict is already in: Not guilty. Forgiven. Clothed in His righteousness.

A New Covenant

The writer of Hebrews provides a powerful picture of our relationship under grace as opposed to the terror-stricken aversion of God that Moses and the Israelites experienced under the Law:

> You have not come to a mountain that can be touched and
> to a blazing fire, and to darkness and gloom and whirl-
> wind, and to the blast of a trumpet and the sound of words
> which sound was such that those who heard begged that
> no further word be spoken to them. For they could not
> bear the command, "If even a beast touches the moun-
> tain, it will be stoned." And so terrible was the sight, that
> Moses said, "I am full of fear and trembling." But you have
> come to Mount Zion and to the city of the living God, the
> heavenly Jerusalem, and to myriads of angels, to the gen-
> eral assembly and church of the firstborn who are enrolled
> in heaven, and to God, the Judge of all, and to the spirits
> of the righteous men made perfect, and to Jesus, the medi-
> ator of a new covenant, and to the sprinkled blood, which
> speaks better than the blood of Abel (Hebrews 12:18-24).

Any church that threatens God's children with hellfire and damna-
tion, laying down the law, is not a New Covenant church. In fact, if you
aren't under the grace of God, you aren't a church at all. "That no one is
justified by the Law before God is evident; for, 'The righteous man shall
live by faith'" (Galatians 3:11). It should be evident to all believers, but
legalism still plagues the church. We must keep in mind these truths:

- "We maintain that a man is justified by faith apart from
  works of the Law" (Romans 3:28).

- "Having been justified by faith, we have peace with God
  through our Lord Jesus Christ" (Romans 5:1).

- "There is now no condemnation for those who are in Christ
  Jesus" (Romans 8:1).

- "The Law was given through Moses; grace and truth were
  realized through Jesus Christ" (John 1:17).

We fear God, but we are not afraid of Him. "There is no fear in love;
but perfect love casts out fear, because fear involves punishment, and
the one who fears is not perfected in love" (1 John 4:18). John didn't

say there is no fear *of* God. But because of God's love, we no longer fear being punished for our sins. The punishment we deserved fell on Christ.

Living under the New Covenant doesn't mean that we no longer fear God. The primordial fear is gone, but the cleansing work of God continues. "Therefore, having these promises, beloved, let us cleanse ourselves from all defilement of flesh and spirit, perfecting holiness in the fear of God" (2 Corinthians 7:1). God is more concerned about church purity than He is about church growth, because church purity is a prerequisite for church growth and bearing fruit. "He has now reconciled you in His fleshly body through death, in order to present you before Him holy and blameless and beyond reproach" (Colossians 1:22). The writer of Hebrews shares what the church can expect and what our response should be:

> See to it that you do not refuse Him who is speaking. For if those did not escape when they refused him who warned them on earth, much less will we escape who turn away from Him who warns from heaven. And His voice shook the earth then, but now He has promised, saying, "Yet once more I will shake not only the earth, but also the heaven." And this expression, "Yet once more," denotes the removing of those things which can be shaken, as of created things, so that that those things which cannot be shaken may remain. Therefore, since we receive a kingdom which cannot be shaken, let us show gratitude, by which we may offer to God an acceptable service with reverence and awe; for our God is a consuming fire (Hebrews 12:25-29).

People will always struggle with fear and anxiety if their trust is in something created that can be shaken. When God shakes the world, those people shake with it! By shaking the world, God is rattling the bars on our "fear cage," exposing our insecurities. Why? So that we will come to understand that we have become prisoners of our own fears and anxieties—and turn to God, who alone can set us free.

The Judgment Seat of Christ

Paul was addressing believers when he wrote, "We will all stand before the judgment seat of God.... So then each one of us will give an account of himself to God" (Romans 14:10,12). This is not a judgment for sins, for we have already been forgiven of all our sins and made alive together with Christ (Ephesians 2:4-5). Jesus "canceled out the certificate of debt consisting of decrees against us, which was hostile to us; and He has taken it out of the way, having nailed it to the cross" (Colossians 2:14). The final judgment of believers will be an evaluation of our works of service on earth, and God will bestow on us various degrees of reward:

> No man can lay a foundation other than the one which is laid, which is Jesus Christ. Now if any man builds on the foundation with gold, silver, precious stones, wood, hay, straw, each man's work will become evident; for the day will show it because it is to be revealed with fire, and the fire itself will test the quality of each man's work. If any man's work which he has built on it remains, he will receive a reward. If any man's work is burned up, he will suffer loss; but he himself will be saved, yet so as through fire (1 Corinthians 3:11-15).

Our eternal destiny was decided the moment we were born again, but how we spend eternity is still to be judged according to our faithfulness. Whatever we have done in the flesh will not last. Work done for our own glory, in our own strength, will be burned up. That which we have done for the glory of God is like gold, silver, and precious jewels. It will stand the test of fire, and we will be rewarded. Knowing that we will be held accountable before God is a powerful motivating force:

We also have as our ambition, whether at home or absent, to be pleasing to Him. For we must all appear before the judgment seat of Christ, so that each one may be recompensed for his deeds in the body, according to what he has done, whether good or bad. Therefore, knowing the fear of the Lord, we persuade men, but we are made manifest to God; and I hope that we are made manifest also in your consciences (2 Corinthians 5:9-11).

I (Rich) admired my father growing up. He was a loving disciplinarian. My father would get paid in cash and give the money to my mother, the family accountant. I saw the roll of $20 bills one evening and quietly took one when no one was looking. I found a white envelope, put the money in it, and took it to the woods where I often played. I dragged the envelope around in the dirt to make it look like it had been there for some time. Then I ran home and announced the treasure that I had "found." My mother was excited for me, encouraging me to use the money wisely.

I never counted on my conscience betraying me. I felt worse and worse. Finally, I couldn't stand it anymore. How could I have stolen from my own parents? How could I have betrayed their trust? I was miserable. I didn't want to face them because I felt such shame, but I knew I had to. When I approached my father, I burst into tears and confessed the crime. He put his arms around me and hugged me. I can still remember the sweetness of being accepted despite my stealing and lying. Then my father said, "Son, your mother and I knew you had stolen the money you said you'd found. We were just waiting for you to come and tell us." That did it. The floodgates of tears blew wide open. I made it my ambition to never do that again.

Love and Discipline

Punishment is retroactive. It is "eye for eye" and "tit for tat." Discipline, on the other hand, is future oriented. Being punished for doing something wrong is very different from being disciplined in order to build character and improve future performance. "Those whom the Lord loves He disciplines.... If you are without discipline, of which all have become partakers, then you are illegitimate children and not sons" (Hebrews 12:6,8). "He disciplines us for our good, so that we may share His holiness. All discipline for the moment seems not to be joyful, but sorrowful; yet to those who have been trained by it, afterwards it yields the peaceful fruit of righteousness" (Hebrews 12:10-11). The purifying work of God should not drive us *away* from Him in fear, but rather *toward* Him in faith. We don't want to stand before God someday and regret the way we lived. We long to see Jesus face to face and hear Him say, "Well done, good and faithful servant! You have been faithful with a few things; I will put you in charge of many things. Come and share your master's happiness!" (Matthew 25:21 NIV).

Loving God and fearing God are not mutually exclusive. Do you love someone who is always truthful? Do you love someone who is big enough to protect you from your enemies? Do you love someone who has the means and desire to supply all your needs? Do you love someone who forgives you when you sin, accepts you for who you are, and loves you unconditionally? Do you love someone who will ensure that justice is done in the end? Do you love someone who volunteers to serve your sentence when you're found guilty? Do you love some-one who cares enough to discipline you so that you don't miss out on your rewards? Do you love someone who sets you free and enables you to become all that you were created to be? Suppose that Someone is so holy and majestic, that to be fully in His presence would require a res-urrected body, and all those who are privileged to see Him can't stop singing His praises. "For as high as the heavens are above the earth, so great is His lovingkindness toward those who fear Him.... Just as a father has compassion on his children, so the LORD has compassion on those who fear Him" (Psalm 103:11,13).

To understand how the fear of God is *the one* fear that can expel all other fears, read the following excerpt of a letter from a psychiatrist and professor of psychology, Philip B. Marquart, MD, to Dr. David Howard, written after a revival at Wheaton College in 1950:

> Now here are some of the astounding psychological facts [coming out of the revival].... Several dozen cases of emotional problems melted away in revival. I lost all my student counseling interviews. One by one they came around and declared that they were cured. So I merely asked them to return once more to give their testimony—which I wrote down in my revival notebook. That means that if we had continuous revival all over the world, believers would need psychiatry much less than they do. I began to wonder whether the Lord wasn't rejecting, for me, the idea of psychiatry of any kind.
>
> Then I began to get an avalanche of new patients. Most of them were under conviction—and in conviction it is possible to get every kind of mental abnormality, as long as they resist.
>
> One student who had scoffed at the revival became beset with a serious phobia—a fear that he might be catching epilepsy. This phobia was the punishment for his scoffing. Secular methods were of no avail.
>
> Finally, I led him to confess to the Lord. Here he resisted. He had scorned the revival in the first place, because he was against confession. As soon as he confessed, his phobia left him.[1]

You can have your own personal revival right now by prayerfully completing *The Steps to Freedom in Christ*. The last Step closes this chapter.

Discussion Questions

1. What is the connection between the Law and the fear of the Lord?

2. Why must judgment come? Why does God wait so long?

3. Why don't most people fear God?

4. What can we learn from Job?

5. Why do people blame God for their mistakes?

6. What does it mean to worship God, and how can we continually do it?

7. How is the fear of the Lord the beginning of wisdom?

8. Why do some run from God and others run toward Him? What is the fundamental difference between the two kinds of people?

9. How does the New Covenant change our orientation toward God?

10. What is the difference between punishment and discipline? How and why does God discipline us?

The Steps to Freedom in Christ

Curses versus Blessings

The Bible declares that the iniquities of one generation can be visited on the third and fourth generations of those who hate God, but God's blessings will be poured out on thousands of generations of those who love and obey Him (Exodus 20:4-6). The iniquities of one generation can adversely affect future ones unless those sins are renounced and your new spiritual heritage in Christ is claimed. This cycle of abuse and all negative influences can be stopped through genuine repentance. You are not guilty of your ancestors' sins—but because of their sins, you have been affected by their influence. Jesus said that after we have been fully trained, we will be like our teachers (Luke 6:40), and Peter wrote that you were redeemed "from your futile way of life inherited from your forefathers" (1 Peter 1:18). Ask the Lord to reveal your ancestral sins, and then renounce them as follows:

Dear heavenly Father, please reveal to my mind all the sins of my ancestors that have been passed down through family lines. Since I am a new creation in Christ, I want to experience my freedom from those influences and walk in my new identity as a child of God. In Jesus's name I pray. Amen.

Listen carefully to what the Holy Spirit may reveal and list anything that comes to your mind. God may reveal cultic and occultic religious practices of your ancestors that you were not aware of. Also, every family has a history of mental illnesses, sicknesses, divorce, sexual sins, anger, depression, fear, violence, or abuse, etc. When nothing else comes to mind, conclude with:

Lord, I renounce <u>name all the family sins that God brings to your mind</u>.

We cannot passively take our place in Christ; we must actively and intentionally choose to submit to God and resist the devil, and then the devil will flee from us (James 4:7). Verbally complete this final step with the following declaration and prayer:

Declaration

I here and now reject and disown all the sins of my ancestors. As one who has been delivered from the domain of darkness and transferred into the kingdom of God's Son, I declare myself to be free from those harmful influences. I am no longer "in Adam." I am now alive "in Christ." Therefore, I am the recipient of the blessings of God upon my life as I choose to love and obey Him. As one who has been crucified and raised with Christ and who sits with Him in heavenly places, I renounce any and all satanic attacks and assignments directed against me and my ministry. Every curse I was under was broken when Christ became a curse for me by dying on the cross (Galatians 3:13). I reject any and every way in which Satan may claim ownership of me. I belong to the Lord Jesus Christ, who purchased me with His own precious blood. I declare myself to be fully and eternally signed over and committed to the Lord Jesus Christ. Therefore, having submitted to God, I now by His authority resist the devil and command every spiritual enemy of the Lord Jesus Christ to leave my presence. I put on the armor of God, and I stand against Satan's temptations, accusations, and deceptions. From this day forward, I will seek to do only the will of my heavenly Father.

Prayer

Dear heavenly Father, I come to You as Your child, bought out of slavery to sin by the blood of the Lord Jesus Christ. You are the Lord of the universe and the Lord of my life. I submit my body to You as a living and holy sacrifice. May You be glorified through my life and body. I now ask You to fill me with Your Holy Spirit. I commit myself to the renewing of my mind in order that I may prove that Your will is good, acceptable, and perfect for me. I desire nothing more than to be like You. I pray, believe, and do all this in the wonderful name of Jesus, my Lord and Savior. Amen.

Incomplete Resolution?

After you have completed the Steps, close your eyes and sit silently for a minute or two. Is it quiet in your mind? Most will sense the peace of God and a clear mind. A small percentage of believers don't, and usually they know that there is still some unfinished business with God. If you believe that you have been totally honest with God and have processed all the Steps to the best of your ability, then ask God as follows:

Dear heavenly Father, I earnestly desire Your presence, and I am asking You to reveal to my mind what is keeping me from experiencing that. I ask that You take me back to times of trauma in my life and show me the lies that I have believed. I pray that You will grant me the repentance that leads to a

*knowledge of the truth that will set me free. I humbly ask that
You would heal my damaged emotions. In Jesus's name I pray.*

Don't spend your time trying to figure out what is wrong with you
if nothing new surfaces. You are only responsible to deal with what you
know. Instead, commit yourself to finding out what is *right* about
you (i.e., who you are in Christ). Some believers can sense a newfound
freedom, and then days or weeks later begin to struggle again. Chances
are God is revealing some more of your past that needs to be dealt with.
God reveals one layer at a time for those who have experienced severe
trauma. Trying to deal with every abuse in one setting may be too overwhelming for some. If we show ourselves faithful in little things, God
will put us in charge of bigger things (see Matthew 25:21). Claim your
place in Christ with the following declarations:

*I renounce the lie that I am rejected, unloved, or shameful. In Christ I am
accepted. God says:*

I am God's child (John 1:12).

I am Christ's friend (John 15:15).

I have been justified (Romans 5:1).

I am united with the Lord, and I am one spirit with Him
    (1 Corinthians 6:17).

I have been bought with a price: I belong to God (1 Corinthi-
    ans 6:19-20).

I am a member of Christ's body (1 Corinthians 12:27).

I am a saint, a holy one (Ephesians 1:1).

I have been adopted as God's child (Ephesians 1:5).

I have direct access to God through the Holy Spirit (Ephesians
    2:18).

I have been redeemed and forgiven of all my sins (Colossians
    1:14).

I am complete in Christ (Colossians 2:10).

I renounce the lie that I am guilty, unprotected, alone, or abandoned. In Christ I am secure. God says:

I am free from condemnation (Romans 8:1-2).

I am assured that all things work together for good to me (Romans 8:28).

I am free from any condemning charges against me (Romans 8:31-34).

I cannot be separated from the love of God (Romans 8:35-39).

I have been established, anointed, and sealed by God (2 Corinthians 1:21-22).

I am confident that the good work God has begun in me will be perfected (Philippians 1:6).

I am a citizen of heaven (Philippians 3:20).

I am hidden with Christ in God (Colossians 3:3).

I have not been given a spirit of fear, but of power, love, and self-control (2 Timothy 1:7).

I can find grace and mercy to help in time of need (Hebrews 4:16).

I am born of God, and the evil one cannot touch me (1 John 5:18).

I renounce the lie that I am worthless, inadequate, helpless, or hopeless. In Christ I am significant. God says:

I am the salt of the earth and the light of the world (Matthew 5:13-14).

I am a branch of the true vine, Jesus, a channel of His life (John 15:1,5).

I have been chosen and appointed by God to bear fruit (John 15:16).

I am a personal, Spirit-empowered witness of Christ's (Acts 1:8).

I am a temple of God (1 Corinthians 3:16).

I am a minister of reconciliation for God (2 Corinthians 5:17-21).

I am a fellow worker with God (2 Corinthians 6:1).

I am seated with Christ in the heavenly realms (Ephesians 2:6).

I am God's workmanship, created for good works (Ephesians 2:10).

I may approach God with freedom and confidence (Ephesians 3:12).

I can do all things through Christ who strengthens me (Philippians 4:13).

I am not the great "I Am," but by the grace of God I am what I am (see Exodus 3:14; John 8:24,28,58; 1 Corinthians 15:10).

Maintaining Your Freedom

It is exciting to experience your freedom in Christ, but what you have gained must be maintained. You have won an important battle, but the war goes on. To maintain your freedom in Christ and grow as a disciple of Jesus in the grace of God, you must continue renewing your mind to the truth of God's Word. If you become aware of lies that you have believed, renounce them and choose the truth. If more painful memories surface, then forgive those who hurt you and renounce any sinful part you played. Many people choose to go through *The Steps to Freedom in Christ* again on their own to make sure they have dealt with all their issues. Often, new issues will surface. The process can assist you in a regular "housecleaning." It is not uncommon after going through the Steps for people to have thoughts like: *Nothing has really changed. You're the same person you always were. It didn't work.* In most cases you should just ignore those thoughts. We are not called to dispel the darkness; we are called to turn on the light. You don't get rid of negative thoughts by rebuking every single one; you get rid of them by repenting and choosing the truth.

In the introduction, you were encouraged to write down any false beliefs and lies that surfaced during the Steps. For the next 40 days, verbally work through that list, saying, "I renounce <u>the lies you have believed</u>, and I announce the truth that <u>what you have chosen to believe is true based on God's Word</u>."

We encourage you to read *Victory Over the Darkness* and *The Bondage Breaker* if you haven't already done so, or to go through the *Freedom in Christ* course. The 21-day devotional *Walking in Freedom* was written for those who have gone through the Steps. To continue growing in the grace of God, we suggest the following:

1. Get rid of or destroy any cultic or occultic objects in your home (see Acts 19:18-20).

2. Be part of a church where God's truth is taught with kindness and grace, and get involved in a small group where you can be honest and real.

3. Read and meditate on the truth of God's Word each day.

4. Don't let your mind be passive, especially concerning what you watch and listen to (internet, music, TV, etc.). Actively take "every thought captive to the obedience of Christ" (2 Corinthians 10:5).

5. Be a good steward of your health and develop a godly lifestyle of rest, exercise, and proper diet.

6. Say the following daily prayer for the next 40 days and the additional prayers as needed.

Daily Prayer and Declaration

Dear heavenly Father, I praise You and honor You as my Lord and Savior. You are in control of all things. I thank You that You are always with me and will never leave me or forsake me. You are the only all-powerful and wise God. You are kind and loving in all Your ways. I love You and thank You that I am united with Jesus and spiritually alive in Him. I choose not to love the world or the things in the world, and I crucify the flesh and all its passions. Thank You for the life I now have in Christ. I ask You to fill me with the Holy Spirit so I can be guided by You and not carry out the desires of the flesh. I declare my total dependence upon You, and I take my stand against Satan and all his lying ways. I choose to believe the truth of God's Word despite what my feelings may say. I refuse to be discouraged; You are the God of all hope. Nothing is too difficult for You. I am confident that You will supply all my needs as I seek to live according to Your Word. I thank You that I can be content and live a responsible life through Christ who strengthens me.

I now take my stand against Satan and command him and all his evil spirits to depart from me. I choose to put on the full armor of God so I may be able to stand firm against all the devil's schemes. I submit my body as a living and holy sacrifice to You, and I choose to renew my mind by Your living Word. By so doing, I will be able to prove that Your will is good, acceptable, and perfect for me. In the name of my Lord and Savior, Jesus Christ, I pray. Amen.

Bedtime Prayer

Thank You, Lord, that You have brought me into Your family and have blessed me with every spiritual blessing in the heavenly places in Christ Jesus. Thank You for this time of renewal and refreshment through sleep. I accept it as one of Your blessings for Your children, and I trust You to guard my mind and body during my sleep. As I have thought about You and Your truth during the day, I choose to let those good thoughts continue in my mind while I am asleep. I commit myself to You for Your protection against every attempt of Satan and his demons to attack me during sleep. Guard my mind from nightmares. I renounce all fear and cast every anxiety upon You. I commit myself to You as my rock, my fortress, and my strong tower. May Your peace be upon this place of rest. In the strong name of the Lord Jesus Christ I pray. Amen.

Prayer for Spiritual Cleansing of Home/Apartment/Room

After removing and destroying all objects of false worship, pray this prayer aloud in every room:

Dear heavenly Father, I acknowledge that You are the Lord of heaven and earth. In Your sovereign power and love, You have entrusted many things to me. Thank You for this place to live. I claim my home as a place of spiritual safety for me and my family and ask for Your protection from all the attacks of the enemy. As a child of God, raised up and seated with Christ in the heavenly places, I command every evil spirit claiming ground in this place based on the activities of past or present occupants—including me and my family—to leave and never return. I renounce all demonic assignments directed against this place. I ask You, heavenly Father, to post Your holy angels around this place to guard it from any and all attempts of the enemy to enter and disturb Your purposes for me and my family. I thank You, Lord, for doing this in the name of the Lord Jesus Christ. Amen.

Prayer for Living in a Non-Christian Environment

After removing and destroying all objects of false worship from your possession, pray this prayer aloud in the place where you live:

Thank You, heavenly Father, for a place to live and to be renewed by sleep. I ask You to set aside my room (or portion of this room) as a place of spiritual safety for me. I renounce any allegiance given to false gods or spirits by other occupants. I renounce any claim to this room (or space) by Satan based on the activities of past or present occupants, including me. On the basis of my position as a child of God and joint heir with Christ, who has all authority in heaven and on earth, I command all evil spirits to leave this place and never return. I ask You, heavenly Father, to station Your holy angels to protect me while I live here. In Jesus's mighty name I pray. Amen.

Chapter Eight

Breaking Strongholds of Fear

*I sought the LORD, and He answered me, and delivered
me from all my fears. They looked to Him and were
radiant, and their faces will never be ashamed. This
poor man cried, and the LORD heard him and saved him
out of all his troubles. The angel of the LORD encamps
around those who fear Him, and rescues them.*

Psalm 34:4-7

Imagine living under the oppressive rule of a godless empire and attending a synagogue where the faithful are waiting for the promised Savior of the world. Then one Saturday in Nazareth, one of your own kinsman stands up to read. He is handed a scroll of Isaiah and reads:

> The Spirit of the Lord GOD is upon me, because the LORD
> has anointed me to bring good news to the afflicted; He
> has sent me to bind up the brokenhearted, to proclaim
> liberty to captives and freedom to prisoners; to proclaim
> the favorable year of the LORD (Isaiah 61:1-2).

This is what Jesus did and read. "And the eyes of all in the synagogue were fixed on Him. And he began to say to them, 'Today this Scripture has been fulfilled in your hearing'" (Luke 4:20-21).

The introduction for the New Covenant came with less fanfare than the introduction for the Old Covenant. Rather than fear of punishment, there was hope for deliverance—but did the people believe Jesus? Do we?

From Fear to Freedom

If you have been totally honest with God and processed all the Steps at the end of the preceding chapters, there is a very good chance wounds have begun to heal, and you have been set free. The Steps don't set you free, nor do they heal your wounds. That is what *Jesus* came to do.

Resolving personal and spiritual conflicts through genuine repentance and faith in God is a beginning, not an end. We are still a work in process and are still being transformed by the renewing of our minds. Some fears have been learned that need to be unlearned. Relying on our own understanding won't enable us to get to the root of the lies behind some phobias. I (Rich) found that out when I tried to discover the basis for the fear that was controlling my son, Brian.

"Brian has been acting a little strange lately," my wife, Shirley, stated once the kids had left the room. I could tell she was concerned. I had just returned from a ministry trip and was getting the usual "state of the family" update.

"In what way?" I replied, putting down the mail I was sorting through. I was concerned too, since our five-year-old son seemed to be vulnerable at times.

"Well, he hasn't wanted to eat anything sweet for a few days. And when he was over at a friend's house, he wouldn't even eat ice cream. At least not until they told him there wasn't any sugar in it." She chuckled a little bit at their success in tricking Brian.

"It sounds like he's afraid of eating sugar. Have they had a dental hygienist or somebody like that at preschool lately?"

Apparently there had been someone talking about "sugar bugs" in his class recently, and that had apparently scared him. We decided to wait and see what happened. That night after dinner, Brian refused the cookie that the others got and opted instead for a banana.

"You know, Brian, bananas have sugar in them too. Natural sugar. It's good for you. In fact, just about everything these days has sugar in it. So to keep from eating sugar, you'd have to stop eating!" I laughed as I finished my "inspired" sermon, fully expecting that Brian would laugh with me and chomp down the banana. I turned back to washing the dishes in the sink, figuring that was the end of this fear-of-sugar nonsense. The whole thing seemed rather silly. After all, most parents would be overjoyed if their five-year-old stopped eating sugary foods.

A minute or so later, I caught a movement out of the corner of my eye. It didn't register at first, but I soon realized that it had been Brian. I turned around to see that he was gone from the kitchen table, and so was his dessert. I looked in the trash can, and there was the uneaten banana.

A little annoyed at Brian's self-will, I marched upstairs to his room. He was sitting on his bed in tears. Softening a bit upon seeing how upset he was, I asked him, "What's wrong, Brian? Why didn't you eat the banana?"

"It has sugar in it."

Frustrated by the irrationality of the whole thing, I left his room, went downstairs, and picked up a banana. I took it up to his room, a "brilliant" plan unfolding in my mind.

"Brian, there's nothing to be afraid of. Watch what I do." Breaking the banana in half, I gave one part to him and kept the other. "Daddy is going to eat half of the banana, and you eat the other half, okay?"

He wasn't impressed. As I enthusiastically wolfed down my half, he gingerly took a microscopic bite and promptly spat it out. By that time, I was really frustrated but still undaunted. I formulated another plan in my mind. I went back to the kitchen and grabbed a candy bar. *There's no way he'll be able to resist that*, I reasoned.

I was wrong. As I chomped down my half, he just stared blankly at me, holding his end of the bargain like it was a mildewed sour pickle. At wits' end, I slunk downstairs to find Shirley. Totally exasperated, I finally got around to doing what I should have done in the first place.

"Shirley, we need to pray. Brian's fear of sugar is real and serious. Something is very wrong. He wouldn't even eat the candy bar I gave him."

As we prayed, I confessed my frustration. God's peace returned. So did wisdom. The Lord clearly directed me to go back and pray with Brian, seeking the root of his problem, just as I would with an adult.

The Lord moved, and Brian was much calmer. He was able to recall some of the things that had scared him. One by one, in his five-year-old way, he renounced those fears. He said, "I say no to the fear of _____!" Heights, fire, bad dreams, and a few other typical childhood fears came to our minds.

Happy for the progress we made, I was still perplexed as to why he was so fearful of sweets.

"Brian, why are you so afraid of eating sugar?"

"'Cause I'll get a cavity," he answered, choking back the tears.

"No, you won't. We'll brush your teeth, and that won't be a problem at all."

I could tell he still was not convinced. "Brian, do you know what a cavity is?"

He shook his head, tears starting to roll down his cheeks. I then hoped that my clear explanation of the nature, origin, and treatment of cavities would do the trick. No dice. So I prayed for more wisdom, and God brought the first breakthrough we needed to help Brian overcome his fear.

"Brian, what do you think will happen to you if you get a cavity?" I asked, sensing that something critical was about to be revealed.

"I'll die."

Bingo! The poor kid had believed the lie that sugar equals cavities equals death. No wonder he was so afraid of sugar! He had likely misinterpreted something that had been said in his school.

I had Brian renounce the fear of cavities, the fear of death, and also the spirit of fear, affirming that God had not given that to him. He announced that God had instead given him power, love, and a sound mind (2 Timothy 1:7).

But that wasn't the end of the battle. In school the next day, he hardly touched his peanut butter and jelly sandwich. Shirley and I prayed again, this time personally dealing with any fears that we and our parents could have passed on to our children. The Lord then led us to help Brian face his fear head-on. The showdown was to be that evening after dinner at the local Dairy Queen.

I could tell that Brian was nervous after we told him where we were going for dessert. "I'm not hungry for any dessert," he lied, hoping we would leave him alone.

Upon arrival, I purchased everyone's ice cream, including a vanilla cone for Brian (his favorite at the time). He watched in silence as everyone else ferociously attacked their dessert. One by one I pointed out to him that his sisters, Michelle and Emily, as well as his mommy and daddy were all eating ice cream—and none of us was getting a cavity. None of us had dropped dead. Still, his dessert sat, melted rivulets of ice cream forming small puddles on the table. The "girls" all finished theirs and headed to the restroom. I felt like I had to press the issue to a crisis point with my son.

"Brian, I know you are thinking that if you eat anything with sugar in it, you will die. There's only one way you'll ever know if that little thought in your head is the truth or a lie."

"What's that?" he asked, turning his sad eyes toward me.

"Take a bite."

Rarely have I prayed so fervently. And rarely have I felt such joy as when he leaned over and took a bite.

Relieved, I said quietly, "Did you get a cavity?"

"No," Brian replied, the faintest smile appearing on his face.

"And did you die?" I asked, grinning from ear to ear.

"No." By this time, Brian was smiling too.

"Then take another bite."

Thankfully, he did. And then he took another and another and another without any coaxing from me. Finally, he turned and said something I'll always remember.

"Daddy, I just felt the fear inside of me snap in two, just like a stick."

And it was over. Really over. Not only was the fear broken, but the lie behind it was overcome by truth. Prior to that incident, Brian was very fearful. Now he is fearless.

Many of the struggles that children have are simply a matter of growth and are better left to the healing power of time. But we cannot assume that every strange or unusual behavior in the life of a child is just a phase that he or she will outgrow. We shared that rather lengthy story to illustrate what is *not* effective in dealing with a stronghold of fear—and to show what *is*. It would seem logical that a phobia rooted in a lie could simply be overcome by identifying the lie and replacing it with truth. In some cases that works, and it is an essential beginning for overcoming phobias. But try reasoning with those who have a fear of flying. Flying is the safest mode of transportation from one city to another. By far, more people are killed in automobile accidents per capita than by flying in an airplane. Rational arguments like that make sense, but a third of our population would still be afraid to fly even when so enlightened. We need the guidance of God to find the root cause of fear, and we need the grace of God to overcome it.

Phobia Finder

If you have successfully resolved your personal and spiritual conflicts by submitting to God and resisting the devil, then you are ready to analyze your fears and work out a responsible course of action according to the following outline:

A. Analyze your fear with God's guidance.

    1. Identify all fear objects. (What are you afraid of?)

    2. Determine when you first experienced the fear.

    3. What events preceded the first experience?

4. Determine the lies behind every phobia.

B. Examine the ways you have been living under the control of fear rather than living by faith in God.

1. How has fear...

a. prevented you from doing what is right and responsible?

b. compelled you to do what is wrong and irresponsible?

c. prompted you to compromise your witness for Christ?

2. Confess any active or passive way in which you have allowed fear to control your life.

3. Commit yourself to God in order to live a righteous and responsible life.

C. Prayerfully work out a plan of responsible behavior.

D. Determine in advance what your response will be to any fear object.

E. Commit yourself to carry out your plan of action in the power of the Holy Spirit.

Analyzing Your Fear

Begin by praying the following prayer out loud:

Dear heavenly Father, I come to You as Your child. I put myself under Your protective care and acknowledge that You are the only legitimate fear object in my life. I confess that I have been fearful and anxious because of my lack of trust and my unbelief. I have not always lived by faith in You, and too often I have relied on my own strength and resources. I thank You that I am forgiven in Christ.

I choose to believe the truth that You have not given me a spirit of fear, but of power, love, and a sound mind. Therefore,

I renounce any spirit of fear. I ask You to reveal to my mind all the fears that have been controlling me. Show me how I have become fearful and the lies I have believed. I desire to live a responsible life in the power of Your Holy Spirit. Show me how these fears have kept me from doing that. I ask this so that I can confess, renounce, and overcome every irrational fear by faith in You. In Jesus's name I pray. Amen.

The following list may help you recognize some of the fears that have been hindering your walk of faith. On a separate sheet of paper, write down the fears that apply to you, as well as any others not on the list that the Spirit of God has revealed to you. As you prayerfully recall your past, write a brief description of what happened (and when) to trigger that fear.

Fear of Satan

Fear of divorce

Fear of death

Fear of not being loved by God

Fear of never being loved by anyone

Fear of not being able to love others

Fear of marriage

Fear of rejection by people

Fear of never getting married

Fear of never having children

Fear of disapproval

Fear of embarrassment

Fear of failure

Fear of being/becoming homosexual

Fear of financial problems

Fear of going crazy

Fear of being a hopeless case

Fear of the death of a loved one

Fear of the future

Fear of confrontation

Fear of being victimized by crime

Fear of losing my salvation

Fear of committing the unpardonable sin

Fear of specific people, animals, or objects

Other specific fears the Lord brings to mind

We all live by faith, but the real question is, "What or whom do we believe?" You could choose to believe that it would be hopeless to even try overcoming your fears, but that's not true. God is the God of all hope, and there is nothing that is too difficult for Him (see Romans 15:13; Jeremiah 32:17). You could choose to believe that it is safer and wiser to avoid certain strong-willed people, elevators in stores, or airplanes. You could believe, like Brian did, that sugar in foods will instantly kill you. But such false beliefs aren't neutral or harmless.

Take as much time in prayer as you need to discern the lies you've believed, because renouncing them and choosing the truth is a critical step toward gaining and maintaining your freedom in Christ. Search the Scriptures for the truth. Seek counsel from mature, godly believers. You have to know and choose to believe the truth in order for it to set you free (John 8:32). Write down the lies you have believed for every fear and the corresponding truth from the Word of God.

Analyzing Your Lifestyle

The next step is to determine how fear has prevented you from living a responsible life, compelled you to do that which is irresponsible, or compromised your Christian witness. Phobias affect how we live, and we need to recognize how they affect us. A timid Christian homemaker who fears her pagan husband will likely compromise her

witness, which will probably lead to irresponsible behavior. An intimidated employee may lie for his boss, even though he knows it is wrong.
Teenagers may compromise their faith and participate in a crime
because they are afraid their friends will reject them.

After you have taken ample time to seek the Lord on these matters,
and you feel you have gained the necessary insights into your fear, it is
time to experience God's cleansing and renewing power through confession and repentance. "If we confess our sins, He is faithful and righteous to forgive us our sins and to cleanse us from all unrighteousness"
(1 John 1:9; see also Proverbs 28:13). It is the kindness of God that leads
you to repentance (Romans 2:4). Confession is agreeing with God that
what you did was sinful or wrong. Repentance is the choice to renew
your mind to the truth of God's Word and to live accordingly by faith.

Express the following prayer for each of the controlling fears in your
life that you have analyzed above:

> *Dear Lord, I confess and repent of the fear of* <u>name the fear you
> identified in your life</u>. *I have believed* <u>state the lie</u>. *I renounce
> that lie, and I choose to believe* <u>state the truth from God's
> Word</u>. *I also confess any and all ways this fear has resulted in
> living irresponsibly or compromising my witness for Christ,
> including* <u>note the ways fear has wrongly motivated you or
> held you back</u>. *I now choose to live by faith in You, Lord,
> believing Your promise that You will protect me and meet all
> my needs. In Jesus's trustworthy name I pray. Amen.*

After working through every fear the Lord has revealed to you
(including their accompanying lies and the resulting sinful behavior),
pray the following prayer:

> *Dear heavenly Father, I thank You that You are indeed trust-
> worthy. I choose to believe You, even when my feelings and cir-
> cumstances tell me to fear. You have told me not to be afraid,
> for You are with me, and not to look anxiously about, for*

You are my God. You will strengthen me, help me, and surely uphold me with Your righteous right hand (Isaiah 41:10). I now ask You to show me Your plan of action for living responsibly and facing my fear. I commit myself to do what You tell me to do, knowing that Your grace is sufficient. I pray this with faith in the name of Jesus, my Savior and Lord. Amen.

Many of the lies we have believed come from living in a fallen world, but we can't overlook the influence of the god of this world, who is the father of lies (John 8:44). You need to renounce his lies, such as: *God isn't going to help you. You don't have what it takes to be brave. You're just naturally a fearful person. You will never get over your fears.* Processing the Steps and using the "Phobia Finder" outline will help you discern what part the devil may be playing in your struggle with fear and anxiety, as the following testimony illustrates.

> Having only been a Christian for five years, I was just coming to understand that many of my experiences of fear and anxiety were not of God, but were of Satan. I couldn't drive over bridges without feeling like I was going to lose control of the steering wheel. I could see myself and my car going over the side, and this totally took over my mind as I came close to any bridge.
>
> I would become almost paralyzed by fear, breaking out into a sweat and almost being unable to breathe. I would call for Jesus to get me over, and He always did; but still, the fear would come back the next time. So I would try and avoid using bridges, or I would just not go where I wanted to.
>
> As a result, I was not enjoying my life to its fullest, as I was living in bondage.
>
> One Sunday in church, a friend of mine came over with a book, plunked it into my lap, and told me to read it. The book was *The Bondage Breaker*. I read through it

and went through *The Steps to Freedom in Christ* in the back.

When I first read it, I didn't sleep very well. That first night I dreamed that Satan was taking me from room to room in a large mansion and was showing me everything he said he owned and how he would make it mine. I woke a number of times and found myself repeating Scriptures out loud and calling on the Lord for help.

The second night, I didn't have the dreams, but I woke up at about 3:00 a.m., shaking violently, as if terribly frightened. I felt no inner fear, only this physical manifestation. I fell back asleep and woke up an hour and a half later. As soon as I awoke, I felt very refreshed and calm and sensed the Lord saying to me, "I told you that I would never leave you nor forsake you."

Soon after that I had to cross a bridge. When I came to within 100 feet of it, I loudly said, "In the name of Jesus Christ, I bind you, spirit of fear. For Jesus is driving this car now, and I am only the passenger!" I sailed over that bridge and talked happily to my daughter, who was in the back seat.

I do not experience that fear any longer, and I know I no longer own it. And it certainly does not own me!

Forming a Responsible Plan of Action

Let's summarize what you have done so far: You have submitted to God and resisted the devil. You have identified your fears and the lies behind them. You understand how those fears have kept you from living a responsible life or compelled you to compromise your witness for Christ. You are now halfway home, because a problem well stated is half-solved.

The next step is to face those fears and prayerfully work out a plan to overcome them. It has been said, "Do the thing you fear the most and the death of fear is certain." When I (Rich) and my wife, Shirley, finally discovered the root of Brian's fear, we knew he had to face it. That's why we took him out for ice cream. He wasn't truly free until he took the first few bites. By his own admission, that's when he felt the fear "snap in two" inside of him.

The woman in the testimony about driving over bridges was exercising faith at the end. By faith she verbally resisted the devil (as Jesus showed us to do when He was tempted in the wilderness; see Matthew 4:1-11), and she declared that Jesus was in charge. Then she drove by faith over the bridge. She broke the back of fear when she called on the name of the Lord and drove across.

Years ago I learned that one of my college students hadn't spoken to her father in six months. The tension in the home was unbearable. I asked her if she would be willing to work out a plan of action to overcome her fear of him. She needed to break the ice, so I asked her what she thought would happen if she just said, "Hi, Dad," when he came home that night. She wasn't sure, so we considered the possibilities. He could get mad; he could say "hi" back; or he could do nothing. It was the latter possibility she feared the most.

We worked out a plan for each possible response from her father. Then I asked her to commit to saying "hi" that night. She agreed to do that and then call me afterward. About 7:30 p.m. I got a call from a joyful young lady, who reported, "He said 'hi' back!" She had faced her fear and broke the control it had over her.

There is a story told of a Coast Guard ship being ordered to sea in the midst of a raging storm. A young seaman cried out, "We can't go out; we'll never come back!" To which the captain replied, "We must go out; we don't have to come back!" Fear is not an obstacle for those who trust God and fulfill their responsibilities.

In Christ we have all been allotted a measure of faith. To exercise that faith, we must have sound judgment. To accomplish the goal of complete freedom, we must take that first step in the right direction.

If your plan to overcome fear includes confronting other people, it is helpful to determine in advance how you would respond to their positive or negative reactions. In other words, the plan shouldn't just include the first step; it should also include possible second and third steps.

For some fears, it is wise to show yourself obedient in little steps of faith rather than leaps of faith. If you are afraid to ride an elevator, you probably shouldn't take you first step by going to the Empire State Building in New York and pushing the button for the top floor. You might want to start with a two-story building that has an elevator. Depending on the severity of your fear, these steps could take place in one day or over a period of days, weeks, or even months. It may be wise to take someone with you as you face your fears. Jesus sent His disciples out in pairs (see Mark 6:7; Luke 10:1). The main idea is to keep moving forward. If you find yourself beginning to balk in fear, exercise your authority in Christ over any attack of the enemy and make the choice to push through the fear, walking by faith in God.

My (Neil's) wife, Joanne, used to have a fear of flying. She took an "overcoming the fear of flying" class. During the instruction phase, the participants were asked, "How many of you think that your worrying will contribute to the safety of the flight?" Everyone raised their hand. Other irrational thoughts often accompany the original lies that cause our phobias.

The class included a short flight from Denver International Airport. Nobody was given a certificate of completion unless they took the flight. "Faith without works is useless" (James 2:20). Joanne did pass the test but didn't want to fly without me for some time, because she believed that I was God's man, and the plane wouldn't go down if I was in it! She overcame that lie, as well.

Most fears are struggles against our own flesh patterns that we developed in the past. But whenever you sense your fear or panic attack is from the enemy, make the following declaration of your authority through Jesus over the devil:

In the name and authority of the Lord Jesus Christ, I renounce Satan and all his works and ways. In the name of Jesus and by His authority, I command all deceiving spirits to leave my presence. I declare that Satan has been disarmed by Jesus at the cross. God has not given me a spirit of fear, but of power, love, and a sound mind. I therefore reject all irrational fears. I choose to walk by faith in the power of the Holy Spirit, live in the light of God's love, and think with the sound mind of Christ.

Facing our fears is a challenge to our faith, but we don't have to face those fears alone. David wrote, "Even though I walk through the valley of the shadow of death, I fear no evil, for You are with me" (Psalm 23:4). The following testimony of victory over deep, long-lasting fear shines with the glory of God:

> My father left home when I was five years old, and so the years that followed were filled with pain and loneliness for me. Our family went to church but didn't know Christ as Savior.
>
> When I was eight, my mother purchased three cottages to rent out at a beach resort. My 16-year-old sister took me swimming whenever we had the chance, and I loved it. It was wonderful to leave the city during the summer months.
>
> Frequently, my future brother-in-law would visit us there at the beach. He enjoyed sneaking up behind me, picking me up, running with me down to the ocean, and throwing me in. Because of the dangerous undertow there, I was terrified. He played this little "game" for many summers, and that is how my fear of water began.
>
> I spent the next 30 years of my life making bad choices, which resulted in painful consequences. But after going to a special church service, the Lord wonderfully poured out His grace and mercy, and I received the Lord Jesus as Savior and was saved.

As I came to know God more and more, I began to realize that a spirit of fear had been with me most of my life. I prayed and prayed, but still I remained fearful.

In the summer of 1998 I was attacked by the enemy like never before. I was afraid to be alone, I trembled every waking moment, and I had constant panic attacks. I even envisioned somebody breaking down my door and harming me. I believed I was losing my mind.

After three months of this, I sought medical help and was put on Prozac. After two weeks, I threw the medication out and cried out to God to help me. I could no longer go on like this! I told the Lord that I was willing to live for Him, and I wanted nothing more than to serve Him and be used by Him. Soon after my prayer, He gave me His answer.

My husband and I had been directed by God to a new church. Soon after our arrival, the pastor's wife invited me to join her board of women's ministry. With a thankful heart, I quickly accepted. God has given me a gift of mercy, and after much prayer, I knew my ministry was to help brokenhearted women.

One of the board's requirements was that I become a member of the church and be water baptized—by immersion! I was certainly willing to become a member, but I knew God was aware of my fear of water and that He would certainly never expect me to get baptized.

Oh, how wrong I was! I was reminded of the words of a pastor who had once told me that God will not do all the work of transforming us. He requires our cooperation and participation. We have a part to play, and that part is to meet Him at the place He is working in our lives.

I shared my fear with a dear, loyal friend, who gave me some godly counsel. She told me about who I am in Christ, and that in Him I had been given authority over

Satan, by the power of the shed blood of Jesus. I was, therefore, free to refuse fear and choose faith. In obedience to my heavenly Father, I made the choice to meet Him at His point of working in my life. I would take a step of faith.

On October 24, I went down into the baptismal pool at my church to be baptized by my pastor. As we stood in the pool, we sang "Amazing Grace." I knew angels were all around us, and as I prayed to Jesus for courage, I was able to go under. Almost. My pastor had graciously not put my head under water, knowing my fears.

But when I came up, my husband, who was snapping pictures, yelled out, "Your hair is dry!" God certainly has a wonderful sense of humor.

I knew, however, that I had to go down again, all the way. And I did! My friend, who was watching, said (during the second time) that I had gone all the way to the bottom of the pool. Total victory!

I had learned that as we draw closer to Christ in total obedience to Him, the enemy tries to intimidate us more than ever. And it is usually at our weakest point. Mine was fear, and it controlled my life.

A few days after my baptism, a peace came over me, and it was then that I knew I had overcome fear and replaced it with faith. I am reminded that 2 Timothy 1:7 says, "For God did not give us a spirit of fear, but of power, and of love, and of a sound mind" [YOUNG'S].

So now, when the enemy tries to have his way, I remind him of who I am in Christ, and I claim the verses in Psalm 91 that say even though a thousand may fall at my side and ten thousand at my right hand, it will not come near me. For I now dwell in the shelter of the Most High [verses 1,7]!

Discussion Questions

1. Why is there less fanfare introducing the New Covenant as opposed to the Old Covenant in the Bible?

2. What did you learn from Rich's story about his son?

3. Why isn't a rational argument enough to convince someone not to fear?

4. What is the first step we should take to overcome our fears?

5. How has fear kept you or someone you know from living a responsible life?

6. How can Satan be the origin of our fears?

7. Why do you need a plan of action?

8. Why is faith useless without following through with what you profess to believe?

9. How can you defend yourself against Satan's fear tactics?

10. What is keeping you from living a courageous life in Christ?

Chapter Nine

Panic Disorder

Anxiety does not empty tomorrow of its sorrows,
but only empties today of its strengths.

Charles H. Spurgeon

I graduated from high school and acquired a good job to start my career in the business world. My life had been normal up to the day I had my first full-blown anxiety attack. I remember it well.

I was working at my bookkeeping machine, entering invoices as usual. All of a sudden, my hands began to shake. I stared at them. *What's wrong with me?* I wondered. *My heart is pounding like a trip-hammer. I can almost hear it. I feel weak! I'm going to faint, I know it. It's hard to breathe! Oh, I need more air desperately! What's wrong? Is this a heart attack? Am I dying? I'm only twenty-five. That's too young to have a heart attack!*

Terror raced through me! I jumped up from my machine. Anything to escape! I staggered out of the office and across the hall to where a friend worked. I sagged into the chair beside her desk.[1]

After about 20 minutes, Bonnie Crandall, the author of *Panic Buster,* began to calm down. Still shaken and frightened, she bravely went back to her office. Too drained and confused to focus on her work, however, she took the rest of the day off. This initial episode was just the beginning, and eventually, Bonnie lost her job, and her world continued to fall apart. Even after finding a new job, she had to quit after a month due to the continued episodes. Doctors prescribed various medications, but she only felt worse. Anxious moments began occurring in other places besides work, including the grocery store. She was becoming increasingly housebound, trapped in a shrinking world that choked off her work, relationships, and sense of worth.

> My world became smaller and smaller. Eventually, I had to quit work completely as I became confined to my home. I had gone from anxiety attacks to agoraphobia, the fear of leaving my home alone. Another three years went by. I simply existed. I felt worthless.[2]

Anxiety attacks (often called panic attacks) are defined in the *Baker Encyclopedia of Psychology* as "very frightening and aversive experiences in which persons are overwhelmed with the physical symptoms of anxiety."[3] Those symptoms generally include some of the following: "racing heartbeat; difficulty breathing, feeling as though you 'can't get enough air'; terror that is almost paralyzing; dizziness, lightheadedness, or nausea; trembling, sweating, shaking; choking, chest pains; hot flashes or sudden chills; tingling in fingers or toes ('pins and needles'); fear that you're going to go crazy or are about to die."[4]

These symptoms are similar to the "fight or flight" body responses to extreme stress and danger. The adrenal glands are working overtime, but there is nothing or nobody to fight, and flight would be anywhere from socially awkward to humiliating. Panic attacks can occur suddenly, without warning, in seemingly harmless situations. They can even occur while an individual is sleeping, as the following account reveals.[5]

> I did not realize I had a problem with fear until I had two surgeries in a short period of time. What a scary time that

was for me. All I knew was that I wanted people praying
for me. My prayer consisted of "Help, God!"

I became agitated and shaky inside. My chest began to
tighten, and as time went by I would wake up every morning at three o'clock with crippling fear. It was as though
my thoughts were out of control. I began to have rushes
go through my body, and then I would collapse in tears.

That sounds like a spiritual attack, and the resolution is to submit
to God and resist the devil, as we explained earlier. Two "scary" surger-
ies can weaken the best of us and leave us more vulnerable than when
we are healthy. Our adrenal glands respond to the external pressures
of life by secreting cortisol-like hormones into our bloodstream. But if
the pressures of life persist too long, the adrenal glands can't keep up,
and *stress* becomes *distress*, leaving us vulnerable to physical illnesses
with little emotional reserve. Stress can lead to cancer and heart attacks.

Bonnie Crandall's story (from the beginning of this chapter) is different, and it would be helpful to know more about the circumstances
surrounding her first episode. Was she under pressure at work and
home? Does she have supportive relationships or dysfunctional ones
with family, friends, and coworkers? Is she physically, mentally, and
spiritually in good health?

From a pastoral perspective, in such cases we would gather that
information and ask the person if they would like to resolve any personal or spiritual conflicts. If they indicate they would, we'd say, "With
your permission, I will lead you through *The Steps to Freedom*. What is
going to happen here today is not what I do, but what you do. You will
be asking God to bring to your mind whatever it is that is keeping you
from experiencing your freedom in Christ." Even if the episodes continue, they are going to have a closer relationship with God, and that
can only help them overcome any other abnormalities or struggles.

If such episodes occur frequently (one or more times during any
four-week period) and involve at least four of the symptoms mentioned

earlier, then the person's affliction is called *panic disorder* by secular therapists.[6] About 75 percent of sufferers are women. It usually has its onset between the ages of 20 and 30, although it can first show up in teenage years or occur in adults over 40. However, it is rare that such episodes occur in old age. Although the first episode may come during a time of unusual stress, victims of this problem are often average, emotionally healthy people. The episodes typically reach maximum intensity within one or two minutes from inception and may last (with slowly diminishing symptoms) from 30 minutes to several hours.[7]

It is common to hear people say that they panicked when confronted by certain fear objects like snakes, or when certain opportunities or challenges are afforded them. *I knew better, but I panicked*, or, *I should have stood my ground, but I panicked*, etc. Those people are experiencing a conscious reaction to the environment, which is different from those who are suddenly overwhelmed by anxiety. There is no identifiable fear object in the latter case, and there seems to be no conscious choice that precipitates the episode. Panic may be the result, but not the cause. Those who struggle with such anxious moments are not helped by dwelling on terms like "panic" and "attack." Therefore, in this chapter we will generally refer to such experiences as "anxiety episodes" or "anxious moments."

The opportunity to stop an anxious moment is when we become aware of the first symptom. Recall that Christians are urged by the mercies of God to present their bodies to Him as a living sacrifice (see Romans 12:1). In a broader sense, we have learned to do this when the first symptoms of the flu, nausea, or a cold occur. We pray, "Lord, I submit my body to You as a living sacrifice, and I ask You to fill me with Your Holy Spirit. In the name and authority of Jesus Christ, I command Satan to leave my presence." That is doing what Scripture instructs us to do: "Submit therefore to God. Resist the devil and he will flee from you" (James 4:7). Of course, not all illness is the direct result of the devil's activities, but what have you got to lose?

It is the same logic as practicing "threshold thinking" when tempted. We have to take the initial tempting thought captive to the obedience of Christ (2 Corinthians 10:5). God has promised to provide a way of escape (1 Corinthians 10:13), but we have to take it when we can, and that is usually right at the beginning. "Therefore, let everyone who is godly pray to You in a time when You may be found; surely in a flood of great waters they will not reach him" (Psalm 32:6). God is always reachable, but the problem is that when people allow themselves to get emotionally overcome, they don't turn to Him. Get bold. Be courageous. Say it out loud. Take your place in Christ.

It is common for individuals, after suffering a number of anxiety episodes, to become increasingly afraid that they are helpless. They start avoiding public places and remain at home whenever possible. The sufferers become more apprehensive and tense, continually guarding against the possibility of another anxious moment.[8] This defensive posture causes them to be even more susceptible to other episodes. Many sufferers still manage to muddle their way through life, coping as best they can, but it is a miserable existence.

The possibility of another episode causes many people to become agoraphobic. Agoraphobia (literally, "fear of the marketplace") can become so severe that sufferers may quit their jobs, stop going to church, avoid grocery stores and banks, and even dread talking on the telephone. In extreme cases, the individual can become housebound for years.[9]

Physiological Considerations

In seeking to overcome anxious and often terrifying moments, it is very helpful to understand how the body works and why certain physical symptoms occur. Often those symptoms are so distressing that sufferers will believe they are in need of emergency medical treatment and will go to the hospital.

There are physical disorders that can cause symptoms that mimic anxious moments; therefore, it is wise to undergo a thorough physical examination. If your physician recommends you see another medical specialist, do so. If a physical condition is diagnosed, follow the treatments directed by the doctor. Drug and alcohol abuse or withdrawal can also have similar physical symptoms to anxiety episodes. The use of stimulants, such as caffeine, could be the culprit, or you could be experiencing the side effects of certain prescription medications. Even pregnancy, premenstrual syndrome, or menopause could be at the root of these symptoms.[10]

If there is a legitimate physiological reason for your symptoms, you need medical help. But if no physical reason exists, it would be wise to explore other possible causes so you can find the psychological and spiritual assistance you need.

Even when there is no physiological cause for anxiety episodes, there are still physical effects on the body due to a person's response. For example, more than 80 percent of sufferers experience a rapid or irregular heartbeat. Any unpleasant sensation in the heart that we can feel is categorized in general as a "palpitation."[11]

Assuming there is no physiological condition warranting medical attention, these critical questions remain: "Why am I having this sensation?" and "How am I going to respond to it?" Let's examine how our body functions. Our nervous system sends a signal from every part of our body to the brain, and the mind interprets the data according to how it has been programmed. The emotional response is immediate. If the mind interprets the data as danger, it immediately sends a signal back to the body. The signal stimulates hormones that engage the sympathetic branch of the autonomic nervous system.[12] The ensuing adrenaline rush is the classic "fight or flight" response protecting us from supposed danger. Physiologically, our blood sugar level increases, our eyes dilate, our sweat glands perspire, our heart rate increases, our mouth becomes dry, our muscles tense, our blood flow decreases in the arms and legs and pools in the head and trunk, and our breathing rate and pattern change.[13]

During an anxious moment, there is no actual physical enemy to fight, so the tension and anxiety we feel continue to build.[14] Eventually, we experience so much pent-up emotional energy that the compelling drive is to flee. In a real emergency, our breathing undergoes a significant change in rate and pattern. That is also true during an anxiety episode. Rather than slow, deep breathing from the lower lungs, we move into rapid, shallow breathing from the upper lungs. During real danger, this natural and necessary process pumps additional oxygen into the bloodstream, while quickly ridding the body of carbon dioxide.[15]

If there is no physical activity taking place at this point in the episode (and there usually isn't), the body discharges too much carbon dioxide, and we experience hyperventilation, leading to an irregular heart rate; dizziness; lightheadedness; shortness of breath; chest pain; blurred vision; numbness or tingling in the mouth, hands, or feet; weakness; confusion; or an inability to concentrate.

The initial physical response to a real or imaginary fear object is to gasp or suck in air. Then, instead of exhaling, we try to suck in more air, but there is no room for it in our lungs. Blowing into a paper bag gets us to exhale and return to a normal process of inhaling and exhaling. It is also helpful to slowly take a deep breath in and then exhale completely.

Knowing that most of the unpleasant physical symptoms are the body's God-created means of coping with a perceived emergency takes a lot of the terrifying mystery out of these episodes. What initially seems to be an overwhelming situation over which we have no control becomes a much more manageable problem if we understand how our bodies are naturally wired to respond to a crisis.

Suppose you have a minor condition of mitral valve prolapse, which is usually a non-life-threatening heart palpitation. Your first experience with it could be frightening, because you don't know what it is. You could think you are having a heart attack. After a thorough physical exam you learn that it is only a minor condition. The next time your heart flutters, your "renewed" mind interprets the data differently, and you experience less angst. Even the first response would be less frightening if your mind had previously been programmed not to fear death.

The Body Responds

Secular therapists talk about the onset of anticipatory anxiety as a key factor in determining whether anxious moments will occur or not. For example, if people have an episode in a grocery store, they will likely struggle with negative thoughts when the need for shopping arises again. The thought process could be something like this:

> I've had an anxious moment before in a grocery store; what's to keep me from having another one? I don't like waiting in lines, especially with people in front of and behind me. What if I become emotionally overcome? I won't be able to escape. I may lose control, and I'll make a total fool of myself and have to run out of the store and leave my shopping cart filled with food. People will think I'm absolutely crazy!

This battle for the mind could go on in the home, while driving to the store, while pulling into the parking lot, or while walking down the aisles. While this person's mind is racing with fearful thoughts and images, what do you think is happening emotionally and physically? Since our emotions are primarily a product of our thoughts, the very same physiological symptoms (pounding heart, rapid and shallow breathing) that accompanied the first anxious moment are already beginning to happen again. Why? Because the body responds to how the mind thinks. The body doesn't distinguish between a real or imaginary threat. To quote Dr. R. Reid Wilson:

> Within the Panic Cycle, it is not the body that responds incorrectly. The body responds perfectly to an exaggerated message from the mind. It is not the body that needs fixing; it is our thoughts, our images, our negative

interpretation of our experiences that we must correct in
order to gain control of panic. If we never told ourselves,
in essence, "I'll lose control in that situation," then we
would not be flipping on that unconscious emergency
switch so often.[16]

Physiological responses to how we think are not foreign to the
Bible. The following verses teach that our thoughts and beliefs do have
an effect on our physical bodies:

- "A joyful heart is good medicine, but a broken spirit dries up
  the bones" (Proverbs 17:22).

- "For as he thinks within himself, so he is" (Proverbs 23:7).

- "Trust in the LORD with all your heart and do not lean on
  your own understanding. In all your ways acknowledge
  Him, and He will make your paths straight. Do not be wise
  in your own eyes; fear the LORD and turn away from evil. It
  will be healing to your body and refreshment to your bones"
  (Proverbs 3:5-8).

- "Beloved, I pray that in all respects you may prosper and be
  in good health, just as your soul prospers" (3 John 2).

Our Adequacy in Christ

We feel anxious when our perceived needs exceed our perceived
resources. We are fearful when we feel helpless and out of control.
Lucinda Bassett, director of the Midwest Center for Stress and Anxiety, shares how her feelings of inadequacy led to crippling fear:

> I'm afraid I'll lose control. I'm afraid of my father, of God,
> of what people will think of me. I'm afraid "it" will catch
> up with me. I'm afraid my parents will embarrass me. I'm
> afraid I'll embarrass myself. My heart will stop. I'm afraid
> I'll throw up in front of everybody, and people will talk
> about me. I'm afraid I'll jump off the balcony. I'm afraid

I'll die. I'm afraid I won't. I'm not good enough for my
friends. I'm not good enough for God. I'll be found out.
I'm afraid of the shadows on the wall. Someone's right
outside my window waiting. I'm afraid of myself. I'm not
talented enough. I'm not pretty enough. I'll panic. I'm
afraid my parents won't love me anymore. I'm afraid I
won't get everything done. I'll choke. I'm inadequate. I'm
afraid I'll go crazy. I'm afraid they'll lock me up and no one
will care anymore. They won't like me if they really know
me. My heart will be broken. I'm not rich enough. I'm not
strong enough. I'm not smart enough. No one [would]
ever be able to love me if they really knew me. I'm afraid
to be myself. I'm afraid I have no self. I'm afraid I might
fail. What if I succeed? What if it doesn't happen? What if
it does? Why am I so afraid?[17]

One of the goals of secular therapy is to convince people that they
are adequate in themselves to handle anxious moments. Without a
relationship with God, they have no other choice but to rely on themselves, but the apostle Paul advocates a different answer for the Christian: "Not that we are adequate in ourselves to consider anything as
coming from ourselves, but our adequacy is from God, who also made
us adequate as servants of a new covenant" (2 Corinthians 3:5-6).

As children of God, we have entered into a New Covenant relationship with our heavenly Father. In the flesh we are weak and helpless,
but "in Christ" we can do all things through Him who strengthens us
(Philippians 4:13). In the flesh we may lose control, but if we walk by
the Spirit we will have self-control (Galatians 5:22-23). "A natural man
does not accept the things of the Spirit of God.... But we have the mind
of Christ" (1 Corinthians 2:14,16). For these reasons, Jesus instructs us
to "seek first His kingdom and His righteousness, and all these things
will be added to you. So do not worry about tomorrow; for tomorrow will care for itself. Each day has enough trouble of its own" (Matthew 6:33-34).

There is one other important spiritual factor that must be considered. Paul says, "Do you not know that your bodies are members of Christ?...Do you not know that your body is a temple of the Holy Spirit who is in you, whom you have from God, and that you are not your own? For you have been bought with a price: therefore glorify God in your body" (1 Corinthians 6:15,19-20). Our bodies are not our own. We belong to God. So we need to be good stewards of our bodies and submit them to Him as living sacrifices (Romans 12:1).

A Time for Medication

Let's review what we have covered so far. The origin of an anxious moment can be a signal to our brain from our physical bodies saying something is wrong. How we interpret that signal is dependent upon how our minds have been previously programmed and what we presently think and believe. The origin can also be a spiritual battle for our minds. In cases other than spiritual attacks from the evil one, how can we overcome anxious moments?

To be good stewards of our bodies, we should live a balanced life of rest, exercise, and maintaining a proper diet. However, living in decaying bodies and a diseased world may require the additional help of medications. We need medical help when there is something physically wrong with our bodies that healthy living cannot correct. Medication can also be helpful in treating symptoms leading up to an anxious moment, as well as the episode itself. Usually this kind of medication is reserved for severe cases and is used to enable patients to have some mental and emotional stability, allowing them to process their issues. In severe cases, people are simply too stressed out to handle the truth without first taking medication.

Many people suffering from anxiety episodes find help in godly counsel and realize complete resolution without the use of medications. We encourage you to seek the Lord for guidance and godly counsel before you consider medication. Then seek the advice of a qualified medical doctor. There are numerous medications (many of which are used in the treatment of depression as well) available for various anxiety disorders. You should ask about possible side effects before agreeing to a particular medication.

After acknowledging that "anti-anxiety medications can be beneficial,"[18] Lucinda Bassett gives the following warning:

> The problem with certain types of anti-anxiety medications is that they give you a false sense of recovery. They alleviate the symptoms, but do nothing to treat the cause, because the cause of your anxiety is very often the way you react and respond to things that are going on in your life.[19]

Medication may bring temporary relief from anxious moments, but it does not eradicate the phobias that may lie behind them, nor does it renew a person's mind. The episodes will likely return when the person stops taking the medication if no attempt is made to get right with God, no cognitive restructuring has taken place, and no physical causes (if any) have been dealt with.

Another potential problem is self-medication. Some chronic sufferers become addicted to prescription drugs or turn to alcohol or illegal drugs to alleviate the emotional pain. Narcotizing one's fears only multiplies the problem, adding another layer to the bondage the individual is already experiencing: chemical dependency. According to an article published in 1996, alcoholism and drug abuse cost businesses $200 billion annually as employees sought to self-medicate their way out of problems.[20] More important than the continued financial cost is the destruction of bodies, marriages, and families. The United States is presently experiencing an unprecedented opioid epidemic.

Street drugs and alcohol have never cured a problem. They only serve to give the illusion of well-being. When the drugs wear off, the harsh realities of life resurface, sending the victim into deeper depression, degradation, and despair. The Bible says, "Do not get drunk with wine, for that is dissipation, but be filled with the Spirit" (Ephesians 5:18). If you or a friend struggle with self-medicating, we encourage you to read Neil's book *Overcoming Addictive Behavior*, which he coauthored with Mike Quarles, or *Freedom from Addiction*, which he coauthored with both Mike and Julia Quarles.

Renewing the Mind

The central nervous system regulates every bodily function according to how the mind has been programmed. In addition to getting proper medical help, we need to be transformed by the renewing of our minds. Anxiety sufferers need to understand how their emotional response is the result of how they think and what they believe. The emotional response of fear is always preceded by a thought, although it can be so rapid that we're hardly aware of the connection.

In addition, certain personality types are more susceptible to anxious moments than others, according to Dr. Edmund Bourne. He describes four subpersonalities that are most vulnerable to serious bouts with anxiety: the "Worrier," the "Victim," the "Critic," and the "Perfectionist."[21] We prefer to think of these four as flesh patterns rather than subpersonalities, because flesh patterns do not define who we are in Christ. That is also why we try to stay away from labels, but for the sake of communication we will use Dr. Bourne's terminology. The Worrier, Dr. Bourne says, is the most common and forceful subpersonality (flesh pattern) in anxiety-prone individuals. He describes the Worrier as follows:

> The Worrier creates anxiety by imagining the worst-case scenario. It scares you with fantasies of disaster or catastrophe when you imagine confronting something you fear. It also aggravates panic by reacting to the first physical symptoms of a panic attack. The Worrier promotes your fears that what is happening is dangerous or embarrassing. "What if I have a heart attack?" "What will they think if they see me?"[22]

Patterns of thinking have been developed over time, and thus it takes time to renew the mind. Worriers find it hard to rest in the loving and protective arms of their heavenly Father. They feel that life's problems present a clear danger that calls for continual vigilance on their part, lest they be caught off guard. Jesus asked, "Who of you by being worried can add a single hour to his life?" (Matthew 6:27). The answer is "none of us," but you can seriously *reduce* the quality of hours by worrying.

Another flesh pattern is the "Victim." The Victim is overwhelmed by a sense of helplessness and hopelessness. Having established a track record of misfortune and failure, this flesh pattern suggests there's no reason why a string of bad luck should end. According to Dr. Bourne:

> The Victim believes that there is something inherently wrong with you: you are in some ways deprived, defective, or unworthy. The Victim always perceives insurmountable obstacles between you and your goals. Characteristically, it bemoans, complains, and regrets things as they are at present. It believes that nothing will ever change.[23]

Though the world may have dealt us a bad hand, we can still be overcomers. "For whatever is born of God overcomes the world; and this is the victory that has overcome the world—our faith. Who is the one who overcomes the world, but he who believes that Jesus is the Son of God?" (1 John 5:4-5).

We overcome the world because Jesus has already done so. We enter into that victory by believing the truth. The person who is convinced that he or she is helpless or hopeless has believed a lie and is consequently unable to walk by faith. How can we be helpless when the Bible says we can do all things through Christ who strengthens us (Philippians 4:13)? How can we be hopeless when the God of all hope is with us, and He is able to fill us with joy and peace (Romans 15:13)?

Playing the role of the victim can become an excuse for not getting well. Jesus encountered such a man one day in Jerusalem:

> Now there is in Jerusalem by the sheep gate a pool, which is called in Hebrew Bethesda, having five porticoes. In these lay a multitude of those who were sick, blind, lame, and withered, [waiting for the moving of the waters; for an angel of the Lord went down at certain seasons into the pool and stirred up the water; whoever then first, after the stirring up of the water, stepped in was made well from whatever disease with which he was afflicted.] A man was there who had been ill for thirty-eight years. When Jesus saw him lying there, and knew that he had already been a long time in that condition, He said to him, "Do you wish to get well?" The sick man answered Him, "Sir, I have no man to put me into the pool when the water is stirred up, but while I am coming, another steps down before me." Jesus said to him, "Get up, pick up your pallet and walk." Immediately the man became well, and picked up his pallet and began to walk (John 5:2-9).

"Do you wish to get well?" That is not a cruel question; it is a very important one. You can't get well unless you desire it and are willing to make the commitment to do whatever it takes. We have all been victimized, and no one can promise that we won't be again. But you don't have to remain a victim for the rest of your life. Nobody can fix your past, but you can be free from it by the grace of God. That wonderful truth is inherent in the gospel.

The third flesh pattern is the "Critic." People with this flesh pattern have overly sensitive consciences that berate themselves and others. Criticizing others is a defense mechanism that doesn't work. Often echoing the voice of a demanding parent, teacher, coach, or employer, the Critic slaps negative labels on our souls, hindering us from experiencing the joy and freedom of being children of God. Faith is drained away, and we feel constantly put down for not being able to overcome our fears and live a normal life.

Closely akin to the "Critic" is the "Perfectionist." The Perfectionist's modus operandi is not to put us down, but to push us to do better and better.[24] The Perfectionist's favorite expressions are "I should," "I have to," and "I must."[25] People with this flesh pattern never have any peace of mind, because they can never achieve perfection. Their overwhelming need to accomplish more and more makes them driven, stressed, and irritable. They are setting themselves up for an anxiety disorder because they can't stand to fail, especially in public.

The Spiritual Battle for the Mind

There are mysteries that the secular world of medicine and psychology have yet to solve. What brings on these anxious moments in the first place? What causes a person who is normally able to handle stress to be suddenly stricken with an anxiety episode? Why do people sometimes awaken terrorized from a sound sleep? And why do Christians often find instantaneous freedom when they call upon the name of the Lord? These questions seemed to be on the mind of someone who contacted our ministry:

> I am wondering if you can help me out with a particular experience that has plagued me and my sleep for the past six or seven years. Although I am a Christian, I have probably experienced about 15 of these panic attacks over the past several years.
>
> They are usually associated with a time in which I've given something over to God or committed my ways to His.
>
> Here is a little history about my sleeping habits. When I was young I would dream very intense dreams about spirits or things related to the spirit world. I'm not sure why, except that I am an artist and have always had a very vivid imagination. Other nights I would dream about the end times and things that happened—very intense dreams also!

As I got older, these dreams would happen less frequently, but when they did come, they came with the same intensity.

When I turned 17, I received a calling from God—a very distinct one. Unfortunately, because of my pride and fear, I did not follow that calling. Through the years since then I have received many opportunities to follow that original calling, and each time I tried, the panic attack would result. Consequently, I would back off from the calling because of the fear of another attack.

The panic attack usually started by waking me out of my sleep to either a rushing sound in my ear, many people talking incoherently, or many people screaming. By the time this ends (usually in about 5 or 10 seconds) an intense, indescribable, mammoth fear envelops my whole body.

I really can't describe how intense this fear is. My body becomes physically paralyzed, no movement. I can't talk. I can move my eyes around and I can hear, though. Finally, a heavy weight seems to rest on my chest and pushes me into my bed. At least that's what it feels like.

This whole experience lasts about a minute, but then I am usually wide awake and scared. I'm not sure what causes this, but I think it may be demonic.

We think so, too. The fact that these attacks occurred around the time she was making a serious move toward God would indicate a spiritual attack. Unfortunately, the scare tactic worked. She backed off from obeying God because of the fear. This is a very common strategy of the enemy, and one we have personally experienced numerous times. Uninformed believers begin to wonder about themselves since nobody talks about these experiences in most of our churches. Those who are enlightened and discerning stand firm in their faith and are not intimidated. They take "every thought captive to the obedience of

Christ" (2 Corinthians 10:5), and they ward off the fiery darts of Satan by holding up the shield of faith (Ephesians 6:16). This is what they receive from Jesus: "Peace I leave with you; My peace I give to you; not as the world gives do I give to you. Do not let your heart be troubled, nor let it be fearful" (John 14:27).

Discussion Questions

1. What is the difference between a pastoral perspective regarding treatment for an anxiety disorder and that of a secular counselor?

2. Why do you think anxiety disorders are more likely to begin when people are in their twenties and healthy, and seldom happen for older people who aren't as healthy?

3. Why is it so important to take corrective action when symptoms first appear or when tempted?

4. What happens if you don't take action right away?

5. If the body is functioning like God designed, then what or where is the source for anxious moments?

6. How can one unresolved anxious moment set you up for others when similar situations arise?

7. What role can medication play?

8. What kinds of subpersonalities/flesh patterns are more susceptible to attacks?

9. Why do some people play the role of a victim?

10. Why should we seek first the kingdom of God?

Chapter Ten

Casting All Anxiety on Christ

When each earthly brace falls under,
and life seems a restless sea,
are you then a God-held wonder,
satisfied and calm and free?[1]

Jesus was traveling with His disciples when they entered a village where Martha welcomed them into her home. She had a sister named Mary, who was sitting at the Lord's feet listening to every word Jesus said. Martha, on the other hand, was distracted by all her preparations. She was the prototype of every modern homemaker who wants to be a good host. It is hard not to sympathize with her. She wanted to keep up appearances and impress her guests, and it upset her that Mary wasn't helping to accomplish her goal. In frustration she said to Jesus, "Lord, do You not care that my sister has left me to do all the serving alone? Then tell her to help me" (Luke 10:40). That is *not* how your cast your anxiety on Christ!

Martha was anxious because her priorities were wrong. Jesus answered her prayer by saying, "Martha, Martha, you are worried and bothered about so many things; but only one thing is necessary, for Mary has chosen the good part, which shall not be taken away from her" (verses 41-42). People everywhere are bothered and worried about so many things, and much of it is due to living our way instead of God's way.

Double-Minded

The primary word for *anxiety* in the New Testament has both positive and negative connotations. Of the 25 uses in the New Testament, 5 of them indicate a sense of caring. If you have an important exam tomorrow, you should feel a little anxious. The proper response is to study. If your child is two hours late, you should feel a little anxious. The proper response is to pray and then take some appropriate action. The other 20 uses refer to a distracting and negative sense of worry. The Greek word for anxiety is a conjunction of two words that by themselves mean "divide" and "mind." To be anxious in a negative sense is to be double-minded, and James says double-minded people are unstable in all their ways (see James 1:8).

Before we were united to Christ, we learned the ways of the world. Let's call those ways "Plan B," which we assimilated from our environment through reason, intuition, and experience. Martha was relying on Plan B to enlist the help of God in living out her own priorities. "Plan A" is God's way, which we choose to believe by faith. God's way is not just a better way to live; it is a living relationship with Almighty God, the creator of the universe. Mary chose Plan A when she sat at Jesus's feet listening to His every word.

Without a knowledge of God's ways, anxiety is inevitable. Without eternal life, how could we not fear death? Unless we are secure in Christ, how could we not be anxious for tomorrow? We would have to live in denial or simply not care. Without God we have no choice but to trust in our own limited resources and the fallen ways of this world.

False Security

Plan B is always lurking in the back of our minds. We have the choice to live according to the Spirit or according to the flesh (see Galatians 5:16-25). These flesh patterns/defense mechanisms will always suggest a way to deal with life's problems on a human level. The anxious Christian asks, "Can I totally trust God, or should I just whisper a prayer and then deal with life as though I am solely responsible for making my own way in this world? Can I cast all my anxieties on Christ, or do I have to retain some worries in order to make sure everything comes out okay?" It is easy to fall back on old ways of coping with life when the pressure is on. Jesus told the Pharisees they were setting aside the commandments of God (Plan A) in order to keep their traditions (Plan B; see Mark 7:9).

Such waffling between Plan A and Plan B creates its own anxieties for carnal Christians. They are double-minded. A natural person could have less anxiety than a Christian who wants to straddle the fence and have the "best of both worlds." The natural person has only Plan B, and some live relatively free of anxiety for a period of time.

For instance, consider a highly educated mathematician who has chosen not to believe in God. He has created his own rationalistic worldview and natural explanation of reality. He doesn't like to be presented with Plan A, because that would create a certain amount of anxiety. He has worked hard to ensure that his family's physical needs and safety are provided for. He doesn't like to think about his purpose for being here or to consider questions about life after death. He has become his own god. Although that will appear to work for a season, the end result is not attractive: "There is a way which seems right to a man, but its end is the way of death" (Proverbs 14:12). What happens when the stock market crashes, health fails, a spouse leaves, an accident happens, or an illness turns out to be terminal? Insecurity is depending upon temporal things that we have no right or ability to control. Security is depending upon eternal life and values that no one or nothing can take away from us.

People are not affected by their environment. They are affected by how they perceive the world and the situation they are in. How they interpret the data their senses are picking up depends upon what they believe. Two people can be in the same situation and respond differently, because they don't have similar experiences, worldviews, or beliefs. One could say to the other, "I don't know what you have to worry about" or "What are you afraid of?"

Suppose you have a very intimidating boss, and you receive word that he wants to see you first thing tomorrow, which makes you very anxious. You don't know why he wants to see you, so your mind begins to entertain several possibilities. *Maybe he is going to reprimand me for that simple little mistake I made last week. Maybe he is going to fire me. That really ticks me off. I think I will quit and not give him the satisfaction. No, he can't fire me, I have been here too long. But what if he does fire me? Where would I get a new job at my age?* The more you entertain such thoughts, the angrier and more anxious you become.

Finally, tomorrow comes after a restless night. You have emotionally vacillated between anger and anxiety. With trepidation you enter his office, only to be greeted by all the top brass, who are there to congratulate you for the promotion you are about to receive. The anger, fear, and anxiety were just a product of your imagination and speculation. You didn't have all the facts, so your conclusion was in error. How would you have felt if you knew the truth that you were being promoted? If what we think or believe does not reflect truth, then what we feel does not reflect reality.

The presence of God affects our total being. "He who raised Christ Jesus from the dead will also give life to your mortal bodies through His Spirit who dwells in you" (Romans 8:11). If we are living by faith according to what God says is true, in the power of the Holy Spirit, our lives will be characterized by "love [the character of God], joy [the antithesis of depression], peace [the antithesis of anxiety], patience [the antithesis of anger], kindness, goodness, faithfulness, gentleness, self-control" (Galatians 5:22-23). The connection between the initiating cause (the Spirit of truth working in our lives) and the end result (self-control) is the mind, which directs the brain that regulates our glands and muscular movements.

Biblical Faith Leads to Wholeness

Jesus asked the blind men, "'Do you believe that I am able to do this?' They said to Him, 'Yes, Lord.' Then He touched their eyes, saying, 'It shall be done to you according to your faith'" (Matthew 9:28-29). The external power of Jesus was made effective in their lives by their choice to believe. In other words, the Lord chose to bring about a physical healing through the channel of belief. Is this not true in every other aspect of life? We are saved by faith (Ephesians 2:8), sanctified by faith (Galatians 3:3-5), and we walk (live) by faith (2 Corinthians 5:7).

God never bypasses our minds; we are transformed by the renewing of our minds (Romans 12:2). He makes possible the renewing of our minds by His very presence in our lives. We respond in faith by choosing to believe the truth and living by the power of the Holy Spirit, not carrying out the desires of the flesh (Galatians 5:16). Jesus is "the way [how we ought to live], and the truth [what we ought to believe], and the life [our spiritual union with God]" (John 14:6). Even the operation of spiritual gifts works in conjunction with our minds. Paul comes to the conclusion, "I will pray with the spirit and I will pray with the mind also; I will sing with the spirit and I shall sing with the mind also" (1 Corinthians 14:15).

The Peace of God

Peace is the antithesis of anxiety. Everybody desires a peaceful life and to be relatively free from anxiety, but there are limits to what a person can hope for in this world. According to Paul, believers have eternal peace with God the moment they are born again: "Therefore, having been justified by faith, we have peace with God through our Lord Jesus Christ" (Romans 5:1). What we need is internal peace, and we can have it if we learn to "be anxious for nothing [don't be double-minded about anything], but in everything by prayer and supplication with thanksgiving let your requests be made known to God. And the peace of God, which surpasses all comprehension, will guard your hearts and your minds in Christ Jesus" (Philippians 4:6-7).

God's peace is present, even when we don't fully understand how things will work out. An awareness of an anxious spirit should drive us to find the peace of God by turning to Him and assuming our responsibility to think as Paul advised: "Finally, brethren, whatever is true, whatever is honorable, whatever is right, whatever is pure, whatever is lovely, whatever is of good repute, if there is any excellence and if anything worthy of praise, dwell on these things" (Philippians 4:8). And as the Bible also teaches, don't just think about these things. Live the truth. Do the honorable, right, pure, and lovely thing. "The things you have learned and received and heard and seen in me, practice these things, and the God of peace will be with you" (verse 9).

We want peace on earth, but we may not always have that. Some things are beyond our right or ability to control. "If possible, so far as it depends on you, be at peace with all men" (Romans 12:18). Let's face it, external peace doesn't always depend upon us. If someone doesn't want to be reconciled with us, it can't be done. We should, however, strive to be peacemakers, because "blessed are the peacemakers, for they shall be called sons of God" (Matthew 5:9). Having internal peace and a sense of worth is possible regardless of external circumstances.

The role of civil government is to keep the peace and create laws that protect us from one another. Even if peace officers were able to maintain law and order perfectly, individuals would still be anxious. The problem is in the heart. Jeremiah recorded God's words, saying, "They have healed the brokenness of My people superficially, saying 'peace, peace,' but there is no peace" (Jeremiah 6:14). Even the Mosaic Law was powerless to give life (Galatians 3:21). The Law was a tutor that was intended to lead us to Jesus, "who is our life" (Colossians 3:4). Jesus said, "Peace I leave with you; My peace I give to you; not as the world gives do I give to you. Do not let your heart be troubled, nor let it be fearful" (John 14:27). But remember, the peace of God orders our internal world, not our external world. In summary:

Eternal . . . . Peace with God . . . . This we have.

Internal . . . . Peace of God . . . . This we need.

External . . . . Peace on Earth . . . . This we want.

The Right Goal

We can't always control other people or the circumstances of life—and, in many cases, we shouldn't even try. The right goal is to become the people God has called us to be. Nothing can grow if there is no life present. Christ is our life, and the Holy Spirit is the sanctifying agent who enables us to be like Jesus. Nothing can stop that spiritual growth from happening except ourselves.

Suppose a mother has adopted the goal of having a loving, harmonious, happy Christian family. Who in that family can block that goal? Every member of the family can, and all of them will at some time. But who could block her goal of becoming the mother and wife that God has called her to be? Nobody! She is the only one. It is a legitimate desire to have a happy and harmonious family, but if her identity and sense of worth are dependent upon achieving that goal perfectly and continually, she is going to struggle with a lot of anxiety and likely become a controller.

A suit salesman attended one of our conferences and shared the following:

> This has been the most liberating week of my life. I have been a Christian for several years, but I have been a terrible witness to my boss. I have continuously struggled with anger and anxiety because of the job. My goal was to sell suits, and whenever I didn't make a sale, I got mad. I started approaching every day with anxiety. *Will I sell my quota, or will this be another frustrating day?* My boss had to talk to me about my anger and attitude.
>
> This week I realized that I had the wrong goal. I learned that I was just supposed to be the suit salesman

that God called me to be. My previous goal was to sell suits and make money. To accomplish that goal, I had learned how to manipulate customers. And to do that, I frequently sold them suits which weren't right for them. This week I started considering the needs of the customer for the first time. I even talked one gentleman out of a sale because it just wasn't right for him.

Last night my boss asked me if I was all right. I was so free from anxiety that he thought I was sick or something. This was the first week I actually enjoyed going to work. Would you believe it? I sold more suits this week than I ever have before.

Where Is Your Treasure?

In the Sermon on the Mount, Jesus teaches that anxious people have two treasures and two visions because they are trying to serve two masters. He goes on to teach that "double-minded" people also worry about tomorrow. Most—if not all—our anxieties can be traced to what we treasure in our hearts and to our lack of faith in God's provision for tomorrow. Jesus said:

> Do not store up for yourselves treasures on earth, where moth and vermin destroy, and where thieves break in and steal. But store up for yourselves treasures in heaven, where moth and vermin do not destroy, and where thieves do not break in and steal. For where your treasure is, there your heart will be also (Matthew 6:19-21 NIV).

Treasures on earth have two characteristics. First, there is the decay of all things physical, which is the law of entropy. This second law of thermodynamics says that all systems become increasingly disorderly and will eventually decay. If rust doesn't destroy it, then moths or termites will. The American dream for some is to have a cabin in the hills and a boat in the marina. It would take a fair amount of energy to keep both in repair. Second, because of the value of earthly treasures, there is always the concern for security. It is hard to be anxiety-free if we are worried about our possessions. The more we possess, the more others might covet what we have. This opens the door for fear about thieves breaking in to steal.

Personal security comes from relationships, not possessions. It is amazing what we can live without if we have meaningful relationships. The critical question is, "What do you treasure in your heart?" Do you spend much time thinking about earthly treasures? Do you worry about your possessions and compare them with what others have? Do you feel prideful when you have more than others? Do you feel jealous when you have less? "Beware, and be on your guard against every form of greed; for not even when one has an abundance does his life consist of his possessions" (Luke 12:15).

There is nothing inherently wrong with owning property. It is the *love* of money, not money itself, that is the root of all sorts of evil (1 Timothy 6:10). Paul's words in 1 Timothy 6:17-19 present the right orientation and balance:

> Instruct those who are rich in this present world not to be conceited or to fix their hope on the uncertainty of riches, but on God, who richly supplies us with all things to enjoy. Instruct them to do good, to be rich in good works, to be generous and ready to share, storing up for themselves the treasure of a good foundation for the future, so that they may take hold of that which is life indeed.

Single Vision

Jesus said, "The eye is the lamp of the body; so then if your eye is clear, your whole body will be full of light. But if your eye is bad, your whole body will be full of darkness. If then the light that is in you is darkness, how great is the darkness!" (Matthew 6:22-23). Ancient tradition viewed the eyes as the windows through which light entered the body. If the eyes were in good condition, the whole body would receive the benefits that light bestows. But if there was something wrong with the eyes, the whole body would be plunged into the darkness, which breeds disease. There is a nuance in this passage that is pregnant with meaning. The "clear eye" is the one with a single vision, which Jesus clarifies in the two verses following this passage: "No one can serve two masters; for either he will hate the one and love the other, or he will be devoted to one and despise the other. You cannot serve God and wealth. For this reason I say to you, do not be worried about your life" (Matthew 6:24-25). There will be no peace in serving two masters. Our only choice is to decide which master we will serve, God or wealth. Whichever master we choose, by that master we shall be controlled.

Jesus said, "If anyone wishes to come after Me, he must deny himself, and take up his cross daily and follow Me" (Luke 9:23). Denying ourselves is not the same as self-denial. Great athletes, politicians, and cult leaders have learned how to deny themselves certain pleasures in order to win or promote themselves and their causes. Self is still the dominate force, though—the one in charge. Denying self is denying *self-rule*. God never designed our souls to function as masters. We are either serving God or mammon at any given time (see Matthew 6:24). We are deceived if we think we are really serving ourselves. Self-seeking, self-serving, self-justifying, self-glorifying, self-centered, and self-confident living is in actuality serving the world, the flesh, and the devil.

We have to die to ourselves in order to live in Christ. We are forgiven because He died in our place. We are delivered because we have died with Him. Paul says, "I have been crucified with Christ; and it is no longer I who live, but Christ lives in me; and the life which I now live in the flesh I live by faith in the Son of God, who loved me and gave Himself up for me" (Galatians 2:20). If we hold on to our natural identity and earthly inheritance, we rob ourselves of an infinitely better spiritual identity and eternal inheritance.

When we pick up our cross daily, we are actually picking up the cross of Christ. There is only one cross. It provides forgiveness for what we have done and deliverance from what we once were—both justification and sanctification. We are new creations in Christ and identified with Him:

in His death (Romans 6:3,6; Colossians 3:1-3)

in His burial (Romans 6:4)

in His resurrection (Romans 6:5,8,11)

in His ascension (Ephesians 2:6)

in His life (Romans 5:10-11)

in His power (Ephesians 1:19-20)

in His inheritance (Romans 8:16-17; Ephesians 1:11-12)

F.B. Meyer said, "Earthly thrones are generally built with steps up to them; the remarkable thing about the thrones of the eternal kingdom is that the steps are all down to them. We must descend if we would reign, stoop if we would rise, gird ourselves to wash the feet of the disciples as a common slave in order to share the royalty of our Divine Master."[2] Jesus said, "Follow Me," at multiple points in the Gospels. Self will never cast out self; we have to be led into it by the Holy Spirit. "For we who live are constantly being delivered over to death for Jesus' sake, so that the life of Jesus also may be manifested in our mortal flesh" (2 Corinthians 4:11). We dare not harden our hearts.

The voices from the world, the flesh, and the devil will scream in our minds, "But it seems so austere. God only wants to control you, and you have to give up everything!" Don't believe that lie, because nothing could be further from the truth. "For whoever wishes to save his life will lose it, but whoever loses his life for My sake, he is the one who will save it" (Luke 9:24). Those who seek to find their identity and purpose for living in the natural order of things will someday lose it. No matter how much we accumulate in this lifetime, it will all be burned up in the final judgment. It is nothing but wood, hay, and stubble (see 1 Corinthians 3:12-13). We cannot take it with us.

A Rewarding Sacrifice

It seems to be the great ambition of humanity to be happy as animals instead of being blessed as children of God. The cross calls us to sacrifice the pleasure of things in order to gain the true pleasures of life. If you shoot for this world, you will miss the next. But if you shoot for the next world, God will provide the good things of this world, as well as make provision for the next. Paul puts it this way: "Discipline yourself for the purpose of godliness; for bodily discipline is only of little profit, but godliness is profitable for all things, since it holds promise for the present life and also for the life to come. It is a trustworthy statement deserving full acceptance" (1 Timothy 4:7-9).

We sacrifice the lower life to gain the higher life. Jesus told the disciples that "the Son of Man must suffer many things and be rejected by the elders and chief priests and scribes, and be killed and be raised up on the third day" (Luke 9:22). "Peter took Him aside and began to rebuke Him, saying, 'God forbid it, Lord! This shall never happen to You.' But He turned and said to Peter, 'Get behind Me, Satan! You are a stumbling block to Me; for you are not setting your mind on God's interests, but man's'" (Matthew 16:22-23).

This memorable rebuke seems mercilessly severe, yet even the crediting of Satan as the source describes exactly and appropriately the character of the advice given by Peter. Satan tempts us, saying, "Save yourself at any rate; sacrifice duty to self-interest, the cause of Christ to personal convenience." This advice is truly satanic in principle, for the whole aim of Satan is to get self-interest recognized as the chief end of man, rather than the fear of God (see Ecclesiastes 12:13). Satan is called the "prince of this world" because self-interest rules this fallen world.

Man unwittingly serves Satan because he is deceived into thinking he is serving self. Jesus counters by sharing the way of the cross, the foundational principle for life in Christ, which is the repudiation of our natural lives.

The cross also calls us to sacrifice the temporal in order to gain the eternal. Martyred missionary Jim Elliot said it well: "He is no fool who gives what he cannot keep to gain that which he cannot lose." We don't have a lack of money in our Western world; we have a lack of contentment. Paul says, "Godliness actually is a means of great gain when accompanied by contentment. For we have brought nothing into the world, so we cannot take anything out of it either. And if we have food and covering, with these we shall be content" (1 Timothy 6:6-8).

Don't Worry About Tomorrow

To help us live anxiety free, Jesus first dealt with our possessions in His Sermon on the Mount. Next, He deals with our provisions. The materialist struggles with the first, the doubter with the second. Can we trust God? Jesus answers:

> I say to you, do not be worried about your life, as to what you will eat or what you will drink; nor for your body, as to what you will put on. Is not life more than food, and the body more than clothing? Look at the birds of the air, that they do not sow, nor reap nor gather into barns, and yet your heavenly Father feeds them. Are you not worth much more than they? (Matthew 6:25-26).

Trusting God for tomorrow is really a question of worth. Birds are not created in the image of God, but we are. Birds will not inherit the kingdom of God, but we (believers) will. If God takes care of the birds, so much more will He take care of us. Observe the lilies of the field: "If God so clothes the grass of the field, which is alive today and tomorrow is thrown into the furnace, will He not much more clothe you? You of little faith! Do not worry then" (Matthew 6:30-31).

God lays His own reputation on the line. If we will trust and obey Him, He will provide. This is a question of God's integrity. Does He care for us, and will He provide for our needs? "Your heavenly Father knows that you need all these things.... So do not worry about tomorrow; for tomorrow will care for itself. Each day has enough trouble of its own" (Matthew 6:32,34). He is asking us to trust Him and take one day at a time.

Essentially, the will of God is to live responsibly today by faith and trust God for tomorrow. Are we people of little faith, or do we believe the fruit of the Spirit will satisfy us more than earthly possessions? Do we really believe that if we hunger and thirst after righteousness, we shall be satisfied (Matthew 5:6)? If we seek to establish God's kingdom, will God supply all our needs according to His riches in glory (Philippians 4:19)? If we believe these things, then we will "seek first His kingdom and His righteousness, and all these things will be added to [us]" (Matthew 6:33). Somebody got the following right:

> There are two days in every week about which we should not worry, two days which should be kept free from fear and apprehension.
>
> One of these days is Yesterday with its mistakes and cares, its faults and blunders, its aches and pains. Yesterday has passed forever beyond our control. All the money in the world cannot bring back Yesterday. We cannot undo a single act we performed; we cannot erase a single word we said. Yesterday is gone.
>
> The other day we should not worry about is Tomorrow with its possible adversaries, its burdens, its large promise and poor performance. Tomorrow is also beyond our immediate control. Tomorrow's sun will rise, either in splendor or behind a mask of clouds, but it will rise. Until it does, we have no stake in Tomorrow, for it is yet unborn.
>
> This leaves only one day, Today. Any man can fight the battles of just one day. It is only when you and I add the burdens of those two awful eternities—Yesterday and Tomorrow—that we break down. It is not the experience of Today that drives men mad. It is remorse or bitterness for something which happened Yesterday and the dread of what Tomorrow may bring.[3]

Casting All Your Cares upon Christ

People consume alcohol, take street drugs, turn to food, have illicit sex, mindlessly repeat mantras, and escape to cabins, boats, or motor homes to reduce their anxiety. One lady told us, "Whenever I feel anxious, I go on a shopping spree!" More drugs are dispensed for the temporary "cure" of anxiety than for any other reason. But when the temporary "cure" wears off, we have to return to the same world, with the added problem of the negative consequences of our escape mechanisms.

The real Healer has invited us to cast all our anxieties on Him:

> Humble yourselves under the mighty hand of God, that He may exalt you at the proper time, casting all your anxiety on Him, because He cares for you. Be of sober spirit, be on the alert. Your adversary, the devil, prowls around like a roaring lion, seeking someone to devour. But resist him, firm in your faith, knowing that the same experiences of suffering are being accomplished by your brethren who are in the world (1 Peter 5:6-9).

Prayer is the first step in casting all your anxiety on Christ. Remember Paul's words: "Be anxious for nothing, but in everything by prayer and supplication with thanksgiving let your requests be made known to God" (Philippians 4:6). Turning to God in prayer demonstrates your reliance on Him. Coming before Him with thanksgiving helps you keep in mind what He has already done for you. God created you, forgave your sins, gave you new life in Christ, equipped you with the Holy Spirit, and prepared an eternal home for you. We suggest a prayer similar to the following:

> *Dear heavenly Father, I come to You as Your child, purchased by the blood of the Lord Jesus Christ. I declare my dependence upon You, and I acknowledge my need of You. I know that apart from Christ I can do nothing. You know the thoughts and intentions of my heart, and You know my*

current situation from the beginning to the end. Sometimes I am double-minded, and I need Your peace to guard my heart and my mind.

I humble myself before You and choose to trust You to exalt me at the proper time, in any way You choose. I place my trust in You to supply all my needs according to Your riches in glory and to guide me into all truth. I ask for Your divine guidance so that I may fulfill my calling to live a responsible life by faith in the power of Your Holy Spirit. Search me, Lord, and know my heart and my anxious thoughts. I want to please You and serve You. In Jesus's precious name I pray. Amen.

The second step is to resolve any personal and spiritual conflicts you may have. Peter instructed us to humble ourselves before God and resist the devil. In other words, we need to make sure that our hearts are right with God. This is the same instruction James gives: "Submit therefore to God. Resist the devil and he will flee from you" (James 4:7). The purpose is to get right with God and eliminate any possible influences of the devil on your mind. Remember, "the Spirit clearly says that in later times some will abandon the faith and follow deceiving spirits and things taught by demons" (1 Timothy 4:1 NIV). You will be a double-minded person if you pay attention to a deceiving spirit. Hopefully you have already resolved these issues by going through *The Steps to Freedom in Christ*. If you have, then "the peace of God, which surpasses all comprehension, will guard your hearts and your minds in Christ Jesus" (Philippians 4:7).

In our experience, most major anxieties are resolved by these first two steps, but you may still have some anxious thoughts about life events. This is common because a little anxiety is normal and should motivate us to live responsibly. If you have successfully completed the first two steps, then work through the following steps, which are summarized in the "Overcoming Anxiety Worksheet" at the end of the chapter.

The third step is to state the problem; a problem well stated is half-solved. In anxious states of mind, people "can't see the forest for the trees," so put the problem in perspective. Generally speaking, the process of worrying takes a greater toll on a person than the negative consequences of what they worried about. *Will my child come home safely? Will I lose my job? Will my spouse remain faithful? Will I pass the test?* If we counted up all the anxious moments that once hounded us and thanked God for every dreaded outcome never realized, we would be forever grateful.

Many anxious people find tremendous relief by simply having their problems clarified and put into perspective. "Will it matter for eternity?" is the important question.

The danger at this juncture is to seek ungodly counsel. The world is glutted with magicians and sorcerers who promise incredible results. Their appearances may be striking. Their credentials may be impressive. Their approach may seem religious and spiritual. Their personalities may be charming, but their characters are bankrupt. "Do not judge according to appearance, but judge with righteous judgment," Jesus said (John 7:24). "How blessed is the man who does not walk in the counsel of the wicked, nor stand in the path of sinners, nor sit in the seat of scoffers!" (Psalm 1:1).

Fourth, separate the facts from your assumptions. Sometimes we're anxious because we don't know what is going to happen tomorrow. Since we don't know, we make assumptions. A peculiar trait of the mind is its tendency to assume the worst. If the assumption is accepted as truth, it will drive the mind to its anxiety limits. Therefore, as best as possible, verify all assumptions and avoid presumptions or whimsical speculations.

Fifth, determine what you have the right or ability to control. Your sense of worth is tied only to that for which you are responsible. If you aren't living a responsible life, you should feel anxious. Don't try to cast your responsibility onto Christ; He will throw it back. But do cast your anxiety onto Him, because His integrity is at stake in meeting your needs—*if* you are living a responsible and righteous life.

Sixth, list everything you can do that is related to the situation under your responsibility. When people don't assume their responsibilities, they turn to temporary cures for their anxiety. Remember, "the work of righteousness will be peace" (Isaiah 32:17). Turning to an unrighteous solution will only increase your anxiety in the future. Doing nothing will not solve the problem either. Passivity only allows problems to worsen while we remain indecisive.

Seventh, follow through and accomplish everything on your list. Then commit yourself to being a responsible person and fulfilling your calling and obligations in life.

For the eighth step, trust that the rest is God's responsibility. Any residual anxiety is probably due to assuming responsibilities that God never intended you to have.

A Peaceful Heart of Gratitude

For the last six years, I (Neil) have been taking care of my wife of 52 years as she slowly declines with agitated dementia. For three years she resided at a long-term skilled nursing facility. I drove 70,000 miles seeing her three times every day to help her to the bathroom, bathe her, and help her eat her meals. I have never sensed the presence and peace of God more than I have these last three years. I wrote a little book about this, entitled *The Power of Presence* (Grand Rapids, MI: Monarch Books, 2016). It is about experiencing God's presence during this time, and about what my presence means to Joanne. My wife is home now with me as I finish the final editing of this book.

I love Joanne more now than I have ever loved her, but not in the same ways as I did at fist. I was attracted to Joanne because she was a classy lady, and I enjoyed being around her. I loved her then because of who she was. Now she can't do anything for me, but thanks to Jesus, I love her now because of who I am. Satan can't touch us; there is no fear of death; and we have learned together to trust God, and not worry about tomorrow. My goal is to love Joanne as Christ loves the church, and make her final days as peaceful as possible in the presence of family.

I believe the secret to contentment is to be forever grateful for the life God has given us. I always try to come before His presence with thanksgiving. Paul wrote, "Give thanks in all circumstances; for this is God's will for you in Christ Jesus" (1 Thessalonians 5:18 NIV). I thank God for the gift of life, for His forgiveness, for meeting all our needs, and for preparing a place for us for all eternity. I'm thankful for the 52 years that Joanne and I had together.

Overcoming Anxiety Worksheet

1. Turn to God in prayer.
2. Resolve all known personal and spiritual conflicts.
3. State the problem.
4. Separate the facts from your assumptions.
    a. List the facts relating to the situation.
    b. List your assumptions relating to the situation.
    c. Verify the above assumptions.
5. Determine your active response.
    a. Identify what you can control as a matter of personal responsibility.
    b. Identify what you have no right or ability to control.
6. List everything related to the situation that is your responsibility.
7. Follow through on your list of responsibilities. Become accountable to someone for fulfilling your goals.
8. Trust that the rest is God's responsibility.

Discussion Questions

1. Why didn't Jesus tell Mary to help Martha? Was it because He didn't care? How will God answer our anxious prayers if we have been living our way instead of His way? Will He bail us out? Why or why not?

2. How can a Christian be double-minded?

3. How is anxiety a product of what we think?

4. Contrast the differences between peace with God, peace of God, and peace on earth.

5. How would you define the right goal for living?

6. What are the potential problems of storing up treasures on earth?

7. What are we sacrificing when we deny self-rule? What are we gaining?

8. How can we keep from worrying about tomorrow?

9. How can we cast our anxiety on Christ?

10. What is your biggest takeaway from studying this book?

Guidelines for Leading This Study on Letting Go of Fear

The normal guidelines for leading a group study apply to this book as well:

1. Encourage participants to come prepared by reading each chapter before the meeting.

2. Create an atmosphere of trust by using the first meeting to get acquainted. Spend some time getting to know one another. Share prayer requests and encourage the group to pray for one another.

3. As best you can, ensure confidentiality.

4. Encourage safe self-disclosure without judgment, but don't permit gossip about others.

5. State at the beginning that everyone's participation is desired, but it is your responsibility as the leader to ensure that no one person dominates the discussion—and that includes you.

6. There are no foolish questions.

7. Everyone's opinion is to be respected.

After you have gone over the discussion questions, finish by leading them through one of *The Steps to Freedom in Christ* (Steps). Each of the first seven chapters is followed by one of the Steps, and the introduction is followed by an introduction to the Steps. Be sure to take the time to read this introduction in your group. The gospel is also explained and followed by a prayer for salvation. If you feel it is appropriate, have the group pray the prayer out loud together. If they are all believers, they will not a have a problem with that. There is also a prayer and declaration at the end of the introduction. Have them pray and make the declaration together out loud.

Each Step begins with a prayer asking God for guidance. These prayers should be said out loud together. After this, give participants several minutes to finish the Step on their own. This is an encounter between themselves and God. They can do it or not do it; it is up to them. Be sure to tell everyone that nobody will be embarrassed or asked to share personal and intimate details of their lives. If anyone is having difficulty with the Steps, talk with them privately. The Steps are not complete until the final Step in chapter 7.

Establishing a Discipleship Counseling Ministry

Very little training is required for mature and biblically literate pastors to lead an inquirer through *The Steps to Freedom in Christ* (Steps). It is actually a self-guided tour that people can process on their own. We have received emails and letters from people all over the world who have processed the Steps on their own. Dr. Wayne Grudem is the most-read systematic theologian in the world today and, in our estimation, a very godly man. In the forward for Neil's book, *Liberating Prayer*, which includes the Steps, Dr. Grudem wrote:[1]

> After living more than 50 years as a Christian, and after teaching more than 25 years as a professor of Bible and theology, I took about two hours to work carefully through Neil's seven "Steps to Freedom in Christ" and apply each step to my own life, reading each suggested prayer aloud. God used that process to bring to mind a number of thoughts and attitudes that He wanted to correct, and then to impart to me a wonderfully refreshing sense of freedom, peace, joy, and fellowship with Himself.

In most cases the leaders just show up, and God sets people free. However, there are difficult cases that require some training. The purpose of Freedom in Christ Ministries is to equip the church worldwide,

enabling them to establish their congregations, marriages, and ministries alive and free in Christ through genuine repentance and faith in
God. We are not a counseling ministry, and we will not do your discipling for you, but we will help you equip godly people in your church
who can help others. We have offices and representatives around the
world who will offer that kind of training for a select few in your
church. Our office in the United States has an online university that
people in your church can enroll in to become part of our Community
Freedom Ministries (see www.ficm.org). There are hundreds of such
associates who are part of CFM in the United States and Canada. We
require three of Neil's books be read by those enrolled: *Victory Over the
Darkness*, *The Bondage Breaker*, and *Discipleship Counseling*. Having
these trained encouragers in a church takes a huge load off the pastor.

For the congregation, we offer a basic discipleship course that
explains creation, the fall, a Christian worldview, how to live by faith,
mental strongholds, the battle for our minds, emotions, forgiveness,
and relational perspectives. The course, entitled *Freedom in Christ*
(Bethany House, 2017), includes a DVD, leader's guide, and participant's guide and concludes with the Steps. This course has been translated into many languages (see www.ficminternational.org). Youth for
Christ in the United Kingdom has partnered with our ministry to produce a youth version that includes a DVD, teacher's guide, and two
choices for a participant's guide (junior high and high school).

The best possible scenario is to plant a church and offer the class for
all new members. Imagine a church where everyone knows who they
are in Christ and have resolved all known personal and spiritual conflicts. However, it is never too late to offer the class in Sunday school,
fellowship groups, and home Bible studies. But it can't be a onetime
offering, because every church has a constant turnover of people. The
class should be continually offered for new members and converts.

Helping members of your church become established alive and free
in Christ is a beginning, not an end. After the basic initial discipleship

class, we recommend the Victory Series, which is a 48-week curriculum based on our identity and position in Christ. It progresses from being rooted in Christ to growing in Christ, living in Christ, and finally overcoming in Christ.

After the basic course, we have resources to help those who have lingering difficulties with depression, anger, fear, anxiety, legalism, broken relationships, and sexual or chemical addictions.

Freedom in Christ Ministries Books and Resources

Core Material

Victory Over the Darkness has a companion study guide and DVD, as well as an audiobook edition (Bethany House, 2000). With more than 1,400,000 copies in print, this core book explains who you are in Christ, how to walk by faith in the power of the Holy Spirit, how to be transformed by the renewing of your mind, how to experience emotional freedom, and how to relate to one another in Christ.

The Bondage Breaker has a companion study guide and audiobook edition (Harvest House, 2006). With more than 1,400,000 copies in print, this book explains spiritual warfare, what our protection is, ways that we are vulnerable, and how we can live a liberated life in Christ

Discipleship Counseling (Bethany House, 2003) combines the concepts of discipleship and counseling and teaches the practical integration of theology and psychology, helping Christians resolve their personal and spiritual conflicts through genuine repentance and faith in God.

The Steps to Freedom in Christ and the companion interactive video (Bethany House, 2017) are discipleship counseling tools that help Christians resolve their personal and spiritual conflicts through genuine repentance and faith in God.

Restored (e3 Resources) is an expansion of *The Steps to Freedom in Christ* with additional explanation and instruction.

Walking in Freedom (Bethany House, 2009) is a 21-day devotional to be used for follow-up after someone has been led through *The Steps to Freedom.*

Freedom in Christ (Bethany House, 2008) is a discipleship course for Sunday school classes and small groups. The course includes a leader's guide, a student guide, and a DVD covering 12 lessons and *The Steps to Freedom in Christ*. This course is designed to enable believers to resolve personal and spiritual conflicts and be established alive and free in Christ.

The Bondage Breaker DVD Experience (Harvest House, 2011) is also a discipleship course for Sunday school classes and small groups. It is similar to the one above, but the lessons are 15 minutes long instead of 30 minutes. It has a companion interactive workbook, but no leader's guide.

Victory Series (Bethany House, 2014-2015) is a comprehensive curriculum, including eight books that follow the growth sequence of being rooted in Christ, growing in Christ, living in Christ, and overcoming in Christ: *God's Story for You, Your New Identity, Your Foundation in Christ, Renewing Your Mind, Growing in Christ, Your Life in Christ, Your Authority in Christ*, and *Your Ultimate Victory*.

Specialized Books

The Bondage Breaker—The Next Step (Harvest House, 2011) includes several testimonies of people finding their freedom from all kinds of problems, with commentary by Dr. Anderson. It is an important learning tool for encouragers and gives hope to those who are entangled in sin.

Overcoming Addictive Behavior with Mike Quarles (Bethany House, 2003) explores the path to addiction and how a Christian can overcome addictive behaviors.

Overcoming Depression with Joanne Anderson (Bethany House, 2004) explores the nature of depression—which is a body, soul, and spirit problem—and presents a "wholistic" answer for overcoming this "common cold" of mental illnesses.

Daily in Christ with Joanne Anderson (Harvest House, 2000) is a popular daily devotional read by thousands of internet subscribers every day.

Who I Am in Christ (Bethany House, 2001) has 36 short chapters describing who believers are in Christ and how their deepest needs are met in Him.

Freedom from Addiction with Mike and Julia Quarles (Bethany House, 1996) begins with Mike and Julia's journey into addiction and codependency and explains the nature of chemical addictions and how to overcome them in Christ.

One Day at a Time with Mike and Julia Quarles (Bethany House, 2000) is a 120-day devotional helping those who struggle with addictive behaviors and explaining how to discover the grace of God on a daily basis.

Setting Your Church Free with Charles Mylander (Bethany House, 2014) explains servant leadership and how the leadership of a church can resolve corporate conflicts through corporate repentance.

Setting Your Marriage Free with Charles Mylander (Bethany House, 2014) explains God's divine plan for marriage and the steps that couples can take to resolve their difficulties.

Christ-Centered Therapy with Terry and Julianne Zuehlke (Zondervan, 2000) explains the practical integration of theology and psychology for professional counselors and provides them with biblical tools for therapy.

Managing Your Anger with Rich Miller (Harvest House, 2018) explains the nature of anger and how to put away all anger, wrath, and malice.

Grace That Breaks the Chains with Rich Miller and Paul Travis (Harvest House, 2014) explains the bondage of legalism and how to overcome it by the grace of God.

Winning the Battle Within (Harvest House, 2008) shares God's standards for sexual conduct, the path to sexual addiction, and how to overcome sexual strongholds.

Restoring Broken Relationships (Bethany House, 2015) explains the primary ministry of the church and how we can be reconciled to God and each other.

Rough Road to Freedom (Grand Rapids, MI: Monarch Books, 2012) is Dr. Anderson's memoir.

The Power of Presence (Grand Rapids, MI: Monarch Books, 2016) is about experiencing the presence of God during difficult times and what our presence means to each other. This book is written in the context of Dr. Anderson caring for his wife, who is slowly dying with agitated dementia.

For more information or to purchase the above materials, contact Freedom in Christ Ministries:

Canada:
    freedominchrist@sasktel.net
    www.ficm.ca

United Kingdom:
    info@ficm.org.uk
    www.ficm.org.uk

United States:
    info@ficm.org
    www.ficm.org

International:
    www.ficminternational.org

Notes

Introduction

1. We encourage you to read Dr. Anderson's book *Overcoming Depression* (Bethany House, 2004) for more information and guidance on this topic.
2. According to the National Institute of Mental Health (NIHM).
3. Edmund J. Bourne, *The Anxiety and Phobia Workbook*, rev. ed. (Oakland, CA: New Harbinger, 1995).
4. Edmund J. Bourne, *Healing Fear* (Oakland, CA: New Harbinger, 1998), 2.
5. Ibid., 3.
6. Ibid., 5.
7. Neil T. Anderson, *Discipleship Counseling* (Minneapolis, MN: Bethany House, 2003).
8. The Board of the Ministry and Healing is chaired by Dr. George Hurst, who previously directed the University of Texas Health Center at Tyler, Texas, george.hurst@uthct.edu. The Oklahoma and Texas data were combined together in a manuscript that was accepted by the *Southern Medical Journal* for publication, Volume: 101, Issue 4 (April 2008).
9. Sherwood Wirt and Kersten Beckstrom, *Living Quotations for Christians* (New York: Harper & Row, 1974), 76.

Chapter 1—Restoring the Foundation

1. Erik Erikson, *Childhood and Society*, 2d ed. (New York: W.W. Norton & Company, 1963).
2. John Dacey and John Travers, *Human Development Across the Lifespan* (Dubuque, IA: William C. Brown, 1995), 289.
3. Ibid.
4. Ibid., 317.
5. Ibid., 50.
6. Ibid., 51.
7. Ibid., 47.
8. "Anxiety Disorders," American Psychiatric Association, 1997, 4-5.

Chapter 2—Fortress of Fear

1. See at www.chapman.edu/fearsurvey.
2. Carlos G. Valles, *Let Go of Fear* (New York: Triumph, 1991), 88.

Chapter 3—Fear of Death

1. As quoted in *USA Weekend*, August 22-24, 1997, 6.
2. Ibid.
3. Ibid., 5.

4. Alison Bell, "The Fear Factor," *Teen*, April 1997, 66ff.

5. Ibid.

6. Ibid.

7. Ibid.

8. As quoted in Everett Ferguson, *Demonology of the Early Christian World* (New York: Edwin Mellen, 1984), 117.

9. Neil wrote *The Power of Presence* (Grand Rapids, MI: Monarch Books, 2016) while taking care of his wife of 52 years, who is slowly succumbing to agitated dementia. The book is about experiencing the presence of God during such times, and what Neil's presence means to Joanne.

10. As quoted in Karen S. Peterson's book *Keeping Kids Safe or Scaring Them to Death?*, as quoted in *USA Today*, August 21, 1995, 4D.

11. Ibid.

Chapter 4—Fear of Man

1. Hannah Hurnard, *Hinds' Feet on High Places* (Wheaton, IL: Tyndale House, 1997), 31-32.

2. Ibid., 32-33.

3. Bill Bright, *Witnessing without Fear* (San Bernardino, CA: Here's Life, 1987), 13.

4. Ibid., 54-65.

5. Adapted from Ibid., 59-61.

Chapter 5—Fear of Failure

1. Adapted from John Pepper, *Detroit Daily News*, August 17, 1997.

2. Theodore Roosevelt, excerpt from his speech "Citizenship in a Republic," given at the Sorbonne, in Paris, on April 23, 1910.

3. Original source of this poem by William Arthur Ward is unknown; the poem was sent to me (Neil) by email many years ago.

4. Susan Jeffers, *Feel the Fear and Do It Anyway* (New York: Fawcett Columbine, 1987), 4.

5. Ibid., 22-23.

6. See at https://quoteinvestigator.com/2012/18/do-good-anyway/.

Chapter 6—Fear of Satan

1. F.F. Bruce, *Commentary on the Book of Acts* (Grand Rapids, MI: Eerdmans, 1954), 114.

2. Ernst Haenchen, *The Acts of the Apostles* (Philadelphia: Westminster, 1971), 237.

3. Martin Luther, *Table Talk*, IV, 5097, as cited in Joseph Turmel [Louis Coulange], *The Life of the Devil* (London: Alfred A. Knopf, 1929), 147. The book includes many references of the devil putting thoughts into the minds of noted saints.

Chapter 7—Fear of God

1. Timothy Beougher and Lyle Dorsett, *Accounts of a Campus Revival* (Wheaton, IL: Harold Shaw, 1995), 67-68.

Chapter 9—Panic Disorder

1. Bonnie Crandall, *Panic Buster* (Jamestown, NY: Hatch Creek, 1995), 9.

2. Ibid., 11.

3. David G. Benner, *Baker Encyclopedia of Psychology* (Grand Rapids, MI: Baker Book House, 1990), 786.

4. "Answers to Your Questions about Panic Disorder," *American Psychological Association*, http://www.apa.org/topics/anxiety/panic-disorder.aspx.

5. Ibid.

6. "Panic Disorder," American Psychiatric Association, 1997, 2.

7. "Panic Disorder," *National Anxiety Foundation*, http://www.nationalanxietyfoundation.org/panic-disorder.html.

8. R. Reid Wilson, *Don't Panic* (New York: Harper Collins, 1996), 32.

9. Ibid., 34.

10. Ibid., 13-14.

11. Ibid., 15.

12. R. Reid Wilson, *Breaking the Panic Cycle* (Phobia Society of America, 1990), 20.

13. Ibid., 21.

14. Ibid.

15. Ibid.

16. Ibid., 18-19.

17. Lucinda Bassett, "Overcoming Your Anxiety and Fear" (video), Midwest Center for Stress and Anxiety.

18. Bassett, "Overcoming Your Anxiety and Fear."

19. Ibid.

20. Bill Hendrick, "Anxiety: New Understanding and Therapy May Help Those Who Cope Every Day," *The Atlantic Journal-Constitution*, December 7, 1996.

21. Edmund J. Bourne, *The Anxiety and Phobia Workbook* (Oakland, CA: New Harbinger, 1998), 175.

22. Ibid.

23. Ibid., 176.

24. Ibid.

25. Ibid., 177.

Chapter 10—Casting All Anxiety on Christ

1. As quoted in L.B. Cowman, *Streams in the Desert*, rev. ed. (Grand Rapids, MI: Zondervan, 1977), 141.

2. Source unknown.

3. The author of this quote could be Robert Burdette, but sources disagree on the attribution.

Appendix B—Establishing a Discipleship Counseling Ministry

1. Neil Anderson, *Liberating Prayer* (Eugene, OR: Harvest House, 2012), 5.

To learn more about Harvest House books and
to read sample chapters, visit our website:

www.harvesthousepublishers.com

HARVEST HOUSE PUBLISHERS
EUGENE, OREGON